FRIENDLY FIRE

FRIENDLY FIRE

THE ACCIDENTAL SHOOTDOWN
OF U.S. BLACK HAWKS OVER
NORTHERN IRAQ

Scott A. Snook

PRINCETON UNIVERSITY PRESS   PRINCETON AND OXFORD

Fourth printing, and first paperback printing, 2002
Paperback ISBN 0-691-09518-3

The Library of Congress has cataloged the cloth edition of this book as follows

Snook, Scott A., 1958–
Friendly fire : the accidental shootdown of U.S. Black Hawks over
Northern Iraq / Scott A. Snook.
p.   cm.
Includes bibliographical references and index.
ISBN 0-691-00506-0 (cloth : alk. paper)
1. Aerial reconnaissance, American—Iraq.   2. Black Hawk (Military
transport helicopter)—Accidents—Investigation.   3. Friendly fire
(Military science)—Iraq.   4. Organizational behavior—Case
studies.   5. Leadership—Case studies.   6. United States Air Force—
Management—Case studies.   I. Title.
UG765.I72 S63   2000
355.4'22 21—dc21   99-041097

British Library Cataloging-in-Publication Data is available

The views expressed herein are those of the author
and do not purport to reflect the position of the United States
Military Academy, the Department of the Army,
or the Department of Defense.

This book has been composed in Times Roman

Printed on acid-free paper. ∞

www.pup.princeton.edu

Printed in the United States of America

10 9 8 7 6 5 4

Dedication _____

THIS BOOK is dedicated to the memory of the twenty-six peacekeepers who died in the friendly fire shootdown over northern Iraq on 14 April 1994:

COL Hikmet Alp	CPT Patrick M. McKenna
Mr. Abdulsatur Arab	Mr. Bader Mikho
SSGT Paul N. Barclay	Mr. Ahmad Mohammad
SPC Cornelius A. Bass	WO1 Erik S. Mounsey
1LT Ceyhun Civas	COL Richard A. Mulhern
SPC Jeffrey C. Colbert	1LT Laura A. Piper
LTC Guy Demetz	SPC Michael S. Robinson
PFC Mark A. Ellner	SSGT Ricky L. Robinson
CW2 John W. Garrett, Jr.	Mr. Salid Said
1LT M. Barlas Gultepe	Ms. Barbara L. Schell
CW2 Michael A. Hall	MAJ Harry C. Shapland
SFC Benjamin T. Hodge	LTC Jonathan C. Swann
Mr. Ghandi Hussein	COL Jerald L. Thompson

It is also dedicated to their families and friends, who continue to wonder how in the world such a thing could have happened. In particular, I owe a great debt to two very special people I met at the congressional hearings. First, to Kaye Mounsey, whose personal courage inspired me to complete this work. Second, to Michael Nye, whose professional courage kept me honest.

Contents

List of Figures _____

Preface

A FUNDAMENTAL assumption of this study is that context and perspective are important. Therefore, it is only fair that I share with the reader—*up front*—my unique background and approach to this research. I do this so that you can more accurately interpret my findings. First, I approach this case from a rather unique perspective. I am not a disinterested observer. I have a very real stake in the organization that I am studying. I am not only a scientist trying to unlock some of the behavioral mysteries of a complex story, I am also a member of the larger organization within which the shootdown occurred. As a commissioned officer in the U.S. Army, I have almost twenty years of experience in uniform. I have fought as a member of a Joint Task Force in combat. Therefore, I did not come to this incident as a complete outsider. However, prior to beginning this project, I had no personal or professional knowledge of the shootdown beyond what I had read in published accounts.

Second, I have an intimate knowledge of fratricide. On 27 October 1983, I was wounded by "friendly fire" from a U.S. Air Force A-7 fighter on the island of Grenada. Thus began my early and painful preparation for writing this book. Curiosity, no matter how perverse, can drive one to great lengths. I have no doubt that this significant personal incident has had an impact on how I view friendly fire and issues of interservice cooperation. Rather than hiding it, I offer my perspective here openly so that you can interpret my work in light of my unique background, rather than in ignorance of it.

Finally, because I approach this case as both a scientist and a practitioner, I have written in an unusually personal and self-reflective style. I do not hesitate to use the "first person," especially when I sense that I am drawing on personal or professional experience. I also openly share my emotional reactions to various revelations as the puzzle unfolds. I do all this to more accurately communicate the very real sense of frustration that such tragedies hold for practitioners, as well as the excitement they hold for scientists.

Acknowledgments ―――――――――――――――――

COMPLEX organizational outcomes cannot be attributed to any single cause; neither can products such as this one. I was fortunate to have enjoyed a large cast of supporting characters. Without the help of insiders such as Colonel (retired) Mike Landrum, Captain Michael Nye (since resigned), John Glaylin, and Kaye Mounsey, I never would have gained access to such a rich set of data. Without the encouragement and insights from my friends and colleagues associated with the Organizational Behavior Program at Harvard— Monica Higgins, Rakesh Khurana, John Kotter, Jay Lorsch, Geoff Love, Peter Marsden, Orlando Patterson, and Don Sull—I wouldn't have had the courage or requisite variety to take on such a challenge.

As this book grew out of my doctoral dissertation, the contributions of three additional scholars mark this work. Nitin Nohria found ideas where there weren't any, provided discipline when I had none, and became a friend when I wasn't looking. Tony Oettinger taught me the perils of "scholar-sh—" and kept my feet on the ground and my eyes on the real world. Richard Hackman walked his talk; he set the conditions that increased the likelihood of success.

One additional person deserves special thanks. In my darkest hours, as I struggled with both the intellectual puzzles of the shootdown and the administrative nightmares of publishing, Charles Perrow took an interest and kept me going. In doing so, he set the standard for academic mentoring by taking an interest not only in my work but also in me. I am most grateful to him for pushing my thinking and my emotions.

None of this would have been possible or even worth doing without the love and support of my family. My parents taught me how to learn, by loving learning themselves. My children kept me sane, by being insane. And my wife showed me how to love, by loving me.

List of Abbreviations _____

AAIB	Aircraft Accident Investigation Board
AAST	Advanced Air Surveillance Technician
ACC	Air Combat Command
ACE	Airborne Command Element
ACO	Airspace Control Order
ACT	Aircrew Coordination Training
AFB	Air Force Base
AGL	Above Ground Level
AIM-9	Air Intercept Missile (Sidewinder)
AMC	Air Mission Commander
AMRAAM	Advanced Medium Range Air-to-Air Missile
ANGLICO	Air Naval Gunfire Liaison Company
ARF	Aircrew Read File
ART	Airborne Radar Technician
ASO	Air Surveillance Officer
AST	Air Surveillance Technician
ATO	Air Traffic Control Order
AWACS	Airborne Warning And Control System
BSD	Battle Staff Directive
BVR	Beyond Visual Range
C3I	Command, Control, Communications, & Intelligence
CDMT	Computer Display Maintenance Technician
CFAC	Combined Forces Air Component
CFACC	Combined Forces Air Component Commander
CINC	Commander In Chief
CRM	Crew (or Cockpit) Resource Management
CTF	Combined Task Force
CW3	Chief Warrant Officer 3
DETCO	Detachment Commander
DOD	Department of Defense
DUKE	Call sign for ACE
Eagle Flight	Name given to Army Aviation Detachment assigned to support OPC; also name used to refer to Black Hawk flights within OPC
F-15	U.S. Air Force air superiority Fighter (Eagle)
FSO	Fire Support Officer
HINDS	NATO designation for Soviet-made attack helicopter
HRO	High Reliability Organization

HUD	Heads Up Display
ICAO	International Civil Aviation Organization
IFF	Identify Friend or Foe
J-3	Joint Staff position for Operations
J-4	Joint Staff position for Logistics
JCS	Joint Chiefs of Staff
JOIC	Joint Operations and Intelligence Center
JSOC	Joint Special Operations Command
JTF	Joint Task Force
JTIDS	Joint Tactical Information Distribution System
MAD DOG	Call sign for Mission Director
MCC	Military Coordination Center
MCC	Mission Crew Commander
MEU	Marine Expeditionary Unit
MG	Major General
NATO	Northern Atlantic Treaty Organization
NCA	National Command Authority
NCO	Noncommissioned Officer
NGO	Non-Governmental Organization
NOTAM	Notices to Airmen
OCONUS	Outside Continental United States
OI	Operational Instructions
OPC	Operation Provide Comfort
OPCON	Operational Control
OPLAN	Operations Plan
OPORD	Operations Order
OPTEMPO	Operational Tempo
OTA	Office of Technology Assessment
PACAF	Pacific Air Force
PVO	Private Volunteer Organization
ROEs	Rules Of Engagement
SD	Senior Director (on AWACS)
SECDEF	Secretary of Defense (William Perry)
SITREP	Situation Report
SOP	Standard Operating Procedure
SPINS	Special Instructions
TACON	Tactical Control
TACSAT	Tactical Satellite
TAOR	Tactical Area of Responsibility
TD	Target Designator
TOC	Tactical Operations Center
UCMJ	Uniform Code of Military Justice
UH-60	U.S. Army Utility Helicopter—"Black Hawk"

UN   United Nations
UNHCR   United Nations High Commission for Refugees
USCINCEUR   United States Commander In Chief Europe
USCINCUSAFE   United States Commander In Chief United States Air
                    Forces Europe
USEUCOM   United States European Command
VID   Visual Identification
WD   Weapons Director

FRIENDLY FIRE

1

Introduction: How in the World Could This Happen?

> For over 1,000 days, the pilots and crews
> assigned to Operation Provide Comfort flew
> mission after mission, totaling over 50,000 hours
> of flight operations, without a single major
> accident. Then, in one terrible moment on the
> 14th of April, a series of avoidable errors led to
> the tragic deaths of 26 men and women of the
> American Armed Forces, United States Foreign
> Service, and the Armed Forces of our coalition
> allies. In place were not just one, but a series of
> safeguards—some human, some procedural, some
> technical—that were supposed to ensure an
> accident of this nature could never happen. Yet,
> quite clearly, these safeguards failed.
>
> *(John M. Shalikashvili, Chairman of the Joint
> Chiefs of Staff)*[1]

ON 7 APRIL 1991, Iraq accepted United Nations (UN) cease-fire conditions and resolutions, thus officially ending Operation Desert Storm and the Persian Gulf War. On the same day, a massive multinational, multiple-agency humanitarian effort was launched to relieve the suffering of hundreds of thousands of Kurdish refugees who fled into the hills of northern Iraq during the conflict. On 18 April, then Lieutenant General John Shalikashvili assumed command of Combined Task Force Provide Comfort. His most immediate concern was to "stop the dying and stabilize the situation" (Scales, 1994: 341). In an ironic twist of fate, almost three years later to the day, a visibly shaken "Shali," the very same General who gave birth to Operation Provide Comfort (OPC), since promoted to the highest ranking uniformed position in the United States military, faced a battalion of media in the Pen-

---

[1] This statement was contained in a cover Memorandum to the Secretary of Defense on 7 July 1994. Included with this summary document were the USCINCEUR's endorsement of and the entire twenty-two volume Report of the Aircraft Accident Investigation Board's findings (Shalikashvili, 1994a: 1).

tagon briefing room to explain how twenty-six peacekeepers had lost their lives in a tragic mishap.

There were three key players in this incident: a U.S. Air Force E-3B Airborne Warning and Control System (AWACS) aircraft, a two-ship flight of U.S. Army UH-60 Black Hawk helicopters, and a two-ship flight of U.S. Air Force F-15C Eagle fighters.

On 14 April at 0736,[2] the AWACS took off from Incirlik Air Base in Turkey as the lead aircraft of 52 sorties of coalition air missions scheduled for that day (see Figure 1.1). Since the mission of the AWACS was to provide "airborne threat warning and air control for all Operation Provide Comfort aircraft," this air-traffic-control-tower-in-the-sky was always the first mission off the ground each day (Andrus, 1994: 2). After leaving Incirlik, the AWACS, with its nineteen-member mission crew, flew to its assigned air surveillance orbit located just outside the northern border of Iraq. From that location, with sophisticated radar and communications equipment, the AWACS would "positively control" all coalition aircraft flying in support of Operation Provide Comfort. The crew reported "on station" at 0845 and began tracking aircraft.

At 0822, two UH-60 U.S. Army Black Hawk helicopters took off from Diyarbakir, Turkey, enroute to the Military Coordination Center's (MCC) headquarters in Zakhu. At 0935, the Black Hawks reported their entry into the no fly zone to the AWACS enroute controller and then landed six minutes later at the MCC. The MCC was located at Zakhu, a small village just inside the United Nations (UN) designated security zone in northern Iraq. There they picked up sixteen members of the UN coalition charged with leading the humanitarian relief effort. Their passengers included five Kurdish civilian leaders, three Turkish, two British, and one French officer, in addition to five U.S. civilian and military officials. At 0954, the helicopters reported to the AWACS enroute controller that they were departing Zakhu enroute to the towns of Irbil and Salah ad Din Iraq for meetings with UN and Kurdish representatives.

Meanwhile, at 0935, a flight of two Air Force F-15C fighter aircraft had taken off from Incirlik Air Base enroute to the air space over northern Iraq designated as the Tactical Area of Responsibility (TAOR). Their mission was to "perform an initial fighter sweep of the no fly zone to clear (sanitize) the area of any hostile aircraft prior to the entry of coalition forces" (Andrus, 1994: 3). At 1020, the F-15C flight lead reported entering northern Iraq to the AWACS controller responsible for air traffic inside the TAOR. Two minutes later, the lead reported a "radar contact on a low-flying, slow-moving aircraft approximately 52 miles north of the southern boundary of the no fly zone (the 36th parallel) and forty miles southeast of his position" (Andrus, 1994: 3).

---

[2] For ease of following, all times referenced in this book are local for the no fly zone.

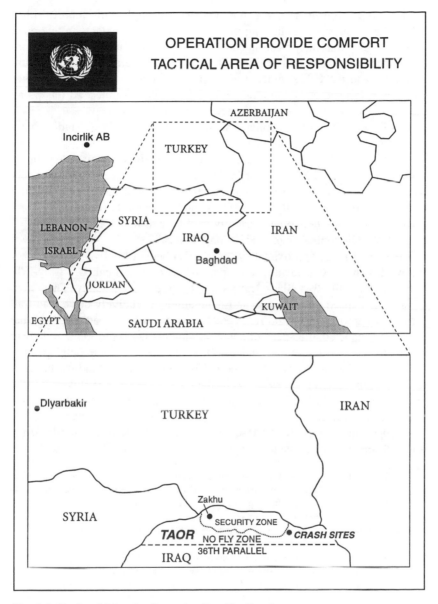

Fig. 1.1. Regional Map for Operation Provide Comfort

The TAOR controller in the AWACS acknowledged this report with a "clean there" response, indicating that he had no radar contacts in that area.

Both F-15 pilots then electronically interrogated the target with their on-board Identification Friend or Foe (IFF) system.[3] These attempts proved unsuccessful and the F-15s initiated an intercept to investigate. Three minutes later, the F-15s had closed to a range of twenty nautical miles. At this point, the lead again reported his radar contact to the AWACS.

This time the TAOR controller responded with, "Hits there," indicating a radar contact at the reported location.[4]

Following established procedure, the F-15s continued their intercept by conducting a visual identification (VID) pass of the contact. Approximately five nautical miles away from his target, the flight lead visually identified a helicopter and called, "Tally 2 Hinds." "Hind" is the NATO designation for a Soviet-made attack helicopter currently in the Iraqi inventory.

The AWACS controller replied, "Copy, Hinds."

The second F-15, approximately three miles behind his lead, immediately followed with a visual identification pass of his own and called, "Tally 2."

By this time the two Black Hawks had entered a deep valley. They were cruising at a speed of 130 knots and maintaining a relatively close lead-trail formation approximately 200 feet above the ground. The lead F-15's visual pass was conducted at a speed of about 450 knots (522 mph), on a glide path approximately 500 feet above and 1,000 feet to the left of the helicopters.

Following their low-level VID, the F-15s circled back behind the helicopters approximately ten miles to begin their firing passes. At this point, the lead notified the AWACS that fighters were "engaged" and instructed his wingman to "arm hot."[5]

At approximately 1030, the lead pilot fired an AMRAAM missile at the trail helicopter from a range of approximately four nautical miles. Imme-

---

[3] The Identify Friend or Foe (IFF) system is an electronic means of identifying individual aircraft or flights. There are two interacting components of the system: a transponder and an interrogator. Each coalition aircraft is equipped with an IFF transponder. When the transponder is interrogated from a ground or airborne source, it will respond with a numerically identifiable pulse. These replies are displayed on the radar scope of the interrogator. (Office of the Assistant Secretary of Defense for Public Affairs, 1994.)

[4] The meanings attributed to the two responses from the AWACS controller are important. The TAOR controller's initial response of "clean there" indicated that he had no radar contacts at all on his screen in the location reported by the F-15s. His response to the lead's second call was, "hits there," indicating that when he looked at that location this time, he saw a simple "blip" on his screen, representing an as yet unidentified radar return. Had he seen a green "H" or a friendly identification number on his screen at that location, the appropriate response would have been, "paint there."

[5] In a two-ship formation such as the one the F-15s flew, there is a clear line of command. The lead pilot is completely in charge of the flight and the wingman takes all of his commands from the lead. The lead's command to "arm hot" instructed his wingman to conduct his own independent targeting.

diately following his lead, the F-15 wingman then fired an AIM-9 Sidewinder missile at the lead helicopter from a range of approximately one and a half nautical miles.[6] Both Black Hawk helicopters were instantly destroyed. All twenty-six people on board perished.

Motivation: To Learn from and Correct Our Mistakes

In a joint letter of condolence to the families of those who lost their lives in this tragic accident, Secretary of Defense William Perry and the Chairman of the Joint Chiefs of Staff General John Shalikashvili expressed their commitment to account for these deaths:

> We believe that actions must speak louder than words. This accident should not have happened, but these brave individuals will not have died in vain if we learn from and correct our mistakes. We are determined to do everything in our power to insure that this type of accident is not repeated. (Office of the Assistant Secretary of Defense for Public Affairs, 1994: 1)

In its purest form, this promise captures the motivation behind this book—"to learn from and correct our mistakes . . . to insure that this type of accident is not repeated."

At a very personal level, friendly fire incidents continue to maintain a perverse grip on the author. On 27 October 1983, along with sixteen other members of the Army's 82d Airborne Division, I was unintentionally wounded in combat by a U.S. Air Force A-7 fighter on the island of Grenada. As I lay in the mud, my first thought was, "How in the world could this have happened?" Just over ten years later, as I read the first press reports of the shootdown in northern Iraq, the same question returned to haunt me. Given all of the recent advances in technical and communications systems and ten additional years of organizational experience, how could such a tragedy occur?

The more I learned, the more puzzled I became. At least in Grenada, the A-7 was flying over a "hot combat zone" during the first confusing days of Operation Urgent Fury. The tactical situation on the ground and enemy threat were in a state of flux. There was an actual shooting war going on and an enemy antiaircraft gun was located in the vicinity of our forces.

The situation in northern Iraq was much different. While the no fly zone was technically declared a "combat zone," no significant enemy action had been detected in the TAOR in well over a year. Pentagon spokesmen acknowledged that the Iraqis "had never violated the nofly zone well north of the 36th parallel" (Aerospace Daily, 1994: 81). There was little in the way of

---

[6] The AMRAAM is a radar-guided Advanced Medium Range Air-to-Air Missile and the AIM Sidewinder is a heat-seeking Air Intercept Missile.

"the fog of war" to blame. It was broad daylight with unlimited visibility and no fighting on the ground.

Both the F-15s and the UH-60s belonged to the same well-established Combined Task Force that had operated without incident for over three years. This same organization had successfully commanded and controlled over 27,000 fixed-wing and 1,400 U.S. helicopter flights since it its inception in 1991 (Andrus, 1994). Dozens of coordinating mechanisms, including weekly meetings, daily flight schedules, operations orders, intelligence briefings, and liaison officers provided redundant layers of cross-checks and communication.

Both flights of aircraft were flying under the "positive" control of the most sophisticated Airborne Warning and Control System (AWACS) in the world. At the time of the shootdown, the highly skilled nineteen-member AWACS mission crew, trained and equipped to track literally hundreds of enemy and friendly aircraft during a high-intensity conflict, had only these four aircraft to control inside the Tactical Area of Responsibility. Both flights had made several radio contacts with AWACS controllers prior to the shootdown.

This was not an emergency. The F-15s had plenty of time to further develop and evaluate the situation. There was little chance that two slow-moving helicopters could have physically "escaped" the jet fighters, nor were they ever a serious threat to the F-15s. As one expert later commented, even if they had been Iraqi Hinds, "a Hind is only a threat to an F-15 if the F-15 is parked almost stationary directly in front of it and says, 'kill me.' Other than that, it's probably not very vulnerable" (Phillips, 1995).

The mission being flown by the Black Hawks was not some obscure training flight. They were not on a routine supply run with food and medical supplies. Instead, they carried sixteen high-ranking VIPs representing most major players in Operation Provide Comfort. This flight was a highly visible priority that required the personal attention and approval of the Task Force Commander.[7]

Both target and shooter aircraft were equipped with sophisticated Identification Friend or Foe (IFF) electronic equipment designed specifically to prevent such accidents. Conservative rules of engagement required a strict sequence of procedures to be followed prior to any coalition aircraft firing its weapons. Both F-15 pilots were highly trained, technically qualified, and well-respected officers with hundreds of hours of experience in their aircraft. The wingman was the F-15 squadron commander and a decorated veteran of the Gulf War. In fact he was even credited with shooting down an Iraqi Hind helicopter during the opening days of that operation.

[7] Brigadier General Pilkington, the Combined Task Force Commander, had personally approved a request for an exception to policy that allowed the helicopters to fly in the no fly zone prior to the fighter sweep.

Given all of the training, experience, safeguards, redundant sophisticated electronic and technical equipment and the relatively benign conditions at the time, how in the world could such an accident happen? This empirical question provides the motivation for this book.

While empirically compelling, not all tragedies are equally interesting in a theoretical sense. Some accidents are easily explained and hence reveal little. For example, if, after some investigation, it was determined that the helicopters had faulty transponders, or the fighters had poorly designed communications systems, or the task force had inadequate written procedures, or the AWACS had faulty radar equipment, or one of the key players was grossly negligent or simply incompetent, or that Saddam Hussein had managed to electronically jam the IFF system, or even if an act of God such as a massive solar flare had caused the systems to fail, then this case wouldn't be a puzzle worthy of theoretical attention.[8]

If, however, after investigating the most obvious possibilities, no simple explanation presents itself, then the case becomes more interesting—more frustrating in a practical sense and more intriguing in a theoretical sense. Theoretically, unusual organizational events and subsequent "incident reviews are central to the systematic development of organizational theory" (Carroll, 1995: 6, Tamuz, 1994). The practical frustration springs from our duty as responsible practitioners to identify a logical source of the tragedy so that it can be isolated and fixed. Such tragic outcomes simply cannot happen without *something* breaking, without *someone* to blame.

In the face of such frustration, our hunger for action is almost palpable. With incidents involving the loss of life, when no compelling account immediately presents itself, we become overwhelmed by the urgent requirement to fix something, anything. Even without a compelling explanation, at every level of command, lists of corrective actions were dutifully compiled and executed. Even at the National Command Authority level, the *Final Report on the Status of Corrective Actions Taken* sent to the Secretary of Defense from the Chairman of the Joint Chiefs of Staff included a tabular listing of the status of 123 specific corrective actions directed as the result of the shootdown (Shalikashvili, 1994b). In addition to this list, each service had its own more detailed "to-do lists" to compile and track for compliance (Office of the Chief of Staff, U.S. Air Force, 1994).

When a single tragic incident such as this one is followed by flurries of wide-ranging organizational action fired in shotgun-sprayed blasts such as these, this suggests that either the conditions contributing to the accident were extremely complex or not fully understood, or both. You shoot with a

---

[8] This list of possible component failures matches loosely Charles Perrow's acronym for multiple failures: DEPOSE: design, equipment, procedures, operators, supplies and materials, and environment (Perrow, 1984: 8). Echoing Perrow, these "conventional explanations for accidents"—while obviously important to practitioners—reveal little of interest to social scientists.

shotgun when you're not quite sure of your target's exact location. By chance, some pellets strike home, while many do not, and the target often survives.

In the case of the shootdown, no single cause was identified. Nothing broke and no one was to blame; yet, everything broke and everyone was to blame—hence, the shotgun and not a rifle. After literally hundreds of thousands of man-hours of investigation by countless teams of technical experts, formal accident investigating boards, autonomous Army and Air Force "tiger teams," investigative reporters, individual commands, criminal and defense investigators and lawyers, congressional staffs, committees and subcommittees, as well as an informally organized but highly motivated group of grieving families, no single compelling explanation emerged to fully satisfy our hunger for closure, to make sense of a seemingly senseless tragedy.

After almost two years of investigation with virtually unlimited resources, we still didn't fully understand why twenty-six people had to die. The complete array of investigative and judicial procedures ran their course. In the end, no one was held criminally accountable. Only one investigation went to court-martial and even it resulted in acquittal. No culprit emerged; no bad guy showed himself; no smoking gun was found. Two friendly fighters destroyed two friendly helicopters and we couldn't point to a single broken piece of equipment, ill-designed procedure, grossly incompetent operator, or act of God to explain the tragedy. What remained was an organizational mystery—a frustrating puzzle—hidden in a massive body of disconnected data, painstakingly compiled at great expense, all gathered in separate unsatisfying attempts to explain a tightly bounded sequence of actions that resulted in a tragic outcome. What remained was not only an interesting empirical case, but also a fascinating theoretical puzzle.

Out of the compelling empirical question, "How in the world could this happen?" grew an equally intriguing theoretical challenge: "What were the organizational and behavioral conditions behind this tragedy?" In this book I take a remarkably rich set of empirical data and search for answers to these two questions. By applying what we know about individual and group behavior in complex organizations, I offer a series of explanations at several different levels of analysis; then I step back, take a more holistic approach, and suggest a grounded theory mechanism that cuts across levels and time.

Theoretical Domain: A Normal Accident in a Highly Reliable Organization

This case could fall almost anywhere among a wide variety of literature, from military doctrine to accounts of airline and industrial safety accidents. Friendly fire—casualties unintentionally inflicted on one's own forces—is not a new problem in the history of warfare. However, until recently, little attention has been paid to studying its causes and possible solutions.[9] After it was revealed that a full 24% of all U.S. combat fatalities in the Persian Gulf War were caused by friendly fire, emphasis placed on what was once viewed as merely an unfortunate "professional hazard" increased dramatically.[10] Congress commissioned the Office of Technology Assessment (OTA) to conduct a study to help it make better informed decisions concerning this issue (U.S. Congress Office of Technology Assessment, 1993). However, neither the OTA study nor more historical treatments of amicicide (Shrader, 1982) are deeply grounded in either behavioral or organizational theories. Conversely, other recent military works that do draw from or attempt to build on such theories (Cohen and Gooch, 1990: 3) do not directly address many critical issues that are central to understanding this particular type of failure.

A growing body of literature that often addresses military failures falls under the general heading of "command, control, communications, and intelligence," or C3I (Allard, 1990, 1995). In this literature, organizational tragedies are usually viewed through either technical or political policy lenses. One noteworthy exception is a thought-provoking summary essay by Anthony Oettinger, who has hosted a seminar on such issues at Harvard's Kennedy School of Government for almost fifteen years now. In a piece titled, "Whence and Whither Intelligence, Command and Control? The Certainty of Uncertainty," Oettinger reminds us that "fallible and resolutely imperfect people are part of command and control systems" (Oettinger, 1990: 5). This book follows Oettinger's lead by viewing a tragic example of command and control failure through an explicitly human behavioral lens.

The application of a human factors perspective to reducing accidents in the aviation industry during the mid-1970s spawned a rich applied body of

---

[9] See Charles R. Shrader's *Amicicide: The Problem of Friendly Fire in Modern War* for one of the first and still most detailed historical reviews of friendly fire incidents (1982).

[10] Most people find a 24% causalty rate from friendly fire shocking. Is this good news or bad news? According to the Office of Technology Assessment report, while difficult to measure accurately, historical estimates of friendly fire casualties have ranged from 2 to 20%. The fact remains that 35 out of the 148 U.S. combat casualties in the Persian Gulf War died at the hands of "friends." The percentage is a bit misleading for two reasons. First, the denominator is so low; this is good news! However, because there were so few casualties in total, due to the "near absolute dominance of the battlefield by the U.S.," this means that "only U.S. rounds were flying through the air and if a soldier was going to get hit by anything, it was likely to be from a U.S. weapon" (Office of Technology Assessment, 1993: 2). Second, the numerator and denominator are interdependent. The denominator was so low largely because we engaged the enemy on our own terms as much as possible. Because we had superior technology, this meant that we fired at the bad guys during times of limited visibility and at the maximum effective ranges of our weapons, most of the time before they even knew we were there. While reducing our exposure to enemy fire, this tactic clearly increased the risks of mistakenly engaging friendly forces since most rounds were directed only at images on a radar or thermal screen.

research that now falls under the broad heading of Crew Resource Management (CRM) (Orlady and Foushee, 1986; Wiener, Helmreich, and Kanki, 1993). John K. Lauber, the psychologist who first coined the phrase, defined CRM as "using all available resources—information, equipment, and people—to achieve safe and efficient flight operations" (Lauber, 1984: 20). The military was a late adopter of CRM training. However, by 1990 all three "services seemed to be firmly committed to a new era in coordination training" (Prince and Salas, 1993: 340). While CRM literature draws from the work of cognitive, behavioral, social, and organizational psychologists, its main focus has been on improving intra-crew coordination and performance. As a result, this perspective does offer some insights into the performance of our AWACS crew. For example, Kanki and Palmer offer some fascinating insights into the "trade-offs between standardization and flexibility" (1993: 133)—a tension that plays a central role in the shootdown. For the most part however, CRM research has paid little explicit attention to inter-crew and organizational phenomena such as those operating at the heart of this accident.[11]

While military doctrine, historical, C3I, and CRM literature each have something to say about this accident, my background is in organizational behavior, hence I draw most of my insights from the behavioral and organizational sciences. Within this general domain, an interesting debate has developed between two apparently opposing camps in the accident literature. On the one side, proponents of normal accident theory (Perrow, 1984; Sagan, 1994) study dramatic failures and emphasize the inevitability of accidents in systems characterized by high complexity and tight coupling. Disciples of this perspective often end up suggesting that perhaps some attempts at organizing high-risk technologies may not be worth the risk. On the other side, high reliability theorists (Roberts, 1989, 1990; 1993; LaPorte, Roberts, and Rochlin, 1989; LaPorte and Consolini, 1991; Weick, 1987; Weick and Roberts, 1993, Weick, 1993b) study unusually successful complex organizations in search of clues to help us better manage them. While both sides admit that failure is unavoidable, one sees the cup as half empty, while the other sees it as half full.

In his book *The Limits of Safety* (1994), Sagan runs a horse race between these two theoretical perspectives. To do this, he lines them up "in a kind of comparative test to determine which provides better insights into the history of U.S. nuclear weapons safety" (Sagan, 1994: 8). In the end, Sagan con-

---

[11] A noteworthy exception to this primarily individual-technical and intra-group approach to safety is James Reason's recent book titled *Managing the Risks of Organizational Accidents* (1997). Drawing primarily from a human factors background, Reason makes the leap up a few levels of analysis and "tries to identify general principles and tools that are applicable to all organizations facing dangers of one sort or another" (1997: xviii). Aimed at practitioners, this book tries to improve the "resistance of complex, well defended systems to rare, but usually catastrophic, 'organizational accidents'" (Reason, 1997: xvii).

cludes that while the "high reliability perspective did lead to a number of useful insights into the problem of nuclear weapons command and control, the historical evidence provides much stronger support for the ideas developed by Charles Perrow in *Normal Accidents*" (Sagan, 1994: 252). In her review of Sagan's work, Rousseau comments on the nature of this debate: "Since each acknowledges the catastrophic potential for failure, what they disagree on is whether the risks are worth it. Such a question is not amenable to scientific test. These so-called competing perspectives are the proverbial 'straw man'" (1996: 201). My experience studying the shootdown largely supports Rousseau's conclusion. It also revealed the value of embracing both approaches rather than adopting one over the other.

The story of Operation Provide Comfort is one of a *normal accident* in a *highly reliable organization*. Combining the two perspectives helped me account for both the long initial period of safe operation as well as the inevitable failure. For over three years, organizational practices and procedures consistent with those uncovered by high-reliability theorists kept Task Force Provide Comfort free from failure. Similarly, conditions described by normal accident theorists ultimately brought down the Black Hawks. Throughout the book, I draw on concepts from both camps to help resolve the apparent contradiction of a normal accident in a highly reliable organization. After all, part of what makes this tragedy so compelling—so disturbing to practitioners and so puzzling to scientists—is the juxtaposition of the shootdown against 50,000 hours of safe flight operations. Had the accident occurred in the heat of battle against a backdrop of 24% friendly fire casualties, while the loss of life would have been no less tragic, such a failure would not have generated the same levels of outrage or bewilderment. When airliners crash they grab our attention not only because of the loss of life, but also because civil aviation accidents are rare; they too are normal accidents in highly reliable organizations. Similarly, when the F-15s shot down the Black Hawks, it grabbed our attention not only because it was a tragedy, but also because the shootdown was an extremely rare event; it was a normal accident in a highly reliable organization.

Another accident that grabbed our attention was the space shuttle *Challenger* disaster. Once gain, by all accounts, NASA was a highly reliable organization. However, as Vaughan emphasizes, "We learn that harmful outcomes can occur in organizations constructed to prevent them, as NASA was . . ." (1996: XV). In the final chapter of her book *The Challenger Launch Decision*, Vaughan examines the *Inevitability of Mistake*, and concludes that "the *Challenger* disaster can justifiably be classed as a normal accident" (Vaughan, 1996: 415), but goes on to emphasize the practical mandate to follow the lessons of high-reliability theorists:

> It goes without saying that managing organizations better can reduce the possibility of mistake leading to mishap and disaster, and that implementing these suggestions

[recommendations uncovered by high-reliability theorists][12] can be beneficial. Every possible avenue should be pursued. However, we should be extremely sensitive to the limitations of known remedies. While good management and organizational design may reduce accidents in certain systems, they can never prevent them. (Vaughan, 1996: 416)

The *Challenger* disaster was also a normal accident in a highly reliable organization. It too is a story that illustrates the value of drawing deeply from both perspectives, of admitting to the inevitability of such tragedies on the one hand, while simultaneously doing everything possible to prevent them on the other.

Acknowledging the value of both schools of thought, I start by following Perrow's lead and take a decidedly systems-oriented approach to the shootdown. Clearly, interactively complex and tightly coupled systems are prone to failure, often in a big way. However, while Perrow's theory would emphasize how the shootdown is *normal*—"not in the sense of being frequent or expected"—but, rather, "in the sense that it is an inherent property of the system to occasionally experience this interaction" (1984: 8), my emphasis and conclusions are slightly different.

While I agree that the cause of normal accidents is found in the nature of the system itself, unlike Perrow, my goal is to better understand the organizational and behavioral dynamics of such systems so as to better design and manage them in an attempt to increase reliability and reduce the likelihood of failure. Accidents may be an "inherent property of the system," but as both a scientist and a practitioner, I am less willing to throw up my hands and wait for the next one. While Perrow's emphasis was on complex technologies and demonstrating the inevitability of such accidents, mine is on uncovering their underlying behavioral and organizational dynamics—on using the case of a dramatic organizational failure as a unique window through which to view more fundamental organizational issues. In this way, my motivations are consistent with those who study high-reliability organizations.

Personal motivations aside, the shootdown itself is largely the story of a normal accident. Perrow classified the organizational world according to complexity and coupling. He even mapped various organizations into four quadrants along these two dimensions. For example, according to Perrow, *military adventures* are both loosely coupled and interactively complex, while *aircraft* and *military early warning systems* are both tightly coupled

---

[12] Vaughan summarizes the following list of high-reliability recommendations: "Safety as the priority objective of organizational elites; effective trial-and-error learning from accidents; redundancy built into both organization and technology to enhance safety; decentralized decision making that enables quick, flexible responses to field-level surprises; and a 'culture of reliability,' built on a military model of intense discipline and training, that maximizes uniform and appropriate responses by those closest to the risky technology" (1996: 416).

and complex (1984: 97). Such a general map of the organizational terrain is useful both as a starting point for future studies and to illustrate the empirical application of the concepts underlying his theory. However, like any model, this matrix is incomplete and can be misleading. For example, our shootdown case involves *early warning systems* for *aircraft* in *military adventures*. According to Perrow's map, this could place our organization in either one of two quadrants. As a result, the very shortcomings of Perrow's matrix highlighted a promising starting point for analyzing this case. While his map offered valuable insights into potentially important system variables and locations of various organizational activities, what it didn't do was capture the dynamic nature of such systems over time or accurately locate an organization such as OPC that contains various aspects of systems that fall into different quadrants. Rather than adding to a static comparative map of many organizations, I built on Perrow's basic insights and analyzed one particularly complex accident in detail, across time, and across levels of analysis. What I found was largely normal people, behaving in normal ways, in a normal organization. Normal, not only in the sense that the accident was an "inherent property of the system," but also in the sense that individual, group, and organizational behaviors central to the shootdown could be explained using generally accepted theories of behavior in complex organizations.

In sum, while Task Force Provide Comfort was a highly reliable organization for over three years, my analysis of the shootdown itself falls within the general domain of normal accidents as established by Perrow—organizational failures that cannot be accounted for by locating a single identifiable precipitating cause. Accidents can occur from the unanticipated interaction of non-failing components. Independently benign factors at multiple levels of analysis interact in unanticipated ways over time, often leading to tragedy. The origins of this accident cannot be traced to any single component failure. By applying what we know about how humans behave in complex organizations, this book attempts to explain how a normal accident occurred in a highly reliable organization.

Data: We Know Exactly "What" Happened

Evidence for this case study comes from a wide range of sources. These sources include official government documents, archival records, interviews, physical artifacts, gun target footage, videotapes, audio tapes, training records, maintenance records, technical reports, trial transcripts, AWACS data tapes, internal Department of Defense (DOD) memoranda, press releases, newspaper clippings, congressional hearings, criminal investigations, conference briefings, flight records, mishap reports, personnel records, military flight plans, oil analyses, medical evaluations, psychological evaluations, human factors reports, optics reports, crash site analyses, equipment teardowns, weather observations, accident site photographs, witness statements, regulations, directives, maps, communications logs, intelligence briefings, task force airspace control orders, pre-mission briefs, flight logs, lists of corrective actions taken, and DOD fact sheets.

The actual shootdown was a very brief event. Only eight minutes elapsed from the time that the F-15 flight lead reported initial radar contact until the time he reported, "Splash 2 Hinds," Within hours, a team of over thirty technical experts—from flight surgeons to F-15 maintenance technicians, from AWACS data analysts to UH-60 avionics specialists—assembled in Turkey to conduct the investigation. A twenty-seven volume *Report of Aircraft Accident Investigation Board* is the primary document detailing the results of this month-long intensive inquiry (Andrus, 1994).[13]

In addition to this basic document, which contains most of the raw data listed above, I collected dozens of internal DOD memoranda concerning the shootdown and its subsequent investigation (e.g., Bliss, 1994; Hall, 1994; Maddox, 1994; Moorman, 1994; Oaks, 1994; Office of the Joint Chiefs of Staff, 1994; Perry, 1994). These letters include executive summaries, analyses of investigations, lessons learned, directives, and conclusions pertaining to the accident.

Additionally, separate service investigations were conducted to examine possible systemic issues relating to the shootdown. For example, the Air Force conducted a multi-command review of the specified and implied deficiencies in training programs. This effort alone involved "over 120 people and 30,000 + man-hours in six Air Force major commands and Headquarters" (U.S. Air Force, 1994: i).

In addition to organizational documents and archival data aimed primarily at determining the cause of the accident for safety reasons, an entirely separate set of data was generated as the result of numerous criminal investigations conducted to establish accountability for the tragedy. A complete series of "investigating officer reports" conducted in accordance with Article 32 of the Uniform Code of Military Justice (UCMJ) provides an entirely different perspective on the accident (Altshwager, 1995; Boykin, 1994a, 1994b; Starr,

---

[13] A portion of the investigation uncovered information that remains classified. Most of this information pertained either to specific capabilities of weapons systems or current operational details—such as the formal rules of engagement. While I personally have the necessary security clearance to gain access to this material, I decided not to take advantage of the opportunity at this point. Final publications have to be unclassified and I did not want to inadvertently prejudice myself with knowledge of information that may creep into my writing. I have been assured by several key informants that the information contained in these classified volumes adds little substance to an understanding of the case. As a final check, after I have completed this book, I will attempt to gain access to this classified data, to confirm for myself that it had no bearing on my findings or conclusions.

1994). As a result of these investigations, only one individual was brought to trial—U.S. Air Force Captain Jim Wang, the Senior Director in the AWACS. The *Record of Trial of Captain Wang's General Court Martial* is a detailed transcript of a twenty-day criminal trial that contains over 2,600 pages of sworn testimony in addition to another 40 volumes of exhibits (Headquarters, 8th Air Force, 1995).

The accident investigation combined with court-martial transcripts provides a remarkably rich set of triangulated data all converging on an eight-minute event. These multiple sources of evidence meet all four types of Patton's (1987) criteria for triangulation when collecting data for case studies: (1) multiple sources, (2) different evaluators/investigators, (3) multiple perspectives on the same data set, and (4) methodological triangulation.

The natural adversarial relationship of a trial presents a unique and powerful method of triangulation. Both prosecution and defense examine the same set of data from diametrically opposing perspectives, constantly challenging each other's sources, interpretations, and arguments. When this transcript was compared to the accident report, lines of inquiry converged. Each source has an explicit perspective for presenting the data in a particular light. Knowing what motivated these different angles shed even more light on my final understanding of the event.

Not only did I analyze converging triangulated secondary reports, but I also gained access to some valuable original multimedia data that brought the accident to life in a way that written words and transcripts could not. I obtained a copy of the F-15 gun-sight-video footage of the shootdown that includes not only video, but also an audio record of the tragedy from the cockpit of the trail F-15 (May, 1994). I also analyzed a copy of video footage taken by a commercial camcorder inside the AWACS (DOD Joint Combat Camera Center, 1994). This camera was focused on an extra controller console in the AWACS during the shootdown and graphically captured the same radar screen information available to AWACS controllers during the incident. Finally, I consulted two commercially produced videos. One is a production-quality videotape taken by an Iraqi news crew on the scene (Amin, 1994). Remarkably, this footage captured from the ground the entire shootdown in vivid detail. I also reviewed a copy of a special investigative report produced by the ABC news magazine *Prime Time Live* that contains several interviews with key players as well as video footage of the inside layout of the AWACS (Phillips, 1995).

One final source of information about this tragedy rounds out my data set. On 3 August 1995, I attended a special Congressional Hearing conducted by the Military Personnel Subcommittee of the House National Security Committee. The expressed purpose of the hearing was to "examine the causes of the accident and assess the effectiveness of all corrective actions with a view toward preventing similar accidents in the future" (Dornan, 1995: 1). This hearing presented three panels of expert witnesses, including testimony from families of the victims (Curry, 1995). This hearing added a political and emotional dimension to my understanding of the tragedy (Mounsey, 1995). Afterwards, I conducted informal personal interviews with several family members, technical experts, and Captain Wang's defense council.

In sum, we know a great deal about this accident. Unlike many complex organizational failures where much of the challenge lies in reconstructing the event itself, there is little doubt about *what* happened here. Such a clear understanding of "what" frees us up to focus instead on the more interesting question of "why." What follows is a short summary of how I went about trying to get my arms around this mountain of data to answer this question. For a more theoretical explanation of this methodology, see Appendix 1.

Analytical Strategy: Constructing a Causal Map

Unfortunately, there is no well-developed methodology for explaining complex organizational events (Rasmussen, 1990; Yin, 1994: 102). My general logic of inquiry was to start at the end and work backwards—moving ever further away in both time and proximity from the actual accident. I followed a five-step process that began with the proximate causes of the tragedy and ventured ever outward in both physical and analytical directions.

The first step was to anchor my analysis onto as objective a foundation as possible. This involved constructing a detailed timeline across subunits of analysis (see Figure 1.2). I started at the end and worked back, detailing each of the critical events and interactions leading up to the actual tragedy. To construct this timeline, I consulted both primary and secondary sources of data. Time-stamped audio, video, and data tapes offered a great start. To this base, I drew from a series of in-depth interviews of multiple informants from various positions in the event space. This allowed me to confirm both reliability and validity by triangulating multiple accounts across sources. It also helped establish just what information was available to whom, and when—setting the stage for step two.

Next, I constructed a rough causal mapping based on formal organizational explanations. Multiple "practical explanations" had emerged from various inquiries. I mapped these accounts onto organizational and temporal space to establish a preliminary "common sense" version of the shootdown. Step one was pure description: "At approximately 1030, the lead pilot fired an AMRAAM missile at the trail helicopter . . ." Step two recounted institutional explanations at the next level of generality: "The accident resulted from a failure to integrate helicopter operations into OPC flight operations." In step three, I asked, "Why?"

To push beyond crude empirical explanations and flesh out the causal

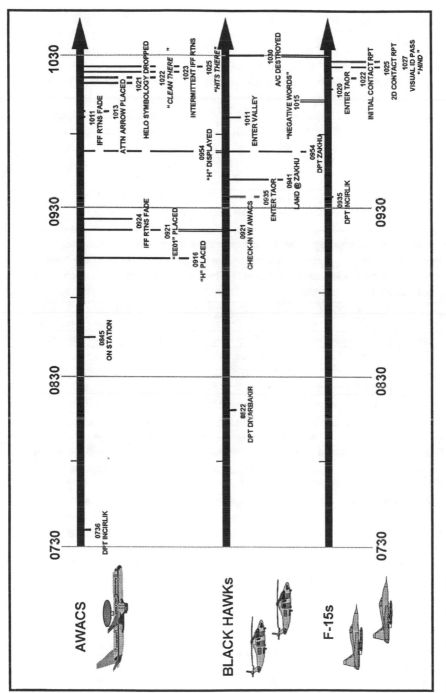

Fig. 1.2. Event Time Line

map, I constantly subjected empirical accounts to the question, "Why?" For example, "Why did the organization fail to integrate helicopter operations into OPC flight operations?" Various answers to this question were again subjected to the "why" test, and so on. With care and repetition, multiple, nested interrogations produced a complex causal web of tentative connections with the shootdown located down in the lower right-hand corner of the map. Leading to this ultimate outcome is an interconnected series of arrows and dotted lines stretching roughly leftward back into time and upward across levels of analysis.[14] My goal at this point was to be exhaustive, to search out all possible interdependencies, to weave a densely woven causal model of the event.

Drawing from a rich set of data, a working knowledge of military organizations, and a broad reading of behavioral science literature, this task involved repeatedly subjecting the causal map to a series of questions aimed at tightening the temporal logic of the diagram. What events could lead to others? What had to logically precede what? Which events could not happen unless something else happened first? What general conditions might contribute to particular events?

As a result of this process, step three not only pushed further away from the incident both temporally and physically, but also conceptually. Hypothesized causal connections began to take shape based on rough open and axial coding of the data.[15] As raw data are broken down and put back together in a systematic way, concepts and categories begin to emerge. Through a process that Strauss and Corbin (1990) label "theoretical sensitivity"[16] and Weick calls "disciplined imagination" (1995: 338), potential conceptual patterns took shape as I grouped emergent concepts into categories. These categories were in turn connected sequentially by both temporal and theoretical links. The analysis conducted in step three resulted in a detailed causal map with tentative links graphically portrayed as an interconnected chain of events across levels of analysis (see Figure 1.3).

Borrowing from sociological literature on narrative explanations (Abbott, 1990; Griffin, 1992, 1993), the next task involved working my way through the temporal map produced in step three—systematically challenging the causal significance of each major fact. To accomplish this, I subjected each critical node in the temporal map to "counterfactual interrogation." Counterfactuals are simply "what if" questions posed by the researcher that conceptually isolate key facts and ask "whether their absence or modification would

---

[14] See Strauss and Corbin (1990: 197–223) for a formal treatment of how to use memos and diagrams to analyze complex qualitative data.

[15] For a detailed description of coding procedures in grounded theory research, see Strauss and Corbin (1990: 57–175).

[16] For a series of techniques designed to "enhance theoretical sensitivity—the ability to see with analytic depth what is there"—see Strauss and Corbin (1990: 75–95).

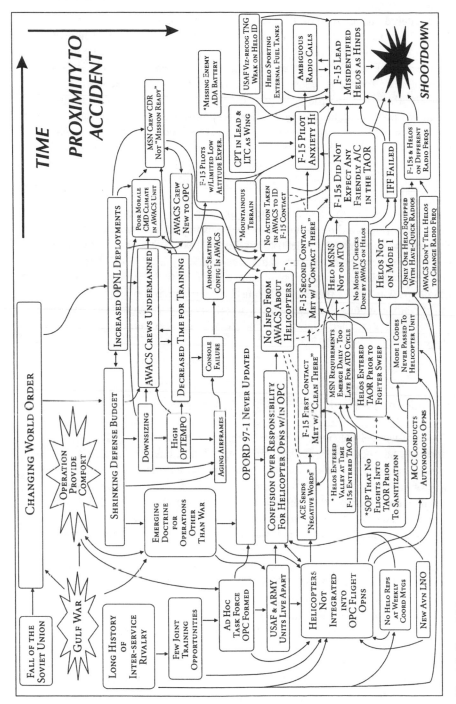

Fig. 1.3. Causal Map

have altered the course of the event as it was recorded" (Griffin, 1993: 1101). For example, a key fact was: "Both F-15s' electronic IFF interrogation of the helicopters failed to indicate a friendly aircraft." An important counterfactual asked: "What if one pilot's IFF received a 'sweet' green [identified as friend] response upon interrogation of the helicopters?" Fortunately, these are just the type of questions asked of major players during extensive post-accident interviews. The response to this question was, "The intercept would have been aborted." As a result, I concluded that the failure of both IFF systems to identify the helicopters as friendly was "essential to the historical configuration as it actually happened and a significant historical cause of what followed" (Griffin, 1993: 1101; Weber, 1949: 166, 171, 180).

After subjecting the tentative causal map to counterfactual interrogation, the final step in building grounded theory was to pick a core category—what Strauss and Corbin call "selective coding" (1990:116)—and systematically relate it to all other categories. This was primarily a process of integration and demanded the formulation of and commitment to a single story line. Finally, it was only a matter of closing the loop and grounding it by validating the story against the data. As I worked my way through these five steps in search of grounded theory, an outline for the book emerged out of the story itself.

Outline of the Book: An Explanation Across Levels

I have organized the book into seven chapters. While I offered a brief summary of the shootdown at the beginning of this one, the detailed case is found in chapter 2: "The Shootdown: A Thin Description." A basic assumption of my analysis is that we cannot fully understand complex organizational events such as this shootdown by treating them as isolated events. Before attempting to explain anything, I wanted to provide enough background so that subsequent analyses made sense—not as isolated explanations, but rather as interrelated accounts embedded in the complex realities of the real world, with a real history. Chapter 2 then is all about description—a story of *what* happened. It sets the scene for the remainder of the book which is devoted to the question *why*.

I preface the four analytical chapters with a brief section introduction: "Multiple Explanations—A Walk Through the Causal Map." Many experts invested a great deal of time and effort to investigate this highly visible tragedy. "Multiple Explanations" reviews these official findings as a natural starting point for my inquiry. After all formal investigations were completed by each of the services and the Accident Investigation Board submitted its report, Secretary of Defense William Perry summarized the accident in four short bullets. According to Perry, the shootdown was caused by:

- F-15 pilot misidentification,
- AWACS crew inaction,
- Task Force non-integration of Eagle Flight, and
- an IFF system failure. (Perry, 1994)

I use Perry's summary to organize my own findings. Each of his four bullets identifies an actor at a conceptually different level of analysis. Each of my analytical chapters explores the shootdown from a different level of analysis.[17]

Starting close to the actual shootdown, chapter 3 addresses the question: Why did the F-15 pilots misidentify the Black Hawks? Here the dependent variable is individual action. How in the world could highly trained American pilots, operating under the control of an AWACS, armed with the best training and most sophisticated equipment in the world, flying in clear skies under relatively benign conditions, mistake a dark green forest camouflaged friendly Black Hawk helicopter with six American flags painted on it for a light tan and brown desert camouflaged Iraqi Hind? Under the broad conceptual umbrella of sensemaking (Weick, 1995), I explain why the pilots saw what they saw, given their strong set of expectations when confronted with an ambiguous stimulus.

Moving further away from the accident and shifting up one level of analysis from individuals to groups, chapter 4 explains why the AWACS crew didn't intervene in the shootdown. Consistent with my premise that context is important, I apply what we know about how groups perform in complex organizations to examine AWACS crew behavior. The dependent variable is group inaction. Our fateful crew suffered from a weak launch and never had a chance to develop into a real team. As a result, when faced with an unfortunate turn of events, critical responsibilities were too diffuse to trigger decisive action. Hence, AWACS crew members did not effectively monitor Eagle Flight and they did not intervene in the F-15's engagement.

Just as a group level phenomenon contributed to the F-15 pilots' misidentification, an organizational factor—helicopter non-integration—contributed to both AWACS crew inaction and F-15 pilot misidentification. The fact that helicopter missions were not well integrated into Task Force flight opera-

---

[17] While Perry identified four bullets, I organize the book around the first three. Clearly the IFF system failed. However, only part of this system failure was technical. Even after extensive equipment teardowns and simulations, to this day the reason that Mode IV of this system failed remains "unexplained"—a technical anomaly. All post-accident information indicates that critical IFF components were operational and Mode IV interrogation should have worked. However, all systems failures are not necessarily caused by technical shortcomings. As a result, human and organizational aspects of the IFF system are addressed throughout each of the three chapters as they influence action at each level of analysis.

tions contributed to the AWACS crew's failure to monitor them and also to the F-15 pilots' misidentifying them. Chapter 5 explores the causes and implications of Eagle Flight's non-integration within the Task Force under the broad framework of differentiation and integration as conceptualized by Lawrence and Lorsch (1967). Given a long history of separate services and highly differentiated tasks, multiple coordinating mechanisms failed to adequately integrate Army Eagle Flight into OPC flight operations. Thompson identifies three types of interdependence and their respective coordinating mechanisms (1967). I use his typology to explain three critical coordination failures in Task Force Provide Comfort. Eagle Flight flying inside the TAOR while squawking the wrong Mode I is explained as a failure to coordinate by standardization. The fact that the F-15 pilots were unaware of the helicopters' presence in the area is explained as a failure to coordinate by plan. Finally, aircraft equipped with incompatible radios and a local policy of "min comm" (minimum communications) hindered attempts to coordinate by mutual adjustment.

Chapters 3, 4, and 5 each explain a separate piece of the puzzle, each at a different level of analysis. Individuals erred; groups floundered; and organizations failed. In contrast, chapter 6 takes a holistic view of the shootdown and presents a cross-level theory of "practical drift" to account for the tragedy. Instead of focusing on the actions or inactions of various players, this chapter points the finger at a seductive mechanism to help explain the shootdown—not as an isolated incident, but rather as a process.[18] Practical drift is the slow steady uncoupling of local practice from written procedure. It is this structural tendency for subunits to drift away from globally synchronized rule-based logics of action toward locally determined task-based procedures that places complex organizations at risk. Practical drift explains the shootdown as a manifestation of a broader organizational dynamic.

Chapter 7 first summarizes some of the lessons learned at individual, group, and organizational levels of analysis. I then extend the nautical metaphor introduced in chapter 6 by suggesting that "practical drift" and "practical sailing" are two sides of the same coin. What appears to be dangerous "drift" from a global perspective, often looks more like adaptive "sailing" from the local perspective of multiple subunits. After a brief discussion on causality, I emphasize the benefits of approaching such complex events from a probabilistic perspective—one that emphasizes the importance of looking across levels of analysis and time—not in search of *the cause*, but rather in search of a broader set of conditions that increases the likelihood of such tragedies occurring. I conclude by exploring some of the practical and theo-

---

[18] For a provocative treatment of the potential power of mechanisms in the social sciences, see Jon Elster's book, *Nuts and Bolts*, in which he argues that "progress in the social sciences consists in knowledge of ever-more mechanisms rather than ever-better theories" (1989: 173).

retical implications raised by this work and calling for the construction of a library of thick descriptions—a collection of detailed case studies of traumatic organizational failures designed to address the broader question: What are the critical design features of a hyper-complex, multilevel, multi-task, organizational system that increase the likelihood of accomplishing the "total task" consistently?

Hannan and Freeman argue that "the distinctive competence of organizations lies in their capacity to generate collective actions with relatively small variance in quality. . . . The modern world favors collective actors that can demonstrate or at least reasonably claim a capacity for reliable performance and can account rationally for their actions" (1989: 73–74). Since a distinctive advantage of organizations is their predictability and accountability, when they fail in either or both of these competencies, such incidents grab our attention.

Organizational tragedies like friendly fire fall squarely into this category. The accidental shootdown of two helicopters by friendly F-15s is a dramatic example of an organization's failure to perform in a predictable, reliable fashion. Ensuing investigations also failed to adequately account for such a failure. A detailed analysis of this single, complex, and compelling case not only reveals practical, methodological, and theoretical insights into our understanding of such organizational tragedies, but it also opens a unique window into the everyday life of organizations.

2

The Shootdown: A Thin Description

I WANT to draw the reader into a world increasingly unfamiliar to most of us, one inhabited by professional warriors. I want to invite you into the strange world of Operation Provide Comfort (OPC), a world in which tigers devour eagles while cougars, dukes, and mad dogs look on.

What follows is primarily description—my own construction "of other people's constructions of what they and their compatriots are up to" (Geertz, 1973: 9). Descriptions come in all shapes and sizes—some are thin, while others are quite thick. I have done my best to separate the thick from the thin by first constructing the skeleton upon which I plan to grow a body of theory. Therefore, this chapter is meant to be skin and bones, to provide the objective scaffolding upon which to hang increasingly thicker, more sophisticated descriptions. Eventually, descriptions will blur into explanations as narration gives way to analysis. Increasingly, the emphasis will shift from what happened, to how it happened, and eventually to suggesting a theory for why. However, for the moment I want to tell a story. This is the story of *what* happened in the skies over northern Iraq on 14 April 1994. This is the story of *how* 26 people died. This is a story that begs us to ask *why*.

Background: Context Is Important

A recurrent theme throughout this study is that we cannot fully understand the shootdown by treating it as an isolated incident or as a string of disconnected events. Context is important. History is important. The actual shootdown lasted only a few minutes; but the trail of experience culminating in this tragedy is long and diffuse. People act in context. Organizations have histories. Therefore, the shootdown must be viewed as it occurred, embedded within a dynamic, complex social milieu. Such a perspective requires a multidimensional description that ranges both across levels of analysis and across time.

To set the stage, I'll briefly review U.S. military involvement in the Persian Gulf from the late 1970s through the shootdown in 1991. Then I will sketch out the origins of Operation Provide Comfort and the general organizational structure of the task force designed to implement it.

A Growing Storm in the Desert[1]

The scene is southwest Asia and we'll join the story in 1979. Our geopolitical curtain rises just as the U.S.-backed Shah of Iran is ousted. Enter the Ayatollah Khomeini followed by the Soviet invasion of Afghanistan. The Ayatollah wanted to punish the Great Satan and the Soviets were heading south toward a warm water port—two potential threats to the world's supply of oil. However, in 1980 Saddam Hussein's surprise attack into Iran and the fierce resistance put up by the Mujahadeen in Afghanistan distracted Khomeini and stymied the Soviets. Kuwait supported Baghdad during Iraq's eight-year war with Iran and paid the price by suffering Iranian attacks on her tankers in the Gulf. The United States responded by providing Kuwaiti ships with limited reflagging and escort service. In 1988, Iran and Iraq ended their war in a draw; the Berlin Wall came down; and the balance of power in the Gulf shifted toward Saddam Hussein, setting the stage for his next adventure.

Just after midnight on 2 August 1990, Iraq invaded Kuwait. Nearly 1,000 Iraqi tanks roared down from the north and west. Simultaneously, special forces units assaulted Kuwait City from the air as seaborne commandos cut off escape routes to the south. It took Iraq less than two days to completely conquer Kuwait. When the dust settled, Saddam's formidable Republican Guard reappeared poised menacingly along Kuwait's western and southern borders facing Saudi Arabia.

U.S. response was swift. Operation Desert Shield began on 7 August 1990. Responding to a Saudi request for assistance, the United States rapidly deployed naval, air, and ground forces to "draw a line in the sand"—to "shield" Saudi Arabia from any further aggression on the part of Iraq. Saddam blinked. World condemnation of the invasion grew and six months of unprecedented multinational mobilization and military buildup followed. The United Nations Security Council set 15 January 1991 as the deadline for Iraq to withdraw its invasion force from Kuwait. The fifteenth came and went; the stage was set for the next act to open with a bang.

At precisely 2:38 A.M. on 17 January, Chief Warrant Officer Tom "Tip" O'Neal of the United States Army fired the first shot of the Desert Storm air war from his Apache helicopter. Coalition air forces quickly achieved air superiority, softened hardened military targets, and systematically destroyed Baghdad's centralized command and control structure. After forty days of aerial bombardment, on 24 February 1991 coalition forces launched the deci-

---

[1] Most of the facts contained in the following summary of the U.S. military's involvement in the Persian Gulf are based on *Certain Victory: The U.S. Army in the Gulf War* (1994). This source was researched and written under the direction of Brigadier General Robert H. Scales by a diverse group of eight Army officers—mostly veterans of the Gulf War.

sive ground phase of the campaign. In less than two weeks, Iraq accepted United Nations conditions and resolutions formally ending the Gulf War on 7 April 1991. The much heralded (at least by the Iraqis) "mother of all battles" was over; however, U.S. military involvement was not. Overnight, the scene shifted from desert battlefields in the south to rugged mountains in the north, as the mission shifted from combat to humanitarian assistance.[2]

Operation Provide Comfort (OPC)

In the confusion immediately following hostilities, Baghdad faced two significant internal threats. In the south, Shiites rebelled against Saddam's Baathist supporters. In the north, the Kurds fought for and briefly gained control of several key cities. Saddam's response was swift and brutal. Neither the lightly armed Shiite rebels nor the Kurdish guerrillas could stand up to the reorganized remnants of Saddam's elite Republican Guard. In the south, American soldiers watched helplessly as Iraqi artillery and gunships slaughtered thousands of Shiites just across the military demarcation line. In the north, "the Iraqi army pushed these people [Kurds] like cattle, packing them against the Turkish border" (Scales, 1994: 340). Out of the 500,000 Kurds forced to leave their homes, an estimated 2,000 refugees died each day from a combination of Iraqi guns and the harsh mountain conditions.[3] Clearly, something had to be done.

Once again, the world community reacted. The United Nations passed resolution 688 condemning Iraqi atrocities and formally establishing a security zone along Iraq's northern border with Turkey (see map in Figure 1.1). The United Nations High Commission for Refugees (UNHCR) helped organize the humanitarian efforts of more than sixty relief agencies from over a dozen nations. On 7 April 1991, the U.S. launched Operation Provide Comfort to ensure the security of relief workers and provide a safe haven for the resettlement of Kurdish refugees. The formal mission statement for OPC read: "[To] Deter Iraqi behavior that may upset peace and order to northern Iraq. On order, respond with sufficient force to protect nation's interests should deterrence fail" (Andrus, 1994: Tab AA).[4]

---

[2] This case deals primarily with operations in northern Iraq (Operation Provide Comfort), but a parallel humanitarian effort also took place in the south (Operation Southern Watch).

[3] In one river valley near Pirinclik, over 20,000 Kurds were packed between two mountains. U.S. special forces soldiers described the scene as a "woodstock without music; the valley was almost too crowded to walk without stepping on someone. Dead animals, garbage, and human waste had turned the ground into a quagmire, fueling outbreaks of dysentery and cholera" (Scales, 1994: 343).

[4] A more detailed mission statement was contained in the original Operations Plan for Combined Task Force (CTF) Provide Comfort, OPLAN 91–7 RESIDUAL FORCES:

Residual forces serve as a symbol of coalition resolve and as a deterrent to Iraqi military

Combined Task Force (CTF) Provide Comfort

From a dead start, an ad hoc task force was organized to coordinate and execute military support for the relief effort in northern Iraq. U.S. Army Lieutenant General Shalikashvili assumed command of Combined Task Force Provide Comfort on 18 April 1991. This was truly a "combined" and "joint" effort. It was combined in the sense that it consisted of a multinational coalition of U.S., British, French, and Turkish forces. And it was joint because the task force was staffed by soldiers, sailors, airmen, and marines from all three military services.

To meet the immediate demands on the ground, "Shali" organized his CTF around two Joint Task Forces (JTFs). JTF Alpha consisted primarily of three battalions of American Special Forces soldiers who were tasked to assist civilian relief agencies in dispensing humanitarian aid to the refugees. JTF Bravo included more combat power. It was originally built around the U.S. 24th Marine Expeditionary Unit (MEU) which came with its own organic service support, aviation squadron, and battalion landing team. Within days, the MEU was augmented by Dutch and Royal marines, as well as miscellaneous combat units from six other countries. With the combined firepower of an army division, JTF Bravo boldly entered northern Iraq. Through negotiation, a show of force, and dogged persistence, they carved out a security zone approximately 160 by 70 kilometers in size. By mid-May 1991, under coalition protection, most of the Kurdish refugees felt safe enough to climb down from the mountains and return home.

In addition to operations on the ground, a major portion of CTF Provide Comfort's mission was to occupy the airspace over northern Iraq. To accomplish this task, a "no fly zone" was established that included all airspace within Iraq north of the 36th parallel. Fighters from U.S., Turkish, British, and French air units patrolled the no fly zone daily to prevent Iraqi warplanes from threatening relief efforts.

By September of 1991, immediate humanitarian and security goals had been met, allowing most CTF ground forces to redeploy. The Combined Forces Ground Component headquarters at Silopi, Turkey, was deactivated and replaced by a much leaner Military Coordination Center (MCC). Figure 2.1 illustrates the organization of CTF Combined Comfort as it operated from September of 1991 through the shootdown in April of 1994.

---

encroachment into the security zone in northern Iraq. Maintain an air presence above the 36 N. parallel as provided by the daily Air Tasking Order. Be prepared to conduct air combat operations over northern Iraq as directed. Be prepared to conduct search and rescue operations and non-combatant evacuation operations of United Nations, nongovernmental organization (NGO) and/or private volunteer organization (PVO) personnel present in the current security zone. On order, conduct limited forced entry operations into northern Iraq to facilitate entry of follow-on-forces. (Andrus, 1994: Tab AA)

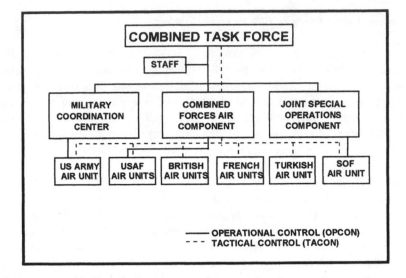

Fig. 2.1. CTF Provide Comfort Organizational Chart

The CTF Commander, a U.S. General Officer, was technically a "co-commander" with a Turkish counterpart. Assisted by his primary staff, he commanded essentially three operational components. The Joint Special Operations Component (JSOC) originally coordinated the activities of special forces units during the relief effort. After September of 1991, JSOC's primary responsibility was to conduct search and rescue operations should any coalition aircraft go down inside Iraq. The Combined Forces Air Component (CFAC) was tasked with exercising tactical control of OPC aircraft operating in the Tactical Area of Responsibility (TAOR).[5] All CTF components, with the exception of those assigned to the Military Coordination Center, lived and operated out of Incirlik Air Base in Turkey. The Military Coordination Center (MCC) worked the ground. In the words of a former MCC U.S. co-commander:

> What it [the MCC mission] all boils down to is to, as we say, see and be seen. Now, there's quite a long mission paragraph that describes that for you. It talks about maintaining contact with regional and local authorities and humanitarian assistance organizations, etcetera, etcetera. But what the MCC is about is to be the physical evidence of coalition commitment to the enforcement of Security Council

[5] Tactical control (TACON) implies a fairly limited scope of authority and involves the detailed and usually local direction and control of movement and maneuvers necessary to accomplish the assigned mission. Operational control (OPCON) implies a broader authority to command subordinate forces, assign tasks, designate objectives and give authoritative direction necessary to accomplish the mission (Office of the Assistant Secretary of Defense for Public Affairs, 1994).

resolutions and cease-fire agreements in northern Iraq, and our job there is see and be seen. (Andrus, 1994: Tab V-100)

To carry out its mission, the MCC operated out of two locations. Their forward headquarters was located in the small village of Zakhu, just inside Iraq. Approximately twenty people worked in Zakhu to include operations, communications, and security personnel, medics, translators, and coalition chiefs. Zakhu operations were supported by a small administrative contingent working out of Pirinclik Air Base, Turkey. Pirinclik is also where the Eagle Flight Platoon of UH-60 Black Hawks was located. The MCC had operational control of Eagle Flight personnel tasked with providing general aviation support to the CTF.

This brief review of U.S. military involvement in the Persian Gulf, along with sketches of Operation Provide Comfort and the task force designed to accomplish it, describes the broad background within which the shootdown took place. However, before describing the incident in detail, or even introducing the central players involved, one critical piece of context is still missing. History and organizational structure are important; but we cannot fully understand the specific untoward actions of a few organizational members without first examining the system of formal mechanisms put in place to communicate and coordinate such action. In military organizations, this topic falls under the general rubric of command and control.

Command and Control: Dense Webs of Crosscutting Guidance

Current U.S. military doctrine identifies four generic processes that must be effectively integrated by senior leaders for successful mission accomplishment: command, control, management, and leadership. Management focuses on resources—planning, organizing, and budgeting to meet unit goals. Leadership emphasizes the exercise of interpersonal influence and motivation to accomplish the mission. While the concepts of management and leadership are useful, for our purposes, the functions of command and control take center stage. According to U.S. Army doctrine, command is "the primary means whereby the vision is imparted to the organization" (U.S. Army, 1987: 41). The command process focuses on communicating intent and providing direction. Control, on the other hand, is a "process used to establish limits and provide structure. Its purpose is to deal with the uncertainties inherent in organizational operations" (U.S. Army, 1987: 41–42). The Army's field manual on *Leadership and Command at Senior Levels* adds the following cautionary note:

> When command is of low quality, control can be overused, creating more tension, centralization of power, and confusion than it reduces. Because it is seen as a way

to reduce risk, its use becomes routine. The control process is characterized by: high-volume, routine communications; coordination activities between elements internal and external to a unit having related responsibilities; structure, which limits uncertainty; and an emphasis on efficiency as a goal. . . . As a process, its effect is to serve primarily as a compensating, correcting device for command. (U.S. Army, 1987: 42)

The twin concepts of command and control and those systems designed to execute these functions structure the formal flow of communication and coordination in complex military organizations. To fully understand any behavior of interest in a military organization—whether it is heroism or friendly fire—we have to first understand how such action is influenced by complex systems of command and control.[6]

Command

The authoritative joint reference of military terms defines command as "the authority vested in an individual of the armed forces for the direction, coordination, and control of military forces" (U.S. Joint Chiefs of Staff, 1986: 74). Unity of command is a fundamental principle of war. In theory, from the lowest private to the Commander in Chief, there exists an unbroken "chain" of command. You can walk into any unit in the military and find a wall in the headquarters building upon which hangs a long line of pictures depicting the entire chain of command—from the local commander all the way through to the President.

Soldiers are constantly tested on knowledge of their chain of command. One of the first lessons drilled into new recruits in basic training is that someone is always in charge. A favorite teaching opportunity for drill instructors is to catch a small group of basic trainees, all privates, off duty, walking to the post exchange for a soda and ask them who is in charge of their group. The appropriate response is for one of the recruits to sound off immediately with his name and rank declaring that he is indeed "in charge"

---

[6] Colonel Kenneth Allard of the National War College emphasizes the directly opposing assumptions about human nature upon which the twin concepts of command and control are based in his insightful book, *Command, Control, and the Common Defense*. Citing an Army doctrinal publication on command and control (U.S. Army, 1985: 3–1, 3–2), Allard conceptualizes command as a "'directive process' for infusing the 'will and intent of the commander' among his subordinates . . . the premise of command rests upon the assumption of 'reliable subordinate behavior.' Control, however, is an entirely different matter: 'Control is a process by which subordinate behavior inconsistent with the will and intent of the commander is identified and corrected. This process is regulatory: its premise is unreliable subordinate behavior. Unreliable behavior in this context . . . will normally be inadvertent, resulting from different perspectives of the battlefield, inattention, and a lack of understanding of the mission or the commander's intent—or the fog of battle'" (Allard, 1990: 185).

of the group by virtue of the first letter of his last name. Given that all members of this group are the same rank, command responsibility is dictated by alphabetical order according to last name. Someone is always in charge; someone is always responsible; and knowing who that is at all times is of utmost importance. Commanders are responsible for everything their units do or fail to do. These are fundamental principles of command and control in the military. Therefore, to fully understand the actions of critical players in this tragedy, we have to first describe the formal command structure within which these behaviors were embedded.

The military operates under a traditional hierarchical command and control structure. Not only are all individual service members assigned a formal and very visible rank that automatically places them at a specific level within a hierarchical pecking order, but units also occupy well-defined niches within the larger organizational pyramid. Just as authority is vested in individuals by virtue of their rank, command authority is dictated by organizational relationships. Privates are subordinate to sergeants, who are subordinate to captains, just as squads are subordinate to platoons, who are subordinate to companies, and so on. Task forces are designed by taking basic unit building blocks and assembling them along hierarchical lines consistent with the demands of the mission and time-honored military traditions of command and control. The combined task force designed to implement Operation Provide Comfort was no different.

CTF Provide Comfort was originally commanded by a three-star Army General. However, since most of the ground forces were withdrawn by the fall of 1991, the mission became primarily an air operation and command eventually fell to a one-star Air Force General. His chain of command ran directly through the Commander in Chief of Europe (CINCEUR), through the Chairman of the Joint Chiefs of Staff,[7] and on to the President (Andrus, 1994: Tab V-033). The fact that this was a CTF—a *Combined* Task Force—threw in an additional wrinkle. Technically, the American one-star was a "co-commander"; he shared command authority with his Turkish counterpart.

Working down from the top, the organizational chart in Figure 2.1 depicts the general command structure of OPC on the day of the shootdown. The task force commander exercised his command responsibilities through his staff, three subordinate commanders, and a complex series of coordinating mechanisms. His staff was structured along traditional doctrinal lines. Under

---

[7] The Chairman of the Joint Chiefs of Staff is not in the legal chain of command; he is the President's principal military advisor. However, the President and the Secretary of Defense work "through" him to command his CINCs—his regional combatant commanders. For example, General Norman Schwartzkopf was the Commander in Chief of the U.S. Central Command (CENTCOM) responsible for commanding U.S. military forces in the Middle East during the Gulf War. He reported directly to the President.

the direction of a Chief of Staff operated five functional cells: a C-1 responsible for personnel issues; a C-2 for intelligence; a combined C-3 and C-5 office for operations and plans; a C-4 to coordinate logistics; and a C-6 to work communications. In turn, component commanders had parallel staffs to assist them in discharging their command and control responsibilities over their subordinate units. While an organizational chart depicts the general hierarchical flow of command authority, for such a complex undertaking an additional set of much more detailed tools is necessary to supplement this structure and coordinate the myriad of diverse day-to-day activities required to execute the mission.

Control

Augmenting the traditional line and staff command structure is a series of supplemental coordinating mechanisms designed to synchronize the complex details of day-to-day operations. In addition to weekly coordination meetings and direct face-to-face communication, several internal task force documents contain critical mission-related information that drives both the operation and synchronization of daily tasks. These documents are also organized hierarchically, from very general guidance that applies to everyone all the time, to more specific directives that change from day to day and even minute to minute, in response to an evolving tactical and political situation. Figure 2.2 illustrates the most important command and control documents in CTF Provide Comfort arranged hierarchically with the most general guidance at the top.

In generic terms, all actions within military organizations are guided by a broad set of doctrine, tactics, techniques, and procedures. JCS Publication 1–02 defines doctrine as those "fundamental principles by which forces guide their actions in support of national objectives" (Wagner, 1990: 8). Tactics "supplement doctrinal principles by describing how to conduct operations in a manner that reflects those principles" (Wagner, 1990: 8). Techniques are the "methods of using equipment and personnel," while procedures are "standard and detailed courses of action that describe how to perform a task" (Wagner, 1990: 9). When military action is placed in context, when an actual organization is assigned a specific mission for a concrete time and place, an additional set of control mechanisms is overlaid onto the generic guidance found in the standard doctrinal pyramid.

Therefore, in April of 1991, when the National Command Authority[8] di-

---

[8] The National Command Authority (NCA) consists of the President and the Secretary of Defense. The NCA is the ultimate legal entity vested with authority to commit U.S. forces. The line of command authority runs directly from the NCA to the unified and specified commanders,

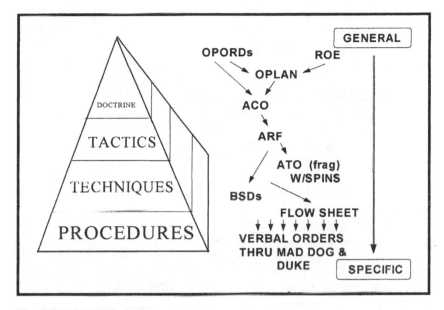

Fig. 2.2. Control Mechanisms

rected the military to conduct Operation Provide Comfort (OPC), the U.S. Commander in Chief Europe (USCINCEUR)[9] directed the creation of Combined Task Force (CTF) Provide Comfort. As a result, four key command and control documents were generated at the European Command level of authority: USCINCEUR Operation Order (OPORD) 002, USCINCEUR OPORD 003, Operations Plan (OPLAN) 91-7, and USCINCEUR OPORD 004. OPLANs and OPORDs are very similar in format and structure. Each document follows the standard military five-paragraph structure for field orders.[10] OPORD 002 defined the initial command and control of CTF forces

---

the four-star combatant Commanders in Chief who are then responsible for executing the military decision directed by the NCA.

[9] Since OPC was to be headquartered in Turkey, and Turkey falls within the European Command's geographical area of responsibility, the U.S. Commander in Chief Europe (USCINCEUR) received this mission.

[10] All military OPORDs and OPLANs follow a standard five-paragraph format. Paragraph 1: Situation, covers the general enemy and friendly situation, to include attachments, detachments, and assumptions. Paragraph 2: Mission, is a clear statement of the explicit tasks required of the organization, and includes answers to the questions who, what, where, and when. Paragraph 3: Execution, has many subparagraphs that all attempt to answer the question how. The main subparagraphs include: concept of the operation (commanders intent, maneuver, fires, etc.), specific subunit tasks, and coordinating instructions. Paragraph 4: Service Support, outlines logistical responsibilities and administrative support plans. Paragraph 5: Command, clearly outlines the chain of command and communications plan.

as running from USCINCEUR to the Commanding General of the CTF. OPORD 003 then directed the CTF Commander to develop an operations plan to govern OPC. OPLAN 91-7, Residual Force, dated 20 July 1991 was then written to delineate command relationships and organizational responsibilities within CTF Provide Comfort. In September 1991, the original organizational structure of the CTF was modified by OPORD 004. In response to the evolving mission in northern Iraq, Serial 004 directed an increase in air assets and the withdrawal of a significant portion of ground forces. However, OPLAN 91-7, as modified by OPORD 004, remained in force as the overarching command and control document at the time of the shootdown.

This series of orders and plans established the general command and control structure of the CTF. It also transmitted sufficient authority and guidance to subordinate component commands and operational units so that they could then develop their own local procedures. Depending on the particular unit or task, these procedures included: OPORDs, Local Operating Procedures, Airspace Control Orders (ACOs), Aircrew Read Files (ARFs), Air Tasking Orders (ATOs), Operating Instructions (OIs), Standard Operating Procedures (SOPs), Battle Staff Directives (BSDs), Flow Sheets, and Checklists.

A few of these local procedures, particularly the ones that relate to the coordination of air operations, are of central importance to the shootdown. The Airspace Control Order for Operation Provide Comfort is a two-volume document that contains the authoritative standard guidance for all local air operations in OPC. The ACO covers such diverse topics as standard altitudes and routes, air refueling procedures, recovery procedures, airspace deconfliction responsibilities, and jettison procedures. All aircrews are responsible for reviewing and complying with information contained in the ACO. Numerous Aircrew Read Files (ARFs) supplement the ACO and are also required background reading for all members of OPC aircrews. ARFs contain classified rules of engagement, changes to the ACO, and recent amplification of how local commanders want air missions executed.

While the ACO and ARFs contain general information that applies to all aircraft in OPC, specific mission guidance is published in daily Air Tasking Orders (ATOs). ATOs contain the daily flight schedule, radio frequencies, Identification Friend or Foe (IFF) codes, and other late-breaking information necessary to fly on a given day. All aircraft are required to have a hard copy of the current ATO with Special Instructions (SPINs) on board before flying. Each morning around 1130, the mission planning cell (or Frag shop) publishes the ATO for the following day. Copies are distributed to all units by late in the afternoon. Any late scheduling changes that do not make it onto the ATO are published in last-minute Battle Staff Directives (BSDs). BSDs are distributed separately and attached to all ATOs prior to any missions flying the next morning. Pilots also fly with Flow Sheets on their kneeboards.[11] These charts are graphical depictions of the chronological "flow" of aircraft scheduled into the no fly zone for that day. Critical information is lifted from the ATO, translated into timelines, and reduced on a copier to provide pilots with a handy in-flight reference.

After taking off, real-time command guidance is passed along to aircrews by radio, through an unbroken chain of command representatives that begins with the Commanding General and runs down through the Combined Forces Air Component Commander (CFACC), through the Mission Director, through the Airborne Command Element (ACE), ultimately to aircraft commanders or pilots. The ACE (call sign DUKE) flies in the AWACS and is the commander's representative on the spot—in the air, armed with up-to-date situational awareness to make time-critical decisions. He is usually a rated pilot with significant tactical experience who monitors all air operations and is in direct contact with the Mission Director (call sign MAD DOG) located in the ground command post. With similar background and training,[12] MAD DOG maintains constant communication links with both DUKE in the AWACS and the CFACC on the ground. He is also responsible for mission execution within a 50-nautical-mile radius of Incirlik Air Base.

This chain of command and series of local procedures not only supplement general command guidance contained in higher level orders and plans, but they also attempt to integrate such broad mission-specific direction with a whole host of existing standard technical publications. Individual service member behavior is not only guided by direct lawful instructions from their chain of command, but also by more task-oriented direction contained in volumes of technical orders, training manuals, service regulations, handbooks, and operator manuals. Some examples of relevant sources of technical guidance influencing actions of key players in this accident include: the UH-60 helicopter operator's manual, the Commander's Handbook on the Law of Armed Conflict, Army Flight regulations, the Tri-Service Mode 4 handbook for IFF operations, the F-15 flight manual, USAF Threat Recognition Training Program manual, the Army's technical manual for the Mark XII IFF system, and the initial qualification training manual for E-3 weapons directors. This is only a partial list; but it illustrates the breadth, depth, and specificity of technical guidance in force at the individual task level of behavior.

Individual action in complex military organizations is synchronized and standardized through a dense web of crosscutting guidance. While attention

[11] Military pilots fly with a small clipboard attached to their knees. These kneeboards contain boiled-down reference information essential to have handy while flying a mission. The daily flow sheet and radio frequencies are two key items usually attached to pilot kneeboards.

[12] In fact, there is a small group of officers who, after completing a standard local training regime, rotate duties. One day they might fly as the DUKE; the next day they might be on the ground as MAD DOG.

tends to focus on the more visible direct exercise of command through the issuance of personal orders, the vast majority of day-to-day individual acts are *in*directly dictated and controlled through a number of standard written procedures. While Figure 2.2 illustrates the hierarchical relationship of most of the specific control mechanisms relevant to the shootdown, Figure 2.3 summarizes how a broad range of formal command and control instruments converge to influence individual service member behavior. From the most general dictates of standard military customs and courtesies (culture)—saluting, proper wear of uniforms, the relationship between officers and enlisted—to the direct verbal orders of local commanders—"about face," "arm hot," or "take the hill"—an individual member of the armed services reacts to a wide range of both general and local formal influence attempts.

The Uniform Code of Military Justice (UCMJ), as well as international laws of warfare such as the Geneva Convention, Presidential Executive Orders, and individual Service Regulations, describe the broad legal framework within which individual military members' actions are judged. Next comes general mission guidance flowing ever downward from the civilian-controlled NCA via an unbroken uniformed chain of command, ultimately finding its way to the individual service member in the field. Such directions carry with them legal authority to use military force within certain clearly specified limits toward the accomplishment of specific national objectives. Such limits are defined in an operation's Rules of Engagement (ROE).

Rules of Engagement are a particularly important set of procedures that are approved at the NCA level, but directly influence individual action on the battlefield. They combine particularly sensitive political considerations with estimates of the local threat and the demands of the mission to guide individual service members in making decisions regarding the appropriate use of deadly force. Because they spell out the detailed procedures that must be followed prior to anyone employing deadly force, ROEs are classified documents. Despite requests by mourning family members to have them declassified, the detailed ROEs in effect at the time of the shootdown remain "secret."

Rules of engagement and other general command guidance are communicated to all subordinate units through a series of operation plans and orders. These documents provide subordinate commanders with the critical information and authority to develop local operating procedures necessary to bridge the gap between general mission orders and specific subunit operations. These local procedures take the form of additional OPORDs, ATOs, ACOs, schedules, ARFs, flow sheets, BSDs, SPINs, checklists, and SOPs—all formal rules designed to coordinate and synchronize the complex actions of various units and individual players. Once published, these written procedures join a whole host of existing technical instructions to guide the ultimate employment of individual weapons and equipment towards the accom-

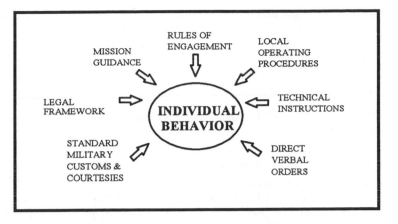

Fig. 2.3. Command and Control Influences on Individual Behavior

plishment of the mission. Finally, real-time verbal and digital information flows through complex systems of command, control, and communications to direct and coordinate the ultimate execution of individual and collective action.

In order to better understand the behavior of central players in the shootdown, it was essential to first introduce the thick, complex, nested, hierarchical command and control structure within which they operate. At first glance, much of this appears a bit overwhelming. However, through almost constant immersion in a "total institution" (Goffman, 1961), systematic socialization through a continuous series of developmental and training experiences, as well as persistent feedback from the ever-present demands of day-to-day practice, most of these influences on individual behavior become ingrained; they become taken for granted. Customs, courtesies, laws, regulations, SOPs, technical instructions, and local procedures quickly fade into the background; they become context—important context nonetheless. Important because individual actions are not isolated events; they do not take place in a vacuum; they are conditioned, shaped, and emerge out of the rich texture of organizational life. Important because what an individual perceives as the subject and the ground, what actions are guided by routine versus conscious decisions, what influences the perceptual difference between novel stimuli and background noise, and where individuals draw the line between context and subject are all important leverage points for analyzing this case. This general insight is not new; however, a particularly unique and powerful aspect of military organizational contexts is the broad framework of command and control relationships within which all individual and collective action is embedded.

This brief summary was meant to set the stage upon which to view the actions of a few critical players in the shootdown. Now it's time to introduce the actors. Moving down a level of analysis and also inching a step closer to the actual event, the following section describes the major players directly involved in the shootdown itself.

The Players: SAVVY, COUGAR, MAD DOG, DUKE, EAGLES, and TIGERS

Embedded within the broad historical and organizational context described above are three primary players: a U.S. Air Force E-3B Airborne Warning and Control System (AWACS) aircraft, a two-ship flight of U.S. Army UH-60 Black Hawk helicopters, and a two-ship flight of U.S. Air Force F-15C Eagle fighters.

There are numerous ways to characterize these players. I just described them as an "aircraft," a "flight of helicopters," and a "flight of fighters." On the radio, during actual operations, they are known as: SAVVY/COUGAR, EAGLE, and TIGER, respectively—their mission call signs. But these "flights" and "aircraft" are operated by individuals and crews; behind each mythical call sign are real people with very real relationships. They live and act within identifiable subunits, nested within ever-larger organizational and societal contexts. This section introduces those individuals, groups, and equipment—the pilots, crews, and their aircraft—which play a central role in the shootdown.

E-3B AWACS: SAVVY, COUGAR, MAD DOG, and DUKE

The acronym AWACS stands for Airborne Warning and Control System. The platform that carries the system is a specially modified Boeing 707 airframe, with its trademark mushroom-shaped radar dome protruding from the top (see Figure 2.4). This aircraft houses a sophisticated system of surveillance, communications, and sensor equipment that literally acts as an "air traffic control tower in the sky." AWACS's formal mission in this operation was to provide "airborne threat warning and air control for all Operation Provide Comfort aircraft" (Andrus, 1994: 2).

The specific model that was on station during the shootdown was a United States Air Force E-3B carrying 19 crewmembers. To accomplish its mission, AWACS personnel were divided into two crews. The flight crew, responsible for the safe operation of the aircraft, consisted of a pilot, copilot, navigator, and flight engineer. These four crewmembers worked as a team on the flight deck at the front end of the aircraft. They responded to the call sign SAVVY. The rear of the aircraft contained the mission crew and their equipment. They responded to the call sign COUGAR. At the heart of the AWACS hums

Fig. 2.4. Eye in the sky: E-3B AWACS Aircraft. Photo courtesy of The Defense
Visual Information Center.

an IBM 4 pi computer that takes raw data from the radar dome, processes it
in accordance with instructions contained in core software, and ultimately
displays tactical information on 14 color consoles arranged in rows throughout the rear of the aircraft (see Figure 2.5).

According to *Multi-Command Regulation 55-33, E-3 Operating Procedures—Aircrew*, the mission crew is "responsible for the command, control, surveillance, communications, electronic, and management functions, to
include: the control and monitoring of assigned aircraft, sensor management,
internal and external communications management, and onboard systems
maintenance" (U.S. Air Force, 1993: 4). To execute these tasks, the mission
crew is organized into three sections under the overall direction of a Mission
Crew Commander (MCC) (see Figure 2.6).

Four equipment technicians operate, monitor, and perform limited in-flight
maintenance of the communications, data processing, display, onboard avionics, and sensor systems, as required. These airmen are busiest early in the
mission as the AWACS "wakes up"—as all of her systems are warmed up,
calibrated, tested, and brought online. However, once all systems are up and
running, and the Mission Crew Commander officially calls "on station," actual
execution of the mission belongs to the surveillance and weapons sections.[13]

---

[13] During sworn testimony, equipment technicians openly admitted to "standing down" once
their equipment was up and running. The computer and display maintenance technician
(CDMT) said, "I tend to sit there and read books more than anything and kind of ignore the net
chatter unless it's actually pointed at me" (Andrus, 1994: TAB V-023, 2). The airborne radar
technician (ART) explained, "I read a lot when I fly. Usually when I hear the word ART, I snap
out of it and answer up. I was reading a book during the time I was sitting on the scope"
(Andrus, 1994, TAB V-024, 2).

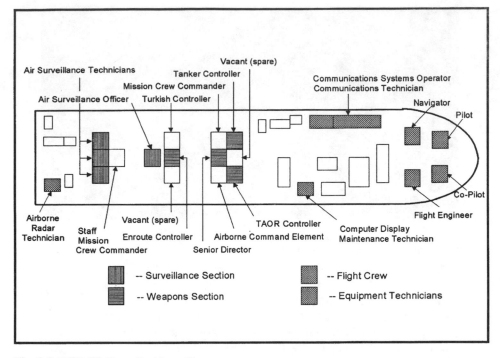

Fig. 2.5. AWACS Crew Positions Chart

The surveillance function is supervised by an Air Surveillance Officer, and carried out by an Advanced Air Surveillance Technician and three Air Surveillance Technicians. According to the regulation, "They [surveillance section] are responsible for the detection, tracking, identification, height measurement, display, telling and recording/documentation of surveillance data" (U.S. Air Force, 1993: 22). In practice, this boils down to handling all non-OPC aircraft detected by AWACS's systems. The surveillance team is responsible for all *un*identified targets that appear on mission crew consoles. As unknown targets appear on their scopes, surveillance technicians follow a detailed matrix to identify the tracks. While responsible for 360-degree coverage, during this particular flight, most of their attention was focused on activity outside the tactical area of responsibility (TAOR), especially contacts south of the 36th parallel.

Under the supervision of the Senior Director (SD), the weapons section is responsible for the actual "conduct of the air battle and for the control of all assigned aircraft and weapons systems in the E-3 area of responsibility" (U. S. Air Force, 1993: 23). For OPC, the weapons section contained an SD (a captain) and three weapons directors (WDs) (all lieutenants). To facilitate communication and coordination, the SD's console was physically located in

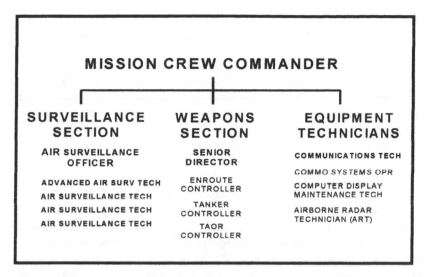

Fig. 2.6. AWACS Mission Crew Organizational Chart

"the pit" right between the Mission Crew Commander and the Airborne Command Element (DUKE) (see Figure 2.5). From this position, through internal radio nets, the SD synchronized the work of the weapons section with that of the surveillance section. He also monitored and coordinated the actions of his three weapons directors to meet the demands of both the DUKE and the MCC.

Each weapons director was assigned responsibility for a specific task. The enroute controller was responsible for controlling the flow of OPC aircraft to and from the Tactical Area of Responsibility (TAOR or no fly zone). He also conducted radio and Identification Friend or Foe (IFF) checks on friendly aircraft outside of the TAOR. The TAOR controller was responsible for threat warning and tactical control for all OPC aircraft within the TAOR. The third weapons director, the tanker controller, coordinated all air refueling operations. Together, the three weapons directors and the Senior Director were responsible for locating, tracking, and controlling all friendly aircraft flying in support of OPC.

In addition to the standard complement of flight and mission crews, due to some unique aspects of the OPC mission, several additional personnel were on board this particular AWACS on the day of the shootdown. To help the crew interface with local air traffic control systems, a Turkish controller flew on all OPC missions. There was also an Airborne Command Element (DUKE) on board representing an immediate line of command to the CFACC through the Mission Director on the ground (MAD DOG). Additionally, since this was the maiden OPC flight for this particular crew, six "instructor" or "staff" personnel also flew on this mission.[14] These "staff" crewmembers belonged to the AWACS support unit permanently stationed at Incirlik Air Base in Turkey. They helped provide continuity for overlapping stateside AWACS crews who periodically rotated through Incirlik on temporary duty status.[15] As one "instructor" testified during the court-martial: "I was on board to be an answer man. To help these guys out since it was their maiden flight this trip. I was there to answer questions about recent occurrences or changes in policy or changes in interpretation that had come about since the last time that they had been in theater" (Headquarters, 8th Air Force, 1995: 1023).

Before leaving the AWACS, here are some brief biographical descriptions of the key players, including the Mission Director (MAD DOG), who operates from the command post on the ground. Descriptions are written "as of" the shootdown.

Mission Director (MAD DOG)—A lieutenant colonel[16] with over 18 years in the Air Force at the time of the shootdown; held a bachelor's degree in recreation and parks and a masters of science degree in aerial space sciences; had logged over 1,000 hours in the F-4 in Europe and an additional 1,000 hours worldwide in the F-15; had served as a liaison officer and most recently in staff positions in Europe and the Air Force Space Command; volunteered to deploy to Incirlik from Guam; arrived in theater on 12 February 1994 and had worked as a certified Mission Director since 22 February; completed his 120-day tour in OPC as the Officer in Charge of Mission Directors and DUKES on 12 June 1994; had flown 25–28 missions in OPC as a DUKE in the AWACS prior to the accident; with 19 years' service, he took advantage of an early retirement option and left the service on 1 October 1994.

Airborne Command Element (DUKE)—A major with 19 years in the Air Force at the time of the shootdown; had perhaps more combat experience

[14] Flying with the AWACS crew on this flight as "staff members" were: an instructor communications technician, an instructor navigator, an instructor communications system operator, an instructor mission crew commander, an instructor weapons director, and an instructor computer display maintenance technician.

[15] Most AWACS crews flying in support of OPC served approximately 30-day tours in Turkey. The particular crew involved in the shootdown was flying its first mission together during this rotation in OPC. They belonged to the 963d AWACS, 552d Air Control Wing, located at Tinker Air Force Base in Oklahoma and departed for Incirlik on 10 April at 0800 local time. Crossing through 8 time zones, they arrived in Turkey on the eleventh at 1400 local time. According to the International Civil Aviation Organization (ICAO) formula for recommended crew rest due to circadian rhythm desynchrony, this crew required 1.8 days of rest time in Turkey prior to flying a mission. According to a technical report filed by the Accident Board Flight Surgeon, each crew member met ICAO requirements (Andrus, 1994: TAB O-7, atch #3).

[16] The rank structure for commissioned officers in the Air Force and the Army is as follows (from most junior to most senior): second lieutenant, first lieutenant, captain, major, lieutenant colonel, colonel, brigadier general (one star), major general (two stars), lieutenant general (three starts), general (four stars).

than anyone else in the Air Force under the age of 40, maybe even 45; had logged over 2,000 total hours of flight time—500 as an instructor and 125 in combat; started his service as an enlisted weather observer/forecaster supporting the Army while on jump status at Fort Bragg for 5 years; earned his bachelor's degree at night; went to Officers Training School and then on to Navigational School—graduated at the top of his class; moved on to Electronic Warfare School and eventually to Fighter Lead-In and survival schools; assigned to fly F-111 bombers; was hand-picked to fly an F-111F bomber in the Eldorado Canyon bombing raid on Libya; became a flight commander; served in the Gulf War—flew 27 combat missions and earned the Distinguished Flying Cross and two air medals for heroism; reassigned for some staff time at Langley Air Force Base, Virginia and then "won the lottery" to come over and represent Langley as a DUKE/MAD DOG in OPC; initially assigned to OPC for three months, but later extended for a full 120 days; at the time of the shootdown, he had worked as a qualified DUKE for four months, with approximately 15–20 sorties as a DUKE prior to the accident.

Mission Crew Commander (MCC)—A major with 15 years in the Air Force at the time of the shootdown; honor graduate of the weapons controller course; had served as a weapons controller in a wide variety of locations for his entire career; had been an instructor weapons controller for three and a half years; graduated with honors from the Aggressors Course; served a tour with the PACAF Aggressors; spent a two-year tour in Korea; opted for a 15-year early retirement and put in his paperwork two months prior to the shootdown; according to testimony, the crew "loved him."

Senior Director (SD)—A captain with almost six years in the Air Force at the time of the shootdown; born in Taiwan; brought to the U.S. by his parents when he was two; graduated from the Air Force Academy in 1988; went immediately into the air controller weapons training program; was then assigned to Tinker Air Force Base in January of 1989 to complete his AWACS Controller Training; upon graduating, was assigned to the 963d AWACS squadron in July of 1989 as a mission-ready weapons controller; became a senior director in October of 1992; this was his fourth deployment to OPC, his second as an SD; was deployed as an SD over 200 days a year and had logged over 2,383 total hours flying time.

Enroute Controller—A first lieutenant with almost four years in the Air Force at the time of the shootdown; graduated from college in May of 1990; started controller school in April of 1991; arrived at Tinker Air Force Base in October of 1991; began AWACS training in December and became mission ready in May of 1992; was almost two years mission ready at the time of the accident.

Tactical Area Of Responsibility (TAOR) Controller—A second lieutenant with over nine years of service at the time of the shootdown; entered the Air

Force in 1985 and served seven and a half years as an enlisted information management specialist; completed his bachelor's degree at night; graduated from Officers Training School in 1993 and went on to Controllers School for six months; assigned to Tinker Air Force Base; at the time of the shootdown, he was a "cherry WD"; had no previous deployments outside of the continental U.S.; became mission ready only two months prior to the incident; was serving his first tour in OPC, first time as a TAOR controller, first time under supervision of this senior director; had only controlled as a mission-ready WD on three previous training flights; considered above average controller by his senior director.

Tanker Controller—A first lieutenant at the time; finished college in 1989; graduated from undergraduate pilot training in late 1991; became a bench pilot (trained, but not flying) and went on to undergraduate controller training through June of 1992; finished controller training in February of 1993 at Tinker Air Force Base; became a mission-ready controller in March of 1993; this was his second tour flying in OPC; considered a very strong controller.

Air Surveillance Officer (ASO)—A captain at the time of the shootdown; mission ready since October of 1992; rated as an instructor ASO; was not a core member of the mission crew; extended a week to cover for the crew's assigned ASO who was upgrading and could not make it to Turkey on time; had already served for five and a half weeks in OPC at the time of the accident; had six missions under her belt prior to the accident; was completing her third trip to OPC; had an extremely high opinion of the Mission Crew Commander; was deployed as an ASO approximately 200 days a year.

On the morning of the shootdown, SAVVY carried the sophisticated eyes and ears of COUGAR to a perch located some thirty-two thousand feet in the skies over eastern Turkey, so that a DUKE could watch TIGERS and EAGLES fly over northern Iraq.

UH-60 Black Hawks—"EAGLE 01/02"

The second major player in this tragedy was the doomed two-ship flight of U.S. Army UH-60 Black Hawk helicopters. The ships belonged to Eagle Flight Detachment, which was under the operational control of the Military Coordination Center. Their mission was to provide general aviation support to the Combined Task Force, particularly the Military Coordination Center. Eagle Flight lived on the U.S. compound at Pirinclik Air Base and flew out of a nearby Turkish airfield called Diyarbakir—a twenty-minute ride from their quarters. Their call signs were EAGLE 01 and EAGLE 02.

Black Hawks were fielded during the early 1980s to replace the Army's aging fleet of UH-1 "Hueys"—the familiar skid-bottomed, all-purpose workhorses of the Vietnam War era. The designator "UH" stands for Utility Heli-

Fig. 2.7. UH-60 Black Hawk with External Fuel Tanks. Photo by Michael Nye.

copter, which is a good description of how these general-purpose aircraft are employed. The Army uses them primarily for troop movement, resupply, and medical evacuation. Powered by twin turboshaft engines, Black Hawks fly at a standard cruising speed of 140 knots (162 mph) for a range of approximately 575 kilometers (360 mi.). When additional range is required, such as was the case on 14 April, external fuel tanks can be mounted on small wing-like sponsons extending from the undersides of the fuselage (see Figure 2.7).

Black Hawks are equipped with a full array of standard avionics. This package includes radios, Identify Friend or Foe (IFF) equipment, and radar sensors. Communications equipment includes FM, UHF, and VHF radios.[17] Each day, a KY58 "gun" is used to key FM and UHF radios with classified codes that allow pilots to "talk secure" in encrypted mode. While UH-60 pilots could talk secure, or "in the green," these two Black Hawks were not equipped with the latest anti-jamming radio called HAVE QUICK. By utilizing an advanced frequency-hopping technology, HAVE QUICK defeated most enemy capabilities to jam transmissions. The AWACS and the F-15s were equipped with HAVE QUICK; unfortunately, the Black Hawks were not. This equipment difference contributed to the shared lack of awareness between F-15 and UH-60 pilots.

In addition to radios, friendly aircraft communicate electronically using Identify Friend or Foe (IFF) equipment. Black Hawks contain an IFF trans-

---

[17] Due to line-of-sight limitations of these radios, the high mountainous terrain in northern Iraq, and the fact that helicopters tried to fly at low altitudes—using the terrain to mask them from enemy air defense radars—all Eagle Flights into the TAOR also carried man-packed tactical satellite radios (TACSATs). These TACSATs were used to communicate with ARROW base (MCC operations) at Zakhu. However, the helicopters had to land to place the TACSATs into operation.

ponder that can be "interrogated" by other aircraft who want to know if it is friendly or not. Friendly radars (located in an AWACS, some fighters, or a ground site) execute what is called a "parrot check" to determine if the target being reflected on their radar screens is either a good guy or a bad guy. The procedure is called a parrot check because once interrogated, the transponder "squawks" back with a secret code—a numerically identifiable pulse that changes daily and must be uploaded onto aircraft using secure equipment prior to takeoff. If the transponder and interrogator are loaded with the proper codes, and the avionics on both ends are working properly, the IFF is the standard means of electronically identifying unknown aircraft.

IFF and radios are for friendly communications. Black Hawks are also equipped with some limited defensive countermeasures. The APR 39 is a system on the aircraft with five antennas mounted left front, right front, left rear, and right rear and on the fuselage bottom to pick up radar signals. These signals appear on a screen along with an audio signature to alert pilots when they are being "painted"—searched or locked onto by another radar. The system also has limited capabilities of defining the type of weapon system that might be doing the tracking, as well as the type of missile being launched. Once the pilots determine that they are being targeted, they have at their disposal an ALQ-144, which is an infrared jammer to throw off heat-seeking missiles, and an M130 chaff dispenser used to throw off radar-guided missiles. As a final safety measure, it was Eagle Flight policy that whenever helicopters were tasked to conduct a mission past Zakhu into the TAOR, they would always fly in sorties of at least two aircraft.

In addition to carrying passenger loads of up to 11 people, Black Hawks normally fly with a crew of four—a pilot, copilot, crew chief, and a gunner. In accordance with a coalition agreement, all OPC aircraft also carried Turkish translators. Pilots are responsible for the safe operation of the aircraft and are either warrant or commissioned officers.[18] The crew chief, a noncommissioned officer (NCO) or senior enlisted soldier, is responsible for the overall maintenance of the aircraft, preparing it for flight, and supervising the duties of the gunner. The gunner assists the crew chief in maintaining the aircraft and its weapons. The standard armament for the UH-60 consists of two

---

[18] There are two distinctly separate groups of service members in the Army—officers and enlisted soldiers. All officers, no matter how junior, outrank all enlisted personnel, no matter how senior. There are two types of officers, commissioned and warrant. Commissioned officers (lieutenants, captains, majors, lieutenant colonels, colonels, and generals) fill leadership and staff positions and outrank warrant officers (warrant officer, chief warrant officer 2, 3, 4, and 5) who primarily fill very specialized roles that require a great deal of narrow technical expertise—such as maintenance technicians, pilots, and administrative specialists. The bulk of the Army consists of enlisted soldiers (private, private first class, specialist). When enlisted soldiers reach the rank of E-5, sergeant, they are then considered noncommissioned officers or NCOs—enlisted positions of leadership (sergeant, staff sergeant, sergeant first class, master sergeant, and sergeant major).

M-60D 7.62mm machine guns, one mounted in each door for local protection.

Personnel and aircraft for Eagle Flight Detachment were supplied by the Fifth Battalion, 158th Aviation Regiment, stationed at Giebelstadt Army Air Field, Giebelstadt, Germany. Normally, a flight platoon of 23 personnel and six Black Hawks from Charley Company in Giebelstadt rotated through the Air Base at Pirinclik, Turkey, to support Eagle Flight's mission. Rotations typically lasted from forty-five to sixty days. At the time of the accident, the detachment was commanded by a captain who was nearing completion of his one-year tour in command. He also flew missions as an aircraft commander and just happened to be the lead pilot, EAGLE 01, on the day of the shootdown. The commander was assisted by a flight platoon leader (usually a lieutenant), an operations officer (who in this case was also the flight instructor), an assistant operations officer, a maintenance officer, a liaison officer (located at Incirlik), and an airfield noncommissioned officer in charge. The remainder of the detachment consisted of aircrews, mechanics, operations NCOs, and administrative clerks. In addition to several military aircraft mechanics, Eagle Detachment was supported by a four-man contract team of SERV-AIR civilian maintenance specialists, who assisted crew chiefs and performed higher-level maintenance and avionics support as required.

The four pilots that flew the two Black Hawks on the morning of the fourteenth used to joke among themselves about how easy a rotation they had, because they were all such proficient and experienced pilots. Chief Warrant Officer 3 Holden, a senior Black Hawk instructor pilot with 19 years service and a member of Eagle Detachment at the time of the accident, commented, "We considered ourselves to be part of the dream team . . . we all had very experienced crews" (Headquarters, 8th Air Force, 1995: 1330). Three of the four pilots had at least five months of experience flying in OPC, with well over 200 hours apiece. The fourth, EAGLE 01, had almost a year of local flying and command experience to draw from on the day he was shot down.

On the morning of the shootdown, under the watchful eye of a DUKE flying in the belly of a COUGAR, two Black Hawks, responding to the names EAGLE 01 and EAGLE 02, carried 26 peacekeepers low and slow over the mountains and valleys of northern Iraq, as two deadly TIGERs prowled the skies above.

F-15C Eagle Fighters: TIGER 01/02

Completing the cast of characters was a two-ship sortie of U.S. Air Force F-15C Eagle Fighters.[19] These aircraft and crews were supplied by the 53d

_____

[19] The potentially confusing use of call signs EAGLE 01/02 and Eagle Flight to refer to Black

Fig. 2.8. F-15 Eagle Fighters on patrol. Photo courtesy of The Defense Visual Information Center.

Fighter Squadron, based in Spangdahlem, Germany. Air crews from "Spang" periodically rotated through Incirlik Air Base in Turkey, serving six-week tours in support of OPC. At the time of the incident, the 53d had nine F-15 pilots flying in OPC. While in Turkey, they flew under the operational control of the Combined Forces Air Component Commander (CFACC) and answered to the call signs of TIGER 01 and TIGER 02.

The F-15 Eagle is an air superiority fighter designed primarily for air-to-air combat. F-15s come in several models. Figure 2.8 depicts the D model two-seat version. On the day of the shootdown, TIGERS 01 and 02 flew single-seat F-15Cs armed with a full complement of ordnance under their wings, including AIM 7, AIM 9, AIM 120, and AMRAAM missiles. AIM is the acronym for Air Interdiction Missile. The designations 7, 9, and 120 indicate various targeting mechanisms. AMRAAM stands for Advanced Medium Range Air-to-Air Missile, a more sophisticated radar-guided missile. When engaging targets, pilots select the ordnance whose characteristics best match the situation.

F-15Cs have a standard avionics package of communications and electronic equipment similar to that of the Black Hawks. However, there are some significant differences. As I have already mentioned, the F-15s were

Hawk helicopters, and TIGER 01/02 to refer to F-15C *Eagle* fighters was not lost on the investigators. One of their recommendations was to rename the helicopter detachment and flights to avoid confusing Hawks and Eagles.

equipped with HAVE QUICK II frequency hopping radios; the helicopters were not. Also, when it comes to IFF equipment, F-15s have transponders that "squawk" codes just like the Black Hawks; however, they also have powerful interrogators that allow them to query unidentified radar contacts. In fact, because the F-15s have this air interrogation capability, it was task force policy for them (or similarly equipped fighters) to be the first mission flown into the TAOR each day.

When conducting combat missions, aerial tactics dictate that F-15s always fly in pairs. There can be two- and four-ship sorties, but each flight starts with the basic building block of two fighters—a lead and a wingman. They fly and fight as a team. The relationship between the flight lead and his wingman is one of the fundamental organizing structures of modern aerial combat. The lead is always in charge. This is one of the few times in the military where formal rank is superseded by functional position. For example, TIGER 01, the flight lead during the shootdown, was a captain and TIGER 02, his wingman, was a lieutenant colonel. Not only did TIGER 02 outrank TIGER 01 by years of service and several ranks, TIGER 02 was also TIGER 01's Squadron Commander, his senior rater, his boss. And yet, because TIGER 02 was flying as the wing, he took all orders from TIGER 01. TIGER 01, because he was the designated flight lead, had command authority over TIGER 02 for purposes of this mission. Due to the nature of high-speed aerial combat, there is no time to question authority. The lead orders and the wing obeys. As TIGER 02 testified, "Rank has no place in the cockpit" (Headquarters 8th Air Force, 1995, vol. 13: 143a.57).[20]

Here are brief career sketches of the two pilots:

TIGER 01—A captain with nine years in the Air Force at the time of the shootdown; graduated from the Air Force Academy in 1986 and went straight to pilot training; completed squadron officers school in residence; spent an unusually large amount of time training with the Army—both as a forward air controller (three years flying OT-37 and OV-10 forward air-control aircraft in support of the Army) and on the ground as an Air Liaison Officer; also parachuted extensively with Army units; wears the coveted gold star on his jump wings in recognition of his combat jump into Panama during Operation Just Cause with the Army's 75th Ranger Regiment; rated as a senior pilot; had flown F-15s for over three years—about 656 hours; is two- and four-ship flight lead qualified; had flown 11 combat missions over

---

[20] During the investigation, a senior pilot testified as follows: "Back in the old days when I was in fighters, we were always taught the scenario about the four into the mountain. If the lead goes into the mountain, you should have II, III, and IV, right into the mountain and you always do what your lead tells you. We also saw that with the Thunderbirds, how four aircraft went in, all into the runway, with four spots all lined up" (Headquarters, 8th Air Force, 1995, vol. 13: 143a.46).

Bosnia[21] and 18 over northern Iraq protecting no fly zones; the mishap occurred on his sixth flight during his second tour flying in support of OPC.

TIGER 02—A lieutenant colonel and 53d Fighter Squadron commander at
the time of the shootdown; held a bachelor's degree in journalism and a
master's degree in administration; had completed military education through
the Air War College in residence; had logged approximately 1,100 hours in
the F-15—a little over 3,000 hours total; was qualified to do everything—
instructor pilot, supervisor of flying, mission commander, and two- and four-
ship flight lead; served in the initial cadre that set up OPC; had flown about
15 flights in northern Iraq; flew combat missions out of Incirlik during Desert Storm; was credited with the only confirmed kill of an enemy Hind
helicopter during the Gulf War—a beyond visual range (BVR) shot—he
never actually saw the helicopter.

Tiger Flight's mission on 14 April was to "conduct a thorough radar
search of the area to ensure the TAOR is clear of hostile aircraft ['sanitize'
the airspace]" (Andrus, 1994: 10). The following passage is taken from
TIGER 01's testimony in which he recounts the portion of his preflight briefing
that not only describes how their radars were employed, but also illustrates
how the two fighters work together:

> Basically, I told TIGER 02 that I wanted to sanitize the entire area, so that he was
> responsible for looking from 20 thousand feet and higher with his radar, and I was
> responsible for putting my radar so it was looking 25 thousand feet and below. We
> had an overlap. I told him that any targets that popped up 25 thousand feet and
> below would be my primary responsibility and I expected him not to initially lock
> the target, but instead to keep sweeping with his radar, looking for some type of
> decoy maneuver, which would mean if we were both locked in there, someone
> could actually come in unobserved to us and shoot us down. (Andrus, 1995: TAB
> V-028A, 11)

On the morning of the shootdown, under the control of a sophisticated
COUGAR, two deadly TIGERs with powerful eyes screamed into the TAOR
loaded for bear in search of prey, while unsuspecting EAGLEs flew close to
the ground, as a DUKE and a MAD DOG watched.

The Shootdown: A Deadly Dance

For the crew of the AWACS, this was their first mission together during this
rotation. They were anxious to get started, eager to show permanent party
staff what they were made of. For Eagle Flight, the fourteenth would also be
an opportunity to demonstrate their competence. They were scheduled to fly

---

[21] His unit in Bosnia actually "intercepted more helicopters than any other unit in the coalition" (Andrus, 1994: TAB V-028: 11).

a very senior group of VIPs deep into the TAOR on an extended village-hopping tour to meet with Kurdish leaders. For our F-15 pilots, every day that someone paid them to fly an advanced fighter was just another day in heaven. TIGER 01 would have an "up close and personal" chance to prove to his boss, TIGER 02, that he indeed had the right stuff by leading not only his squadron commander—his wingman—but also the entire flow of 52 coalition aircraft into the TAOR for that day.

The Prelude

All of our central players rose early on the fourteenth.

SAVVY and COUGAR. Each record member of the AWACS woke up on the morning of the fourteenth between 0430 and 0540 hours (Andrus, 1994: TAB O-6 atch 4).[22] They were picked up by a crew bus at their billets around 0600 and transported to the airfield. At the airfield, they drew their equipment and received three standard briefings: one from the staff, one from the pilot and Mission Crew Commander, and a short intelligence update. They then boarded the AWACS just after 0700. While the flight crew prepared the aircraft for take off, the mission crew stowed their equipment and strapped in. They were scheduled for a 0750 start, with a 15-minute window. All went well during preflight checks and the AWACS lifted off early at 0736 (see Figure 1.2).

After taking off, SAVVY flew the aircraft to a "wake up orbit." They climbed to 32,000 feet and flew a 010 radial approximately thirty-five miles from Incirlik. This local orbit was required for the mission crew's equipment technicians to bring COUGAR's systems on-line. If everything goes well, it takes approximately thirty minutes to warm up the radios, tune the radars, and establish the JTIDS downlink.[23] During the investigation, the staff mission crew commander commented on the wake up: "This was one of the smoothest flights to date . . . it was going extremely well" (Andrus, 1994: TAB V-013: 5). All of the systems came up quickly and the Mission Crew

---

[22] For ease of understanding, I will refer to all times as local for the TAOR. Incirlik was one hour behind to the west. Therefore, these crews actually woke up between 0330 and 0440 local for where they lived. For example, sunrise in Incirlik on 14 April was 0606 hours (local), 0536 (Incirlik local) in the TAOR.

[23] JTIDS stands for Joint Tactical Information Distribution System and is a central component of theater command and control. JTIDS provides ground commanders with a real-time downlink of the current air picture from AWACS. This information is then integrated with data from other sources to provide commanders with a more complete picture of the theater. Establishing the JTIDS link was such a critical task in OPC, that if for some reason AWACS was unable to make the connection during their wake-up orbit, they would abort the mission and launch another aircraft.

Commander called "systems ops"—which means all mission critical equipment was operational.

This "thumbs up" from the back signaled SAVVY to leave her wake up orbit and press eastward. COUGAR had good eyes, but SAVVY had to carry them closer to the action.[24] AWACS left the local airspace and headed for ROZ 1 (restricted operating zone)—the airspace designated for SAVVY's holding orbit—a fairly narrow racetrack that AWACS would fly for the remainder of the day. Once SAVVY reached its air surveillance orbit, DUKE called MAD DOG and reported "on station" at 0845—indicating to the mission director on the ground that AWACS was operational and in position; he could launch the fleet.

EAGLES.[25] Meanwhile, the crew of Eagle Flight woke up around 0515 hours, made the twenty-minute ride to Diyarbakir, and reported to operations at 0710. At this point, EAGLE 01—the air mission commander—conducted an aircrew briefing. As always, he began by taking attendance. All pilots were required to attend. Following roll call, he covered crew coordination, updated the intelligence situation, briefed codes, formations, altitudes, air speeds, and reporting responsibilities. After the briefing, EAGLE 01 dropped off his flight plan[26] at Turkish Base Ops and the crews headed for their helicopters. On the way out to the flight line, crew chiefs stopped by the security police building to draw their weapons and ammunition.[27]

Once they arrived at their helicopters, pilots and crew chiefs preflighted their aircraft according to the operator's manual. Meanwhile, each crew cleaned and prepared their helicopters. This included removing tie downs, cleaning the windows, mounting the M-60s, and installing the intercom headsets. After preflight and a crew brief, the pilots then entered their birds to complete their checklists. At around 0815, they called the tower to request clearance for takeoff. This was the signal for the Turkish liaison officers (LNOs) to board the aircraft. According to a coalition agreement, no passenger-capable American military aircraft would fly in Turkey without a Turkish officer on board. With four-man crews and Turkish LNOs, the two

---

[24] The actual ranges and capabilities of AWACS systems are highly classified.

[25] Since all members of Eagle Flight died in the accident, the following chronology of events was pieced together from interviews with various operations and support personnel who participated in the preflight and launch activities on the morning of the fourteenth.

[26] The contents and dissemination of information contained in this plan became an important issue during the investigation. The Black Hawks' flight plan contained their scheduled takeoff time, low-level transit routes between Diyarbakir through Gate 1 to Zakhu, and return time. Because the crews rarely knew exactly where they would be going within the TAOR until after they were briefed by their customers/passengers at the Military Coordination Center, most flight plans only indicated that Eagle Flight would be "operating in and around the TAOR" (Headquarters, 8th Air Force, 1995: 1269).

[27] Each crew drew two M-60 machine guns, two M-16 rifles, and a 9mm pistol for each member of the flight crew.

Black Hawks of Eagle Flight lifted off at 0822 from Diyarbakir Air Base heading east into the rising sun. They climbed to an initial altitude of 3,500 feet. About five miles out, EAGLE 01 contacted BATMAN, the Turkish flight following facility, and requested clearance to climb to 7,500 feet. BATMAN then cleared Eagle Flight to continue on their planned low-level transit route to the Iraqi border.

Almost an hour out of Diyarbakir, at 0921, the Hawks checked in with AWACS on the enroute frequency as they prepared to enter the TAOR through Gate 1: "Anyone, this is EAGLE 01." The AWACS enroute controller replied, "EAGLE 01, COUGAR copies." Five minutes prior to this radio check, the "friendly general" track symbology and track designator "TY06" that the surveillance section had originally assigned to the Black Hawk flight was replaced by a more precise "H" character—indicating friendly helicopter. After EAGLE 01 checked in on the radio, the Senior Director changed the track designator from "TY06" to "EE01"—for EAGLE 01.[28] Three minutes later, apparently due to terrain masking, the Black Hawks' IFF returns faded at 0924. At this point, the helicopter symbology was suspended; which means that it was graphically maintained in the vicinity of Zakhu, even though it was no longer attached to an active signal.

Flying at an altitude of 7,500 feet, Eagle Flight crossed the border into Iraq at 0935 and immediately executed a spiral descent into Zakhu.[29] They landed at 0941 in the small village of Zakhu, shut down their engines, and reported to Military Coordination Center headquarters (forward) to meet their passengers. The mission commander, EAGLE 01, then conducted a short ten-minute briefing to confirm the passenger manifest—who would sit where, cover security requirements, the purpose of the mission, and route of flight. After this briefing, eighteen passengers—all VIPs, including both the Turkish and U.S. Military Coordination Center co-commanders, boarded the two helicopters and strapped in. At 0954, Eagle Flight reported their departure from Zakhu to AWACS: "COUGAR, EAGLE 01 is enroute WHISKEY to LIMA." Whiskey and Lima were delta code letters for Zakhu and Irbil, respectively. As they left Zakhu, the Black Hawks also contacted Arrow Operations at Maverick Base (Military Coordination Center main headquarters) on their VHF radio, informing them that they had departed.

Zakhu was located in a wide open valley very close to the convergence of

[28] By reviewing the AWACS's mission data tapes it was possible to accurately re-create the exact sequence of events and symbology just as they appeared on crew screens the day of the shootdown.

[29] As they approached Gate 1, Eagle Flight helicopter pilots would have preferred to fly "on the deck" (approximately 200–300 feet above the ground) for better tactical protection; however, Turkish controllers insisted that they remain at 7,500 feet as they crossed into the TAOR. Turkish liaisons inside the helicopters actually took note of the altimeter reading as they crossed the border.

the Tigris and another smaller river. As the helicopters flew to the southeast, the ground elevation increased steadily. After about twenty minutes, they were flying over extremely rugged mountainous terrain. Initially, these ranges run primarily east to west. Gradually, they turn, so that as Eagle Flight flew further to the east, the direction of the mountain ranges shifted to north-south. Approximately twenty minutes east of Zakhu, at 1011 hours, they entered a deep valley and dropped off AWACS's scopes.

Two minutes later, at 1013, the Air Surveillance Officer placed a computer generated "attention arrow"[30] onto the SD's radar scope in an attempt to query him about the lost helicopter symbology that was now floating unattached to any track in the vicinity of the last known location of Eagle Flight. No action was taken at this time and the arrow automatically dropped off the screen after sixty seconds. At 1015, the Air Surveillance Officer adjusted the AWACS's radar to a low-velocity detection setting in an attempt to improve the system's capability to detect slow-moving targets.

TIGERS. Both F-15 pilots woke up at 0630 hours, had cereal and juice for breakfast, and rode in the duty vehicle together to the squadron. They arrived at their squadron at 0730 and checked the weather (SKC—sky clear all the way down the slide) and Notices to Airmen (NOTAMs). Brief time was scheduled for two hours prior to takeoff; they started on time at 0735. The first part of the brief is always intelligence. To get the latest update, TIGERS 01 and 02 stopped by the intel office and were briefed by the squadron intelligence officer. This update lasted about 10 minutes. Highlights included the number and type of Iraqi fighters and sorties flown the previous day, a change in the surface-to-air missile battery order of battle (overnight they had lost track of an enemy Roland surface-to-air missile site), the search and rescue words for the day (a number and letter code used in case they had to eject), and then some current intel about the turmoil in Rwanda following the shootdown of their president.

After leaving intel, both pilots sat down together and began their tactical brief at approximately 0745. They went through the FRAG (Air Tasking Order) line by line, reviewing the flow of aircraft scheduled into the TAOR that day. They briefed go/no-go items. For example, if, after ground testing, they were unable to either squawk or interrogate all IFF modes, they would "step" to a spare aircraft. They reviewed their communications plan—covering radio sets, frequencies, check-in time tables, and procedures. They talked briefly about the threat—what sort of enemy aircraft and missiles they might face. Finally, TIGER 01 walked through what he called the "meat of the entire briefing"—how they would conduct various intercepts. He briefed three options: a high fast flyer, a medium or low fast flyer, and a low slow target

---

[30] The attention arrow is also accompanied by a blinking alert light on the Senior Director's console.

(Headquarters, 8th Air Force, 1995: 143.9). For each scenario, TIGER 01 described the tactical formation and strategy that they would use to intercept potential targets. He then covered the split of high-low radar sweep responsibilities and his plan for clearing his wing to shoot in accordance with standing Rules of Engagement. The tactical briefing ended at around 0820 with a short discussion of how the two F-15s would "merge"—rejoin formation and continue the mission after passing a target—following an engagement.

At this point, they had twenty minutes until "step time." Step time is when pilots climb, or "step" into the truck that takes them out to their aircraft. This twenty minutes was spent attending to personal business, sanitizing (removing all personal identification items—wedding bands, patches, pictures, and money—except military ID), suiting up (at "life support" they were issued a G-suit, survival vest, harness, helmet, 9 mm pistol, 15 rounds, two clips, and a global positioning system receiver), and signing for four mission items at the operations desk (a video tape for heads up display [HUD] filming, an unclassified pilot aide, a classified aid that included silhouettes of helicopters and aircraft, and an escape and evasion kit complete with "blood chits"—papers promising potential captors that they would be rewarded for the safe return of downed pilots).

At 0840, TIGERS 01 and 02 "stepped" into the truck with the duty supervisor of the day, who was responsible for preflighting the spare aircraft, and drove out to the flight line together. At the aircraft, they met their crew chiefs, checked the maintenance forms, loaded their video tapes, and conducted a "walk around" check of the aircraft. It is during this time that the crew chiefs actually set the IFF codes on their aircraft and loaded the encrypted communications information so that their pilots would be able to talk secure. Finally, assisted by their crew chiefs, both pilots climbed into their F-15s and strapped in.

Fighter pilots pride themselves in hitting their scheduled "start time." So, just prior to 0900 hours, TIGER 01 counted down, "three, two, one, start engines." Both aircraft started at exactly 0900 hours and TIGER 01 reported, "MAD DOG, Tiger 1 is engine start, words." By saying "words," TIGER 01 prompted the Mission Director for any last minute changes to the FRAG that may have occurred since they stepped. MAD DOG replied with, "The combat divert is BATMAN, the altimeter there is XXXX, and negative words." This information told the pilots where to fly, should they not be able to return to Incirlik and perhaps more important, that MAD DOG had not received any new information since the ATO (FRAG) was published. Both pilots then completed their BIT checks—internal tests of critical electronic systems such as IFF and radar. Everything checked normal.

At 0920, they taxied out to "arming," where the safety pins were pulled from their missiles; the aircraft were "armed hot." Also at this point, a technician used a hand-held interrogator to check their Mode IV IFF. Once again, both aircraft checked normal and they continued taxiing to the end of runway four north, where they received clearance from the tower. Tiger flight took off right on schedule at 0935 hours.

Following two separate full afterburner takeoffs, the F-15s turned east toward Iraq. About 10 miles from the field, they did a systems check on each other. TIGER 02 first interrogated 01 on all four modes. He then pulled past him, allowing 01 to check his IFF. Both aircraft checked out on all four modes and rejoined a spread formation flying about 2,000 feet apart at an altitude of 27,000 feet. Fifty miles out of Incirlik, both TIGERs switched over to channel eight on their main radios so that they could monitor COUGAR on the enroute control frequency. At K-town (the first visual checkpoint enroute to Gate 1) the lead checked in with AWACS: "COUGAR, TIGER 01, K-Town, as fragged, flight level two seven zero." This call tells COUGAR and DUKE that all is well; they have two aircraft with ordnance just as described in the FRAG. COUGAR responded with, "Roger"—simply indicating that he copied the transmission.

Seventy-five miles later, or halfway between K-Town and Derek, both pilots switched their radios to secure auxiliary and checked in with each other one final time to see if they were experiencing any problems with critical aircraft systems. "TIGER 01 is negative alibis." This call by the lead told his wingman that he had no problems. The word "alibis" is a standard brevity code word for "problem." His wing responded with, "TIGER 02, negative alibis," indicating that he too was fully operational.

At Derek, the second checkpoint, both aircraft did a HAVE QUICK check. The two pilots spoke to each other on their HAVE QUICK frequency-hopping radios to make sure that they worked and were set to the same key. The lead then called, "COUGAR, TIGER 01, check-in HAVE QUICK." COUGAR responded with, "Loud and clear." This confirmed that all three aircraft could speak to each other on the radio and frequencies they planned to use once they entered the TAOR.

The next task was for TIGER 02 to complete a "cons check." As the first aircraft flying into the TAOR that day, the fighters wanted to determine the altitudes at which contrails found. A contrail is that telltale streak of white condensation clouds that stream out from behind jet engines under certain temperature and humidity conditions. For fighters, contrails are important, because they work like a big neon sign alerting enemy gunners to your presence. To do this check, TIGER 02 dropped down to the floor and then climbed steadily, while 01 watched and called out to him when his contrail started and when it stopped. While climbing, TIGER 02 marked the range of these altitudes by monitoring his altimeter. F-15s left contrails that day between 31,000 and 35,000 feet. Both pilots made a note to avoid flying at that height.

The final checkpoint is called "jump," because it is the jumping-off point for aircraft entering the TAOR. Jump is located 40 miles northwest of Iraq, just outside of Gate 1. The time was 1015. At this point, TIGER 01 switched to channel 9 on his main radio and called, "DUKE, TIGER, as fragged, words." Again, he was telling DUKE that he had two aircraft configured as depicted on the ATO with no problems. He was also asking DUKE if he was aware of any changes in the situation since his last check-in. DUKE responded with, "BATMAN is the combat divert, altimeter is XXXX, negative words"—indicating that he had nothing new to add; to his knowledge, the situation had not changed in any significant way.

After this check with DUKE, both pilots "fenced in." Just prior to entering the TAOR, they turned on all of their combat systems that they normally do not fly with over civilian territory. Fencing includes activating their ability to dispense chaff and flares and turning on their internal electronic system that jams enemy threats. The only combat switch that remains closed is the master arm. This is not turned on until fighters are actually engaged and the lead directs, "arm hot."

The final critical preparation for entering Iraq was to switch their IFF Mode I code from 43 to 52. All friendly fixed-wing aircraft flying in Turkey on the fourteenth flew with Mode I coded 43; once they entered the TAOR, both TIGERS 01 and 02 switched over to 52. After fencing in and switching IFF codes, both aircraft were fully configured to enter the combat zone over northern Iraq. TIGER 01 adjusted his airspeed slightly so that he would hit Gate 1, the actual border between Turkey and Iraq, at exactly the planned time. At precisely 1020, the F-15 flight lead called, "COUGAR, TIGER on station."[31]

SAVVY had COUGAR on station. Two EAGLES flew low and slow. Two TIGERS entered the gate. The scene was set. The deadly dance was about to begin.

The Dance

Up to this point in time, our three main players were all going about their business as usual. The weather in eastern Turkey was beautiful; visibility was "a million plus." All systems on all platforms had checked out perfectly. Members of the AWACS crew were drinking their first cup of coffee, looking forward to controlling a string of some fifty coalition aircraft during their shift. The two Black Hawks of Eagle Flight were full of VIPs enjoying a low-level tour of the region.

At 1020, the helicopters had just dropped down out of very rugged terrain,

---

[31] For operational security reasons, he actually used a code word to indicate their status as "on station."

with 7,000-foot mountains and almost vertical relief. They were flying at 130 knots in a straight line approximately 200 feet above ground level (AGL), heading down a small river valley between two high mountain ranges. The F-15s were crossing the border into Iraq to begin their sweep.

At 1021, the AWACS Mission Crew Commander was in the middle of a discussion with the flight engineer and another crew member about trying to get the temperature a little warmer in the back compartment. Meanwhile, the enroute controller dropped the helicopter symbology from the scopes, removing the only visual reminder to the AWACS crew that there were Black Hawks inside the TAOR. Each crew member simultaneously monitored several radio frequencies, as well as internal communication nets.

As TIGER 01 entered the TAOR, he was sweeping low, as briefed. Immediately, he picked up a blip—a contact approximately 40 nautical miles ahead to the southeast. As his radar swept back and forth, small green rectangles—"hits"—appeared on his scope, indicating that he was getting returns from something flying at that location. On his auxiliary radio, he alerted his wingman and then locked onto the contact. Locking onto a target takes all of a radar's energy, normally diffused across a sweep, and focuses it onto one specific point in the sky. This allowed TIGER 01 to obtain speed and altitude information about the contact. His lock reported a target flying on a heading of 100 degrees at approximately 130 knots, very low to the ground. In fact, as it often does with helicopters, it registered some negative altitude readings.

At this point, TIGER 01 held his radar lock and used the F-15's air-to-air interrogator to query the target. The first mode he checked was Mode I—the general code that all OPC aircraft should be squawking while flying in the TAOR. Initially, he checked with his switch set to "CC," which tests only for the "correct code"—in this case code 52. If this was a friendly aircraft, he should squawk Mode I, code 52 when interrogated in this manner. There was no response. While in the sweep mode, the contact appeared on his scope as a rectangle. When he locked onto it, the rectangle changed into a star with a vector stick (indicating speed, altitude, and direction). When he interrogated it, there was no change; it remained a star. Had it been squawking code 52, the star would have changed into a diamond. It didn't.

TIGER 01 then reached down and flipped his interrogation switch from "CC" to "auto." Set this way, his radar would interrogate continuously Mode IV, which is the second mode that all coalition aircraft should be squawking. If his target was squawking the correct Mode IV, the star should change into a circle. What happened at this point is important. Since this chapter is about pure description, I'll let TIGER 01 explain:

> Initially, when I pressed down on the air-to-air interrogator, that star did turn to a circle. It lasted for about one second, then the circle just disappeared and went

back to a star. Normally, when we interrogate we hold the interrogation down 5 to 6 seconds to be sure that we're doing continuous interrogation. There are anomalies with the jet that cause the initial interrogation to come up as a false reading. So right now I don't know for sure what that's telling me. All I know is I've seen that before in the aircraft, it's given me false information before, but I'm going to have to check it again. It only lasts for a second and goes away. For the remainder of the interrogation, 4 to 5 seconds, it's a star and it's showing me that he's not squawking Mode IV. (Andrus, 1994: TAB V-029, 19)

Meanwhile, his wingman, TIGER 02, has rolled his own radar down to check the target and reported to his lead, "Hits there." This verification confirmed for TIGER 01 that it wasn't just his aircraft that was picking up a return.

At 1022, TIGER 01 called, "COUGAR, TIGER's, contact, Bull's Eye, zero three zero for fifty low and slow." "Bull's Eye" is a classified geographical reference point in Iraq that everyone in the coalition knows about. All contacts are fixed off that point. Therefore, any friendly listener to TIGER 01's call could locate his contact by starting at the agreed upon location for the Bull's Eye and then moving off it thirty degrees (northeast) for fifty miles.

The enroute controller responded with, "Clean there"—indicating that he had no radar contacts in that location. A replay of AWACS data tapes confirms that in fact there were no radar or IFF returns at that location, at that time. However, approximately one minute later, at 1023, as Eagle Flight flew into a wider valley, AWACS began to receive intermittent IFF signals in the area where the F-15s had called their contact. The "H" character also reappeared on the Senior Director's scope at 1023. These intermittent IFF returns strengthened until 1026, when they became solid and remained present without interruption, until 1028.

Meanwhile, after making his initial report to COUGAR, TIGER 01 broke his radar lock and returned to the sweep mode to search his area for other targets. He wanted to make sure that no one was sneaking up on him while his attention was focused on the one return. He also checked his map and noticed that a road ran through the area where he had made contact. "Sometimes our radar locks onto road traffic pretty successfully. . . . Granted, most of the roads down there are not autobahns like they are in Germany, so no one should be traveling at 130 knots. But the radar can lie to you" (Andrus, 1994: TAB 029, 20).

To follow up on this thought, TIGER 01 contacted his wingman and raised the possibility of the contact being road traffic. He did this by making a second contact call over the main radio at 1025, repeating the location, altitude, and heading of his target. TIGER 02 replied that he showed the target at 300 feet—indicating that he didn't think that it was on the ground. This time the enroute controller responded with, "Hits there"—indicating that he also had radar returns on his scope corresponding to the spot where the F-15s were looking. The actual wording of COUGAR's response to these calls is important. A "hit" is normally used to describe a blip—any radar return that pops up on a scope. The term "paint" is normally used when referring to an IFF-type of return. The data tapes show that at 1025, IFF returns were intermittent; at 1026, they were clearly visible on AWACS's scopes.

While not quite as dependable, F-15 radars can also interrogate while in the sweep mode. During this time period, TIGER 01 made a second check of Modes I and IV. Again, he received no response.

Having already confirmed through electronic means that his target was apparently not friendly, in accordance with the rules of engagement, it was time to execute a visual identification (VID) pass to confirm that it was hostile. TIGER 01 then reapplied his lock onto the target and began to descend. As he broke from an altitude of twenty-seven thousand feet, his target was still between twenty and thirty miles away. Once again, TIGER 01 recalls:

> I lock the target again with my radar, and again I interrogate Mode I, Mode IV, and EWWS—a classification [sic] system. Each interrogation is about 5 to 6 seconds long, and all of them are negative. So I get no Mode I reply; it doesn't turn to a diamond. I get no Mode IV reply; it doesn't turn to a circle, which tells me that he is not squawking friendly Mode I or Mode IV. (Andrus, 1994: TAB V-029, 21)

Passing through ten thousand feet and closing quickly to ten nautical miles, TIGER 01 located his contact in the target designator (TD) box of his heads up display. His onboard computer automatically positions whatever he is locked onto into this box and holds it there. Once again, he sees the target lined up with the road through his display. Once again, he tells his wingman that his "TD is on the road."

By 1026, TIGER 01 had closed to seven nautical miles when his TD finally came off the road. But, as he recalls, "I'm seven nautical miles away; the ground is green; I still can't see anything out there" (Andrus, 1994: TAB V-029, 21).

At 1027, TIGER 01 finally picked up a helicopter in his TD box approximately five miles out. He made the call, "TIGER 01 is tally, one helicopter, standby VID." At the same time, the enroute controller initiated an "unknown pending unevaluated" track symbology in the area of the helicopters' radar and IFF returns.

The following sequence of events happened very quickly. But, as TIGER 01 lamented during his testimony, while they "all happened at the same time, I can only talk about them one at a time" (Andrus, 1994: TAB V-029, 22).

At a speed of approximately 450 knots, TIGER 01 flew by his target from above and behind. As he passed, he could see the helicopter through his canopy—approximately five hundred feet below and about a thousand feet offset to his right. Immediately upon drawing even with the helicopter, he pulled up hard, looked over his shoulder, and spotted what looked initially like a shadow; but it was too far back. A closer look revealed that what he had spotted was not a shadow at all, but rather a second helicopter flying in trail behind the first.

At 1028, TIGER 01 tried to report what he saw: "VID Hind—correction, Hip . . . no Hind." Hip and Hind are both NATO designations for two different types of Soviet-made helicopters. While making the call, TIGER 01 pulled out his "goody book" with aircraft pictures in it and actually checked the silhouettes.

Meanwhile, as briefed for low slow intercepts, TIGER 02 performed an "S" to put some distance between him and his lead. From this separation, TIGER 02 picked up two radar returns and interrogated both of them. According to his testimony, "Lead [TIGER 01] turned to a diamond indicating friendly, while the other reply remained negative friendly" (Andrus, 1994: TAB V-028, 10). He then locked onto the second contact.

TIGER 01 called, "ID Hind, Tally two, lead trail, TIGER 02, confirm Hinds." COUGAR responded with, "Copy Hinds."

Following his lead's direction, TIGER 02 replied, "Stand by," as he closed in on the trail helicopter. Initially he picked up only a single shadow. Then, as he passed by at fifteen hundred to two thousand feet to their right, he saw two helicopters and pulled up quickly calling, "Tally two."

Following their initial fly-by, both F-15s pulled up hard and flew back around to the northwest. The helicopters were still flying southeast. After about ten nautical miles, the F-15s turned around again and pointed back toward their targets. At this point, TIGER 01 called, "COUGAR, TIGER 02 has tallied two Hinds, engaged." The call "engaged" implied that the fighters were preparing to employ ordnance.

The lead then directed, "TIGER arm hot"—clearing his wingman to shoot as long as he met the rules of engagement.

The next call came quickly, "TIGER 01 is in hot"—indicating that the lead F-15 had armed his missiles and was proceeding to engage a target. He then called to his wingman, "We're coming in behind them; there's two of them in lead trail; I'm going in first, TIGER 01 is going in first, so I will shoot the trailer and then you will shoot the leader" (Andrus, 1994: TAB V-019, 24). At this point, TIGER 02 turned on his video camera and recorded the actual engagement from his cockpit.

When he turned back toward the helicopters, TIGER 01 had switched his radar to the auto acquisition mode, which caused it to automatically relock onto the targets. Focusing on the target designator box of his heads up display, he looked for the helicopters. As he closed in on them, he could see both birds—confirming that he was indeed locked onto the trailer. He then did one final Mode I check, received a negative response, and then "pickled." Once again, I'll let TIGER 01 explain this final deadly sequence:

I pickled, which means I pressed the button that expends ordnance. . . . It's a habit pattern. Always before—in training at all times before we press the pickle button, we always—we call it "hammering down." We always interrogate to give the— any type of—one last chance to see if there's [sic] any systems that would tell us something different. But it is a normal everyday occurrence. It's almost—you don't even think about it; it just happens. You just lock a target and automatically interrogate, and that's what I did. (Andrus, 1994: TAB V-039, 24)

From a range of about four miles, TIGER 01 released a radar-guided, Advanced Medium Range Air-to-Air Missile (AMRAAM). It dropped off the aircraft, climbed initially, disappeared for an instant as the booster motor ran out; and then, about seven seconds after it was launched, there was a large explosion in the vicinity of the target.

TIGER 01 noticed that after the trail helicopter went down, the remaining one made a hard left-hand turn into a ravine. The F-15 lead immediately pulled off to the left and initiated the following sequence of calls (Andrus, 1994: TAB N, 1):

F-15 Lead: TIGER 01, splash one Hind. TIGER 02, you're engaged with the second one. He's off my nose two miles, right past the fireball. Two, call in. One's off left.

F-15 Wing: In hot.

F-15 Lead: Copy. TIGER 01, splash one Hind. TIGER 02 is engaged, COUGAR.

AWACS: COUGAR copies. Splash one Hind.

F-15 Lead: He's in a left-hand turn, low.

TIGER 02 closed to within two miles of the remaining helicopter, selected an AIM-9 Sidewinder, heat-seeking, Advanced Intercept Missile, uncaged the seeker head, and fired from a distance of nine thousand feet. According to TIGER 02, "The missile grabbed a large amount of lead and then corrected back towards the target. A fireball engulfed the aircraft and the wreckage fell along the north side of the valley" (Andrus, 1994: TAB V-028, 11).

F-15 Wing: TIGER 02, splash second Hind.

F-15 Lead: Splash two, TIGER 02, come off south.

F-15 Wing: Stick a fork in him; he's done!

By 1030, it was all over. There were no survivors. All 26 souls on board the Black Hawks perished instantly. On 14 April 1994, in clear skies over northern Iraq, two hungry TIGERs devoured two defenseless EAGLEs, while a COUGAR, DUKE, and MAD DOG looked on.

Multiple Explanations:
A Walk Through the Causal Map

CHAPTER 2 describes "what" happened; the next four examine "why." We begin with the hard-won fruits of expert analysis. While this book is premised on the very assumption that prior investigations fail to tell the entire story, clearly there is much to learn from such laboriously generated findings. Therefore, we turn to the conclusions reported by the accident investigation team as natural points of departure for our own analysis—as practical guideposts to mark our way on an explanatory journey.[1]

What follows then is a "walk through the causal map"—a systematic stroll through a densely woven web of causality. At the end of her historical ethnography, *The Challenger Launch Decision*, Diane Vaughan argues that, "What matters most is that we go beyond the obvious and grapple with the complexity, for explanation lies in the details" (1996: 463). If explanation lies in the details, so surely does confusion. As we begin to pick our way through the details of this explanation, you may find it useful to refer to Figure 1.3 The Causal Map. General Andrus, President of the Investigation Board, concluded that the shootdown was "caused by a chain of events" (Andrus, 1994: 1). Figure 1.3 maps out these events both temporally and logically in relation to each other—and ultimately, to the shootdown itself. Keeping it handy will help you maintain your analytical bearings as we attempt to disentangle the interconnected threads of causality.

Multiple Explanations

On 14 April 1994, twenty-six people from five different countries lost their lives in an instant. Many people wanted to know why; and, they wanted to know quickly.

[1] While I do draw heavily from information generated by the original Air Force accident investigation and court-martial of Captain Wang, I should note that several accident victims' family members have voiced concerns about the adequacy of this investigation. As a result of these concerns, the House of Representatives' Subcommittee on Military Personnel, Committee on National Security requested the Office of Special Investigations of the U.S. General Accounting Office (GAO) to "determine if the Air Force's subsequent Aircraft Accident Investigation Board investigation of fratricide had met its objectives" and "to consider concerns voiced by victims' family members and others" (U.S. General Accounting Office, Office of Special Investigations, 1997: 1). With a few exceptions (that I include later), the GAO found that the "Aircraft Accident Investigation Board was properly convened and met the objectives set forth in Air Force Regulation 110–14" (U.S. General Accounting Office, Office of Special Investigations, 1997: 6).

The Experts

On the day of the shootdown, the United States Secretary of Defense
(SECDEF), Dr. William Perry, directed the United States Commander in
Chief, Europe (USCINCEUR) to "conduct an investigation into the facts and
circumstances" surrounding the accident (Andrus, 1994: 1). The USCIN-
CEUR ordered the Commander in Chief, United States Air Forces Europe
(CINCUSAFE) to convene an Aircraft Accident Investigation Board
(AAIB). Literally overnight, a distinguished group of aviation, technical,
medical, and legal experts from around the world converged on Incirlik Air
Base to receive their charter. On 15 April, President Clinton and Secretary
Perry directed the AAIB to conduct a "thorough, deliberate, and exhaustive
investigation to *determine every one of the causes* that contributed to this
tragedy" (emphasis added) (Shalikashvili, 1994b: 1).

For six weeks, board members evaluated training and readiness programs;
performed technically sophisticated equipment "tear downs"; analyzed all
sorts of physical evidence; formally interviewed over 120 witnesses; conducted detailed reviews of local directives, operating procedures, crew quali-
fications, communications logs, crash site photographs, and maintenance records; examined optical, medical, and human factors issues; and
reconstructed event time lines from all manner of voice, video, and digital
tapes. On 27 May 1994, Major General Andrus, President of the Aircraft
Accident Investigation Board, forwarded his findings to the Pentagon.

Not surprisingly, the AAIB had chased the attribution rabbit back into all
the familiar holes. In his seminal study of *Normal Accidents*, sociologist
Charles Perrow lists the following "conventional explanations for accidents":

> operator error, faulty design or equipment, lack of attention to safety features, lack
> of operating experience, inadequately trained personnel, failure to use the most
> advanced technology, and systems that are too big, under financed, or poorly run.
> (1984: 63)

A rough coding of the Board's findings confirms Perrow's insights. In the
concluding paragraph of the *Report of Investigation*, General Andrus covered all the bases. He cited at least one example of each of Perrow's "conventional explanations":

- **Operator error**—"The F-15 flight lead misidentified the U.S. Black
  Hawk helicopters . . . the wingman did not notify the flight lead that he
  had been unable to make a positive identification, and allowed the en-
  gagement to continue."
- **Faulty design or equipment**—"The reason for the unsuccessful Mode
  IV interrogation attempts cannot be established, but was probably at-

tributable to one or more of the following factors: incorrect selection of interrogation modes, faulty air-to-air interrogators, incorrectly loaded IFF transponder codes, garbling of electronic responses, and intermittent loss of line-of-sight radar contact."

- **Lack of attention to safety features**—"There was a general misunderstanding throughout OPC organizations regarding the extent to which the provisions of the Airspace Control Order applied to MCC helicopter operations."
- **Lack of operating experience**—"The AWACS mission crew commander on 14 April 1994, who had flown only one sortie in the previous three months, was not currently qualified in accordance with Air Force regulations."
- **Inadequately trained personnel**—"OPC personnel did not receive consistent, comprehensive training to ensure they had a thorough understanding of the USEUCOM [United States European Command]-directed ROE [rules of engagement] . . . and neither F-15 pilot had received recent, adequate visual recognition training."
- **Failure to use the most advanced technology**—"The helicopters were unable to hear the radio transmissions between the F-15 flight and AWACS because they were on a different radio." This is because the Black Hawks were not yet equipped with the more advanced HAVE QUICK frequency-hopping radios, while the F-15s and the AWACS were.
- **Systems that are too big, under financed, or poorly run**—The shootdown "was caused by a chain of events which began with the breakdown of clear guidance from the Combined Task Force to its component organizations."

These multiple explanations are extracted from the Executive Summary of the Aircraft Accident Investigation Board Report (Andrus, 1994: 4–6).

Several weeks later, after reviewing all 21 volumes of this report, the Chairman of the Joint Chiefs of Staff, General Shalikashvili, endorsed the findings of the AAIB in a cover memorandum to his boss, the Secretary of Defense. In this memo, the Chairman recommended that Secretary Perry "approve the findings of fact and opinions related to the cause of the subject incident" (Shalikashvili, 1994a: 1). Notice what he endorsed: "findings of *fact* and *opinions* . . . *related to* . . . the *cause*." He did not endorse the Board's conclusions as an *explanation*, or even as *the cause*; but rather as some combination of "facts and opinions" that are in some way "related to" the cause of the shootdown. This is a carefully worded summary of the Board's work. Since we will pick up where the board left off, we should be clear exactly what type of information we are starting with.

The Answers

Five days later, Doctor Perry sent a memorandum back to the Chairman and all of his Service Secretaries and Chiefs. In this document, he officially approved the Board's findings and concluded that

> After three months of inquiry, we now have answers to many questions, and they are profoundly disturbing. The accident was the result of errors, omissions, and failures in the procedures of Operation Provide Comfort, the performance of air units involved, and the operation of equipment used. (Perry, 1994: 1)

Later in the same communiqué, he summarized the "errors, omissions, and failures" into a short list of bullets:

* The F-15 pilots misidentified the Black Hawks.
* The AWACS crew failed to intervene.
* Eagle Flight and their operations were not integrated into the Task Force.
* The Identification Friend or Foe (IFF) systems failed.

Having received the final institutional stamp of approval, these four "causes" have since been generally accepted within the military community as "the explanation" for the shootdown.

In the end, Secretary Perry concurred with the findings of the Board and reported that "we now have answers to many questions." Once again, notice the Secretary's carefully chosen words. The board's investigation answered "many," but apparently not "all," questions.

The Questions

In the following chapters, we examine each of these "answers" in detail. Then, we turn them on their heads. By transforming each answer into a question, we take advantage of the expertise and labor of others and then push one step further. Mechanically, this is a simple process. By asking *why* each of Secretary Perry's bullets occurred, we swim one stroke further up the causal stream in hopes of gaining a deeper understanding of how and why the tragedy occurred.

In sum, we start with a set of "conventional explanations"—accounts provided by subject matter experts that are tightly linked to the raw data. From this concrete base, we push off in the direction of more abstract theory. And, we will do this in a very systematic way, hoping to nourish the raw seeds of descriptive data sown in chapter 2 into seedlings of explanatory theory sprouting in chapter 6. Chapters 3, 4, and 5 then are analytical bridges that span the gap between description and theory.

Across Levels and Time

In chapter 2, the case was presented along two lines of logic—temporal and levels of analysis. We started with the broadest context and oldest history and then systematically worked our way ever closer to the accident—from the general geopolitical context of U.S. military involvement in the Gulf on down through organizational, group, and individual player actions. In the following chapters, we simply reverse the order. Starting with the most immediate causes—individual actions—we then push further and further away from the shootdown, both across time and levels of analysis.

Notice that at the heart of each of Secretary Perry's four answers lies a different actor. In fact, each cause points directly to a conceptually different level of analysis: pilots (individual/dyadic), crew (group), task force (organizational), and IFF system (technical):

Individual. At the level of individuals and dyads, the focus is on the immediate actions of the F-15 pilots. Two individuals, flying as a pair, shot down the helicopters. Chapter 3 explains why.

Group. Airmen in the AWACS operate as a team whose task explicitly requires them to interact with other individuals and groups. Hence, Perry's second bullet is aimed squarely at the crew of the AWACS—a shot that begs analysis of both intra- and inter-group phenomena. Chapter 4 draws from what we know about the behavior of groups in complex organizations to explain why the AWACS crew failed to adequately track helicopters and intervene in the shootdown.

Organizational. Highlighting the failure to integrate Eagle Flight into the broader Task Force shifts our attention up one more notch to organizational-level challenges. Here I highlight issues of organization and structure—those formal coordinating mechanisms designed to synchronize complex actions of multiple subgroups within the task force. Chapter 5 accounts for the Task Force's failure to adequately integrate Eagle Flight into its air operations as well as the failure of its leadership to notice such a serious disconnect.

Technical System. Finally, while IFF system failures are identified as a separate "technical" cause by both Secretary Perry and the AAIB, for the moment suspend your judgment of this "system failure" until we examine this critical link in greater detail. Clearly, the IFF played a central role in the shootdown. However, just because advanced technical components lie at the heart of this system, it doesn't necessarily follow that this was a purely "technical" breakdown. Also, while not formally a *level* of analysis, technology and the technical-human interface are so central to this incident and others like them, that we'll treat them as they occur in practice, woven into and across all other hierarchical "levels." Hence, you'll find references to how IFF information influenced individual pilot actions in chapter 3, how helicopter IFF interrogation responsibilities were perceived by AWACS crew members in chapter 4, and how intraorganizational breakdowns in the co-ordination and dissemination of IFF codes contributed to the accident in chapter 5.

We explore each of these multiple explanations in detail, starting with the individual-level proximate cause: two F-15 pilots misidentified their targets.

3

Individual-Level Account:
Why Did the F-15 Pilots Misidentify
the Black Hawks?

THERE IS NO denying that the pilot of the lead F-15 mistakenly identified the two friendly Black Hawks as enemy Hinds. At 1028 on 14 April, TIGER 01 keyed his main radio and tried to report what he saw:

"VID Hind—correction, Hip . . . no Hind."

Later, during the investigation, TIGER 02 testified:

> Human error did occur. We misidentified the helicopters; we engaged them and we destroyed them. It was a tragic and fatal mistake which will never leave my thoughts, which will rob me of peace for time eternal. I can only pray the dead and the living find it in their hearts and their souls to forgive me. (Andrus, 1994: TAB V-029, 13)

In subsequent testimony,[1] a visibly shaken TIGER 01, specifically selected, trained, and promoted for his self-confidence and decisiveness, did his best to recount what he had *seen* and *done* during those few critical seconds of the visual identification pass (VID). Variously contorting his arms and hands to help tell the story, and periodically closing his eyes to concentrate, TIGER 01 replayed for investigators those few tense minutes of the intercept, as seen through his mind's eye:

> My pass past the helicopter is approximately 500 feet higher than him and about a thousand feet offset to the side. So,—and he's off to my right. So, basically, as

[1] Much of what I argue in this study is based on the premise that context is important. Not only is context important to understand the shootdown, but it is equally important to understand raw data such as quotations taken from informant interviews. Therefore, whenever I present lengthy transcriptions, I will try to communicate as best I can their context—the social situation in which they were constructed. For example, the following passage was transcribed from audiotaped testimony of control witness #26—the F-15 Flight Lead—on 23 April 1994. It is important to note that for this particular accident, the Air Force made the rather unusual decision to treat the investigation not as a "safety mishap"—where the primary aim is to *learn* from the accident, hence witness testimony cannot be used against them for any criminal proceedings—but, rather, as an "accident investigation." For example, prior to consenting to this interview, TIGER 01 was advised that he was suspected of the following offenses: "dereliction in the performance of duties . . . and involuntary manslaughter" (Andrus, 1994: TAB V-029, 2). In spite of the pending charges, he waived his right to remain silent, and answered all questions asked by investigators. His testimony was made under oath, with counsel present.

I'm coming down on him, he's out in the front of my canopy, and then as I pass him on his left side and high, he moves across the front to the right, and I'm looking down through my canopy off to my right side. Okay.

What I *see* [emphasis added] is a Hind Helicopter. I knew this 'cause it had a tapered empennage—which is just basically that the tail section from the bubble part to the tail is tapered, it gets slimmer as it goes back. The vertical tail is sloped so it goes backwards. It doesn't go straight up in the air. It actually, it's slanted towards the rear of the aircraft, the vertical tail. He has sponsons on both sides. Sponsons, basically—some people call them wings. It's the—it's the part of the aircraft that they attach their . . . to put ordnance on. But, because I'm above them, I can only see the tip and the tail of the ordnance, not the actual ordnance, coming out from each side of the sponson. There's no markings and it is a dark camouflaged green blended in very well with the green ground below it.

I'm doing about 450 knots at this point, and he's doing 130, so I'm going to pass him fairly quickly. So, once I get to the side of him—the one place I worry about, especially with a Hind helicopter shooting ordnance, is out in front of his nose, level to below . . . so, I'm going to pull high over top of him, right over top of the helicopter.

I say on the radio, "VID Hind, no Hip." So it actually changed from a Hind to a Hip. I don't remember the exact wording. My thinking at that time was, I was positive of the aircraft I was looking at, but I was not sure that I was saying the right designation for it. So, as I'm pulling up over the top I actually pull out the guide that we have that has the silhouettes of the helicopters, and confirm that the helicopter that I'm looking at is indeed a Hind.

So I come back on the radio and say something to the effect that, "Disregard Hip, VID Hind." Again, my reasoning—I knew what kind of helicopter I was looking at. Due to the speed that it happened and adrenaline at the time, I couldn't remember whether it was called a Hind or a Hip. So I had to look in my book to tell. (Andrus, 1994: TAB V-029, 21–22)

This passage reveals an understandably shaken individual struggling to re-construct what happened during a few fateful moments. This is an example of an individual trying to *make sense* of a seemingly senseless act—to some-how make sensible that which, on its face, makes no sense at all.

On its face, what appears to make little sense is how a highly respected and experienced American pilot, operating under the control of an AWACS, armed with the best training and most sophisticated equipment in the world, flying in clear skies under relatively benign conditions, could mistake a dark green, forest-camouflaged, friendly Black Hawk helicopter with six red, white, and blue American flags painted on it for a light tan and brown, desert-camouflaged Iraqi Hind (see Figure 3.1).

Even if the targets had been Iraqi Hinds, they posed no serious threat to the safety of the F-15s, and there was virtually no chance that such slow

Fig. 3.1. Helicopter Comparison: UH-60 *(top)* vs. Mi-24 Hind *(bottom)*. Photos by Michael Nye.

flying helicopters could have escaped two supersonic jet fighters in the open terrain of northern Iraq. And yet, within the space of eight minutes—from the time of initial radar contact, until the time that both aircraft were destroyed—TIGER 01 and TIGER 02 detected, reported, interrogated, intercepted, visually identified, and shot down two friendly aircraft filled with high-ranking VIPs. How do we make sense of this? Why did the F-15s misidentify the Black Hawks and shoot them down so quickly?

The standard attribution is "pilot error."[2] Clearly, the F-15 pilots "erred"[3]

[2] Perrow estimates that between 50 and 70% of aircraft accidents are attributed to "human error" (1984: 133). Reason concludes that for most people the "oft-repeated statistic that human errors are implicated in some 80–95% of all events generally means that individual human inadequacies and errant actions are the principal causes of all accidents" (1997: 223).

[3] The notion of "human error" is a slippery concept. Jens Rasmussen has investigated this topic extensively and concluded that "errors are, basically, defined as being human acts which

when they misidentified the helicopters. However, Perrow warns us that while *most* "accidents are attributed to 'operator error' or 'human error' . . . there is a growing recognition that this is a great oversimplification" (1984: 67). A brief glance at the lower right-hand corner of the Causal Map (Figure 1.3) seems to confirm Perrow's suspicions. The flurry of causal arrows aimed at the box containing the misidentification event seems to suggest that there is nothing "simple" at all about this particular pilot error.

These two F-15 pilots did not wake up on the fourteenth itching to go out and shoot down some friendly helicopters. There was no malice or evil intent. However, were they negligent? If, after some digging, we were able to determine that they were under the influence of drugs or alcohol, technically unqualified, grossly negligent, disregarding standard procedures, incompetent, or acting just plain stupid,[4] then perhaps a simple conclusion of "pilot error" would make sense. We could stop our swim back up the causal stream secure in the knowledge that "to err is human" and, on this particular day, these pilots may have been a little "more human" than others.[5]

However, apparently this was not the case. After extensive investigations by both safety experts and criminal prosecutors, no charges were filed against the pilots.[6] By all accounts they were technically qualified and com-

---

are judged by somebody to deviate from some kind of reference act" (1992: 1). Psychologists "interested in errors as windows to the mind" have differentiated errors based on an actor's intention: "*slips* and *lapses* depend on wrong execution of a proper intention, whereas *mistakes* depend on proper execution based on the wrong intention" (Rasmussen, 1992: 4). For a thorough treatment of this topic, see Rasmussen, 1990 and Reason, 1990, 1997.

[4] For example, in a series of investigations published in 1995, it was reported that outrageous behavior on the part of some U.S. Air Force pilots contributed to several accidents. One fighter jet apparently crashed as the pilot was trying to "moon" his compatriots through the canopy. In another incident, a cargo aircraft reportedly crashed with the pilot's wife sitting at the controls.

[5] See Rasmussen (1992: 2–9) for a detailed discussion of the nature of human error in causal explanations. For example, in this passage he discusses the nature of determining how far to swim back up the causal stream:

> In causal explanations of an accidental occurrence, its origin will be backtracked upstream the course of events to find the "cause." No objective stop rule can be devised to terminate the search. It is always possible to go one more step backwards in the search and the decision to stop and to accept an event as "the root cause" depends on the discretion of the analyst. The immediate implication is that the choice depends on the perspective of the analyst. Sometimes the search is terminated when an event or act is found which appears to be a familiar explanation, sometimes it stops when a cure to prevent an event is known, and sometimes simply because the causal path disappears. (Rasmussen, 1992: 3)

[6] During emotionally charged investigations, there is always the chance for innuendo and rumor to surface. A letter from Senator Strom Thurmond, the Ranking Republican Member of the Senate Armed Services Committee, to the Secretary of Defense cited an anonymous source who charged that TIGER 02 had previously received a negative evaluation report characterizing him as a "trigger-happy" pilot who should be separated from the service for "dangerous flying and lack of judgment." Subsequent investigation by the SECDEF failed to substantiate these allegations.

petent fighter pilots who appeared to have followed standard procedures on the morning of the fourteenth. In TIGER 02's words:

> I want to remind you that our mission and our intentions on 14 April were honorable. My flight leader and I were and are two well trained, highly experienced pilots trying to perform our mission to the best of our abilities. That mission was not conducted haphazardly, but it was performed in a disciplined manner as planned and as briefed. (Andrus, 1994: TAB V-029, 13)

If they were not grossly negligent, if a pack of investigators under strong pressure to hold someone accountable were unable to indict them based on a reasonable-person standard, then where does this leave us? The pilots still misidentified the helicopters. They still made a mistake; they still erred.

> But human error is a consequence not a cause. Errors . . . are shaped and provoked by upstream workplace and organizational factors. Identifying an error is merely the beginning of the search for causes, not the end. The error, just as much as the disaster that may follow it, is something that requires an explanation. Only by understanding the context that provoked the error can we hope to limit its recurrence. (Reason: 1997: 126)

This chapter attempts to follow Reason's logic, to provide a better understanding of the context that "provoked" the error, to examine the "upstream workplace and organizational factors" that "shaped" what TIGERs 01 and 02 saw during their visual identification pass, to answer the question: Why did the F-15 pilots misidentify the Black Hawks?

Making Sense: Seeing Through the Mind's Eye

Asking why the F-15 pilots shot down the Black Hawks is, in the following sense, more a question of meaning than of deciding. Disaster literature pays much attention to decision making (Allison, 1971; Janis, 1982; Vaughan, 1996). It often places less emphasis on the generation of meaning. Rather than framing the puzzle as, "Why did they *decide* to shoot?" instead, I side with Weick, who prefers to ask: "What's going on here? That's not so much a question of what decision to make as it is a question of what meaning is appropriate so we can then figure out what decision we need to make" (1987: 123). Our pilots had to first determine "what's going on," before they could decide "what to do." I take a decidedly constructionist approach to my individual-level analysis. By treating the ultimate shootdown as a flow of experience to be interpreted, rather than as a decision to be analyzed, I deliberately direct us away from the more common strategy of examining disasters through rational decision-making lenses.

We are constantly engaged in a personal and collective struggle to make sense—"people interacting to flesh out hunches. . . . The image here is one of people making do with whatever they have, comparing notes, often imitating one another directly or indirectly, and then operating as if they had some sense of what was up, at least for the time being" (Weick, 1995a: 133). How TIGERS 01 and 02 "interacted to flesh out hunches," how they "made do with whatever they had," how they "compared notes," how they "made sense of what was up," how they personally and collectively constructed reality on the morning of the fourteenth is central to solving the mystery of misidentification.

"Seeing is not necessarily believing; sometimes we must believe before we can see" (Perrow, 1984: 9). Often even when we see, we do not believe. By the time TIGER 01 looked down through his canopy at 1028, he couldn't help but *see* a Hind helicopter. The Hind was constructed in his mind's eye at the intersection of a sufficiently ambiguous stimulus, a strong set of expectations, and a perverse desire to see an enemy target. This is the short answer to the misidentification question.

Ambiguous Stimulus: What Did They Actually See?

What was actually "out there" for TIGER 01 to see when he flew by on his visual identification pass?[7] Two UH-60 Army Black Hawk Helicopters (50′ × 20′ × 9′), painted with dark forest green camouflage infrared suppressive paint, outfitted with external fuel tanks, also marked with six red, white, and blue American flags, (3′ × 1′10″)—one on each cabin door, one on each auxiliary fuel tank, one on the nose, and one on the fuselage belly. The helicopters were flying approximately 200 feet above the ground at a speed of 130 knots. The F-15s flew by at approximately 450 knots, approaching the helicopters from above and behind. The slant distance of TIGER 01 was approximately 1,100 feet, while TIGER 02 closed to within about 1,500 feet.

An extensive human factors vision evaluation was conducted by technical experts from the Visual Psychophysics Branch of the Armstrong Laboratory,

---

[7] Weick warns that we should "beware of Cartesian anxiety" (1995a: 37)—a dilemma defined by Varela, Thompson, and Rosch as "either we have a fixed and stable foundation for knowledge, a point where knowledge starts, is grounded, and rests, or we cannot escape some sort of darkness, chaos, and confusion. Either there is absolute ground or foundation or everything falls apart" (1991: 140). I should warn you that the philosophy of Descartes in no way makes me anxious, and similarly, I have no problem with a hazard that Burrell and Morgan have identified as "ontological oscillation" (1979: 266)—the free movement back and forth between a concrete, objective world and one that is subjectively constructed. "People who study sensemaking oscillate ontologically because that is what helps them understand the actions of people in everyday life who could care less about ontology" (Weick, 1995a: 35). What was actually "out there" were two friendly Black Hawks; what TIGER 01 "saw" was an enemy Hind. I have no problem with this.

at Brooks AFB in Texas. The expressed purpose of this evaluation was to "provide information concerning the physical and psychophysiological factors that influenced the visibility of the two UH-60 Black Hawk helicopters preceding the accident" (Andrus, 1994: TAB O, 1). Based on recovered technical data, visual angles of the helicopter and U.S. flag markers were calculated assuming several different flight geometries. Applying extensive optical modeling techniques and accepted visual standards, this information was analyzed to determine the range of contrasts of the helicopters against the Iraqi terrain and to predict whether the helicopter and flags were above identification thresholds—given flight geometries, visual acuities of the pilots, absorption properties of USAF sun and "shooter" visors, and optical distortions in the F-15 canopies.

Even this sophisticated analysis yielded equivocal results. While investigators concluded that the speeds and ranges of both F-15s during their VID pass were neither too fast nor too distant to preclude the pilots from optically distinguishing the relevant outline features of the Black Hawks, due to a host of additional "unknown factors," they were unable to confidently predict whether or not the pilots *should* have accurately detected and identified them under the actual conditions of the intercept.[8]

In the final paragraph of their report, these expert analysts, with Ph.D.s in physiological optics, list several potentially powerful "other factors that influence target detection and identification" (Andrus, 1994: TAB O, 12). For example, "visual acuity drops dramatically as fixation shifts from the fovea.[9] If [the pilots] had to rely on peripheral viewing for their recognition or identification of the helicopters or their marker features, their visual performance capabilities would be lower than expected when foveal viewing was used. The magnitude of these potential effects is impossible to predict without knowing which portion of their visual field was used and for which visual tasks" (Andrus, 1994: TAB O, 12). Foveal fixations are not the only unknowns.

In addition to purely physio-optical factors, the human factors report listed two additional influences that would have had a significant impact on the pilot's visual perceptions: previous training and individual expectations. First, they raise the issue of visual recognition training. "The features of a friend or foe aircraft of which the pilots were trained to make identifications will also influence how the targets are identified" (Andrus, 1994: TAB O, 12). Recall TIGER 01's detailed retrospective account of what he *saw*: "I knew this [that it was a Hind] 'cause it had a tapered empennage. . . . The

---

[8] These same calculations did, however, predict that it was very unlikely that either pilot could have identified the U.S. flag markings, given their speeds and distances.

[9] The fovea centralis is a small depression in the retina that provides the most distinct vision. Visual resolution drops with more eccentric viewing. "Visual acuities, such as 20/20, are typically only representative of foveal vision, which corresponds to the center of the visual field" (Andrus, 1994: TAB O, 12).

vertical tail is sloped so it goes backwards. . . . He has sponsons on both sides" (Andrus, 1994, TAB V-029, 21). During visual recognition or "viz-recce training," pilots are taught that three distinguishing features of Hind helicopters are their tapered empennage, a rear-slanting tail, and ordnance-carrying sponsons. Coincidentally, Black Hawks also have narrowing tail sections, back-sloping vertical tails, and, from the top, UH-60 external fuel tanks resemble the ordnance-laden wings found on a Hind. TIGER 01 explains: "But, because I'm above them, I can only see the tip and the tail of the ordnance, not the actual ordnance, coming out from each side of the sponson" (Andrus, 1994, TAB V-029, 21).

Due to the range, angle, and speed of the fighters' VID pass, the objective visual stimulus was ambiguous. However, experiments consistently show that when our senses don't supply complete information, we do our best to "fill in the gaps"; we draw from context to "read between the lines"; we match sketchy input with available cognitive schemas to "complete the picture" as best we can. Bruner explains how what we perceive is influenced by what we expect:

> Perception is to some unspecified degree an instrument of the world as we have structured it by our expectancies. Moreover, it is characteristic of complex perceptual processes that they tend where possible to assimilate whatever is seen or heard to what is expected. . . . What human perceivers do is take whatever scraps they can extract from the stimulus input, and if these conform to expectancy, to read the rest from the model in their head. (1986: 47)

While Bruner has us reading from models in our heads, Weick reminds us that we "interact to flesh out hunches"; we "make do" with whatever we have. All TIGER 01 had was "whatever scraps [he could] extract from the stimulus input"—a split-second view of "the tip and the tail of the ordnance," as seen through the canopy of his jet, speeding by at a relative speed of 320 knots. There were, no doubt, a few gaps to fill in, some lines to read between, and several missing pieces of the picture to complete.

With the help of his silhouette book and guided by his expectations, TIGER 01 "made do" with what he had; he "read the rest from the model in [his] head"; he pulled it all together and made the fateful call: "VID Hind—correction, Hip . . . no Hind." Unfortunately, making do with what he had was not good enough. But what exactly was it that he had to "make do" with?

Responsibility for Air Force threat recognition training is delegated to wing commanders. "Both pilots received only limited visual recognition training in the previous four months" partly due to the disruption of normal training caused by the Wing's physical relocation from one base to another in Germany (Andrus, 1994: vol. 2, 43). The last training they received prior to the accident was in December of 1993. This training consisted of viewing "beer shots"[10] of enemy and friendly aircraft projected on a screen from a 35mm projector. Only 5 percent of the slides depicted helicopters and, not surprisingly, almost all of these photos were taken from the ground looking up. Not only is this the most convenient angle to photograph, but it is also the angle of most interest to the Army—the service that supplied the photos, a service that generally doesn't see helicopters from above. Most photos in the deck showed either the front, bottom, or side of the aircraft. None were taken from the above aft quadrant—the position from which the F-15s intercepted the Black Hawks, the position from which most fighters would view a helicopter. Also, there were very few slides of U.S. Black Hawks in the "training decks," and apparently none with wings and auxiliary tanks attached. Additionally, none of the F-15 pilots' intelligence briefings or "spin up" training[11] ever covered the camouflage scheme of Iraqi helicopters—light brown and desert tan.

Interviews with other fighter pilots reveal that even when viz-recce training is timely, and even when slides portray more appropriate viewing angles, in general, an F-15 pilot's helicopter recognition skills are limited. This is primarily because most F-15 pilots consider helicopter recognition to be a relatively unimportant skill. With the possible exception of F-16s, which routinely fly at low levels, most air superiority fighters spend relatively little time flying "on the deck"—down in helicopter territory.[12] Their primary mission is air-to-air combat against other fast movers. Next to surface-to-air missiles (SAMs), an F-15's greatest threat is another fighter. Hence, as a matter of survival, and as a result of having most of their operational training focused on high-altitude aerial combat, most F-15 pilots' attention during recognition training is focused on accurately identifying their most likely contacts, their most dangerous threats—other high-altitude friendly and enemy fighters—not relatively harmless helicopters that fly low and slow.

In addition to recognition training, the second critical unknown raised by the Board's experts on human factors was the F-15 pilots' expectations, their mindsets at the time of the VID:

---

[10] Pilots refer to such training slides as "beer shots" because many of the aircraft photos appear as they might to someone who was drunk. The photos are deliberately blurred to make them more difficult to identify, to more nearly simulate flight conditions under which pilots will be required to make the actual call.

[11] All personnel and units that rotated through OPC received various forms of "spin-up" training to prepare them to operate out of Turkey into northern Iraq. A portion of this training was conducted at their home station, while much of it was provided by the permanent party staff at Incirlik during their first days in-country.

[12] Even though he was technically certified to fly as flight lead on missions as low as 500 feet, TIGER 01 had flown only two air-to-air training sorties below 1,000 feet above ground level (AGL) prior to the incident. This is out of a total of three and a quarter years of flying as a qualified F-15 pilot. TIGER 02 had not flown a low-altitude sortie since 18 November 1993 and was only current to perform missions down to 1,000 feet AGL.

The expectation set of the F-15 pilots at the time of the target identification could also influence their visual perceptions. For example, if the Black Hawk helicopters were flying in an area where they were not expected to be, the F-15 pilots' visual perception of them may have been biased by their expectations of the types of aircraft they would likely encounter in that area. The information briefed to the F-15 pilots prior to their mission, as well as their experiences on previous missions, could also influence their visual perceptions. (Andrus, 1994: TAB O, 13)

Based on their previous experience and the information they received that morning, what did the F-15 pilots expect to see?

Expectations: What Did They Expect to See?

"The more expected an event, the more easily it is seen or heard" (Bruner, 1986: 47). What did TIGER 01 *expect to see* when he looked through his canopy that morning? He (his mind) expected to see an enemy helicopter. What he (his eyes) saw—the objective sensory input he received—was ambiguous. The combination proved lethal.

There is little doubt that what the F-15 pilots expected to see during their visual pass influenced what they actually saw. "Beliefs affect how events unfold when they produce a self-fulfilling prophecy. In matters of sensemaking, believing is seeing" (Weick, 1995a: 133). By the time TIGER 01 *saw* the helicopters, he already *believed* that they were enemy. All that remained was for him to selectively match up incoming scraps of visual data with a reasonable cognitive scheme of an enemy silhouette. As he flipped through the photos in his onboard "goody book," the ordnance sponsons of the Hind were too easy a match with the top view of UH-60 external fuel tanks. His book contained no photos of Black Hawks. In his own words:

> I had no doubt when I looked at him, that he was a Hind. . . . The Black Hawk did not even cross my mind when I made that visual identification, perhaps, in fact, the only helicopter that crossed my mind was the Hind. (Andrus, 1994: TAB V-030, 44–45)

Believing *is* seeing. Expectations color reality. "When perceivers act on their expectations, they may enact what they predict will be there. And when they see what they have enacted, using their predictions as a lens, they often confirm their prediction" (Weick, 1995a: 152). Given the situation, TIGER 01 expected to see an enemy helicopter. During his VID pass, he then enacted what he predicted would be there; he *saw* an enemy helicopter. When he *saw* what he enacted, using his predictions as a lens, he confirmed his prediction. "If the expectations are accurate enough (satisficing), people gain confidence in their situational assessment and treat it as the definition of the situation" (Weick, 1995a: 146).

The question still remains: Why did he *expect* to see an enemy helicopter? Why did he *believe* that they had to be enemy? Notice TIGER 01's words: "Black Hawks did not even *cross my mind* . . . the only helicopter that *crossed my mind* was the Hind." What influences what *crosses our minds*? What influenced TIGER 01's expectations?

People create their own environments which then constrain their actions (Weick, 1979). Together, the two F-15 pilots created theirs out of the general preflight context, actual mission events, and social interaction just prior to the shootdown. It was this socially constructed, emerging frame of reference that then constrained their actions during the intercept. It was within this subjective mental framework that ambiguous visual stimuli were interpreted.

Preflight Context

What the F-15 pilots expected to find in Operation Provide Comfort (OPC) emerged gradually over a long period of time. In part, it grew out of their past experience in the region. Both pilots had served in the area before. TIGER 01 flew 12 missions on a previous OPC tour, and this was his sixth flight of his second rotation. His wingman had flown approximately 15 missions out of Turkey into Iraq prior to the incident, a few during Desert Storm and several more during the first few days of Operation Proven Force—the predecessor to OPC. Their expectations also grew out of their general knowledge of the political and military history of northern Iraq. TIGER 02 recalls some of the background information that helped set the preflight context for him:

> The baggage that I carried with me that day, we had Intel briefs, an article was in the paper that happened earlier in that week that talked about Iraqis moving a hundred thousand troops into northern Iraq, including elements of the Republican Guard. We had Intel briefs that had taken place the week prior about a German journalist who had been assassinated in Irbil, and the word was coming through Intel channels that Saddam Hussein was very upset with the status of the UN sanctions staying in position and so consequently, he was interested in—in, I believe the term the Intel guy used was whacking a UN worker, they were fair game and he was willing to pay bounties on them. (Andrus, 1994: TAB V-029: 31)

This was the general mindset of our two pilots when they rotated down to Incirlik from Germany. According to TIGER 02, this was "the baggage" he carried with him that day.

The TAOR was technically designated as a "combat zone"; and to a U.S. pilot "suffering through peacetime," combat flights were a rare commodity not to be taken lightly. Even though there hadn't been a confirmed "no fly zone violation" since January of 1992, when an F-16 shot down a MIG-23, the mission on the fourteenth was still no run-of-the-mill training mission. This was serious business and these TIGERs came "loaded for bear." Once again, TIGER 02:

> We come down here, we load up live ordnance, we fly in unfriendly skies, at times flying in surface-to-air missile rings . . . and it's still—it's an unfriendly neighborhood out there and you have to keep that in mind every time you go out there. (Andrus, 1994: TAB V-029: 43, 56)

Mission Events

Building on this general notion of flying a combat mission in unfriendly skies, the specific sequence of events experienced by our pilots on the morning of the fourteenth did nothing to detract from the overall serious tone of the flight. Instead, almost everything they did that morning further reinforced the message that this was no routine training flight over the Nevada desert. Drawing personal sidearms with live rounds, removing wedding bands and all other personal items that could be used by potential captors, and carrying "blood chits" offering substantial rewards for returning downed pilots, all served to drive home the message that the bad guys were real, and the potential for running into them was not insignificant.

As we retrace the critical events of the morning, each one contributed in its own way to the overall construction of a frame of reference within which the fateful VID was embedded, a frame that filtered a sufficiently ambiguous set of inputs in such a way as to "allow" TIGER 01 to see what he saw—a prophecy self-fulfilled:

> Self-fulfilling prophecies need not be simply inadvertent by-products of expectations imposed unsystematically on the world. Instead, given the preoccupation of organizations with foresight, strategic planning, prediction, and extrapolation, we might find that self-fulfilling prophecies become commonplace, deliberate tools when people focus on the future. As they dwell on what might happen, people's expectations become better articulated, stronger, and potentially more capable of being a potent force in their own validation. (Weick, 1995a: 134)

There is little doubt that military organizations are preoccupied with "foresight, strategic planning, and prediction." Military planners constantly "focus on the future." The whole function of military intelligence is to provide commanders with as complete and accurate a picture as possible about current and predicted enemy behavior. The morning of the fourteenth was no different. TIGER 01 explains:

> First thing we do at brief time is talk to Intel. So we went into the Intel office, intelligence office. Our squadron intelligence officer briefed us on—first thing he briefs us on is the number of sorties flown the day previous by Iraqi fighters and

helicopters. . . . That day there was a Roland [surface-to-air battery] at a previous site that was no longer there. So it hadn't yet to appear at a different site, so we didn't know where it was. (Andrus, 1994: TAB V-030, 7)

Plenty of information was briefed about potential threats. Nothing at all was briefed about friendly helicopters.

After the Intel briefing, both pilots sat down together in a quiet room and "game-planned" their flight. This is called the tactical briefing, because its design requires pilots to collectively step through each phase of their upcoming flight, to mentally walk through each step of the mission, to discuss contingency plans for things that might go wrong, to anticipate the unanticipated. As TIGER 01 explains, this includes potential enemy contacts: "We cover in extensive detail during the brief what type of threat we can expect to see, what the ranges are they're going to shoot, and how we're going to handle that" (Andrus, 1994: TAB V-030, 10). Following a standard checklist, in systematic detail, TIGER 01 walked his wingman through the entire flight as he envisioned it would take place. They discussed each step of the mission: preflight and takeoff procedures, friendly air flow, communications and electronics checks, go/no-go items, expected threat, arming procedures, rules of engagement, and intercept tactics. By the end of the tactical brief, each pilot had a "mental picture" of exactly how the mission would flow.

The explicit purpose of this briefing is to build a shared set of expectations, to construct a base framework of beliefs about the predicted events of the morning. Weick was right: "Self-fulfilling prophecies need not be imposed unsystematically. . . . Instead, . . . [such] prophecies become commonplace deliberate tools when people focus on the future." What could be more systematic than TIGER flight's preflight sequence of briefings deliberately designed to anticipate and predict future events? Their tactical briefing was in fact a systematically imposed self-fulfilling prophecy, a "commonplace deliberate tool" used to prepare for the future.

Like world-class athletes visualizing their routines prior to performing, our pilots prepared by imagining; they gamed; they predicted; they anticipated; they planned; they expected. Paraphrasing Weick: "As they dwel[t] on what might happen, [their] expectations bec[a]me better articulated, stronger, and potentially more capable of being a potent force in their own validation." Two coordinating mechanisms became particularly "potent" in this process: the Air Tasking Order (ATO) and the "flow sheet." Not only were these two documents reviewed in detail during the tactical briefing, but the flow sheet itself was carried with the pilots on their kneeboards as a primary reference for the mission. TIGER 01:

The source document for our planning is the ATO [Air Tasking Order]. They use this to assist us—the flow sheet that's in the front of this—but where I would really expect to find out, no kidding, what's happening with the Black Hawks would be in the ATO. If it's not there, it shouldn't be happening. (Andrus, 1994: TAB V-029)

No takeoff times were listed in the ATO for Eagle Flight on the fourteenth.

Recall that the flow sheet is an unclassified portion of the daily ATO (or FRAG) that graphically portrays the scheduled flow of all friendly aircraft into the TAOR. Two aspects of the flow sheet were particularly potent forces in the formulation of TIGER flight's expectations. First, there were no helicopters mentioned anywhere on the flow sheet. Second, TIGER flight was listed as the very first mission into the TAOR. All other OPC aircraft are listed below them. All other aircraft are scheduled to follow them into the TAOR.

According to written guidance in the Airspace Control Order (ACO), the two-volume definitive aerial coordination document for the Task Force: "No aircraft will enter the TAOR until fighters with AI [air interrogation] radars have sanitized the TAOR" (Andrus, 1994: TAB AA-1, 8). This was TIGER 01's interpretation:

> The ACO . . . says that aircraft with AI radars will be the first people to enter the AOR each day to sanitize. So, my understanding is, if you're the first F-15 flight of the day, and right now the F-15s are primary air-to-air, so they're going to go in with their AI radars, if you're the first F-15 flight of the day, which we were, you will be the first one in the area. No one else will be allowed in until you ensure there are no Iraqis in the area. And that's according to the ACO. (Andrus, 1994: TAB V029, 35)

Given their understanding of the ACO, reinforced by their being listed on the first line of the flow sheet, with no mention anywhere of helicopters, TIGERS 01 and 02 expected to see no friendly aircraft in the TAOR as they crossed into northern Iraq. They expected no friendlies to enter the TAOR until after they had completely swept it, until the area was sanitized.

However, tactical situations can change quickly. There is always the possibility that an urgent late-breaking mission might not make it into the FRAG or onto the flow sheet. There is always the chance that someone might have approved a last-minute exception to the ACO policy allowing an aircraft to enter the TAOR prior to the initial fighter sweep. These were experienced pilots. They understood how fluid combat situations and complex air flows can be. They also knew that there were several systems in place to pass along such late-breaking news in the event that something important had changed since the ATO was published the prior afternoon, since their flow sheet was run off, since their morning Intel brief.

In fact, prior to "stepping" out to their aircraft, they received one such update in the form of a Battle Staff Directive (BSD). Recall that BSDs are handwritten sheets that contain last-minute changes to information published in either the ATO or Aircrew Read Files (ARFs). On the morning of the incident, both pilots received a three-page BSD with updated missions and call signs. Sure enough, the situation was fluid and the system in place to handle last-minute changes seemed to be working.

But critical information can change even after you "step" to your aircraft. That's why TIGER 01 called MAD DOG—the mission director on the ground—right after engine start. He wanted to make sure that nothing important had changed from the time that he had left base ops until he climbed into his fighter on the flight line. TIGER 01 explains:

> We called him (MAD DOG) regularly after engine start. I told him—the gist of the conversation was, "MAD DOG, TIGER 01 is engine start, words." When we say "words," it means—it's just a short term asking him to give us any information that changed in the ATO, the FRAG order, the weather, the combat diverts, airfield statuses, all that kind of stuff, that we didn't know when we stepped. He knows what information we have when we brief and we step. If any of that changed he would tell us at that time. That's what I'm asking him when I say "words." His reply was, "The combat divert is Batman. The altimeter there is"—I don't remember what it was, but he gave me an altimeter setting to set in my altimeter. He said, "negative words," which means that he has no information that he knows of that I need to know that popped up since the time the ATO came out. (Andrus, 1994: TAB V029, 13–14)

At the final jumping-off point prior to entering Iraq, just 40 miles northwest of gate 1, by design, TIGER 01 again checked in. This time he called DUKE in the AWACS, his airborne link to the ground chain of command. The F-15s were about to enter the TAOR, and the lead wanted to make sure that he was aware of any last-minute changes that may have arisen since taking off, since last talking to MAD DOG. TIGER 01:

> I say, "DUKE, TIGER, as fragged, words." So again, I'm telling him that I have two aircraft as the ATO depicts, with no problems, and I'm asking him if he has any additional information that I need to know that's changed since my brief time. His response again is, "Batman is the combat divert, the altimeter is this, area altimeter in Iraq is this"—and he said, "negative words," which, again, means that he has no information to pass to me that would be any different than the information I had in front of me at brief time. (Andrus, 1994: TAB V029, 17)

So far, so good. Everything was going according to plan. The F-15s switched their IFF Mode I from 43—the peacetime code for Turkey—to 52, the one designated for combat flights inside the TAOR. They "fenced in"—turning on and checking all combat systems.

Try to put yourself in TIGER 01's shoes. You're in the lead F-15, fully armed; you have good communication with both the AWACS and, through DUKE, to your ground command post. Apparently, nothing important has changed since your initial mission briefing earlier in the morning. You are confident that everything is going according to plan. You make some final adjustments to your airspeed so that you cross the international border exactly on time. At precisely 1020, you report to the AWACS (call sign COUGAR):

"COUGAR, TIGER is on station." Usually at this point, if there is any air-to-air activity anywhere in Iraq, COUGAR will give us a "picture call" that tells us what he sees. An example that I had seen a couple days prior, there were actual fighters flying down at K-West air field in central Iraq—or north central Iraq, and he would tell me where their location was and the fact that they were flying. So, he's supposed to give me the "picture" of any aircraft in the area. He says,—he just responds, "Roger," with no picture calls. My assumption is that there is no air activity in the AOR at this time. (Andrus, 1994: V029, 18)

At this point, the AWACS mission crew *was* aware that Eagle Flight was flying inside northern Iraq. By this time, the Black Hawks had already checked in with the AWACS on three separate occasions. Approximately twenty-five minutes prior to the fighters crossing into Iraq, Eagle Flight had reported their departure from the MCC enroute to their first village. And yet, when the fighters reported, "on station," they received no picture call from the AWACS controller. (I examine AWACS's inaction in the next chapter.) Meanwhile, the F-15s were ready to sanitize the airspace over northern Iraq, totally unaware of the two friendly helicopters operating inside the TAOR ahead of them.

Once again, place yourself inside the head of TIGER 01 and try to "make sense" of your situation as you receive bits and pieces of information over the next ten fateful minutes. Be sensitive to your growing expectations as mission events unfold. What do you expect to see in the TAOR as you consult with others trying to make sense of what is going on?

At precisely 1020 you cross the international border. Immediately, you pick up radar hits just off your nose approximately 40 miles out. You see a blip, a green rectangle on your radarscope, as it sweeps back and forth. Something is out there. Could it be? You call your wingman to see if he sees what you do. Meanwhile, you "lock onto" the target—taking your radar out of the sweep mode and focusing all of its energy onto the contact. The lock reveals that yes, something appears to be flying out there on a heading of 100 degrees at approximately 130 knots, very low to the ground. Your wingman confirms the contact with a call of "hits there"—indicating that his radar is also displaying returns in that location.

With your right thumb, you depress a small red button on your control stick—electronically interrogating the contact with your IFF system. You check Mode I first. No response. Whatever's out there, it's not squawking Mode I, code 52, like it should be if it was a friendly flying in the TAOR. You reach down and flip the switch to "auto," which interrogates continuously Mode IV, the other code that all friendlies should be squawking. This time, you get a momentary "sweet" friendly response. But it only lasts about one second, then disappears. Very strange. . . . But, you've seen this before, where an IFF interrogation has given you momentary false readings. You try again. This time, you get another short positive, followed by four to five seconds of negative.

You make the call to AWACS and tell them that you have a contact at a specific location. You wonder if their powerful systems have also picked up your contact. COUGAR responds with, "Clean there"—indicating that he has no returns of any kind at that location. Perhaps the mountainous terrain could be masking COUGAR's line-of-sight radar.

Once again, you call your wingman. You suggest that it could possibly be road traffic. You also try your IFF again. This time, they all check out negative. So, you still can't confirm that he's a friendly. You call the AWACS again and report the target's altitude, location, and heading. TIGER 02 responds first. He tells you that he reads the target with an altitude of about 300 feet; he doesn't think it's road traffic. This time, COUGAR responds with, "Hits there"—indicating that the AWACS's radar has also picked up some returns at that location. But the fact that COUGAR responded with, "Hits there," and not "Paint there," indicates that he too has an unidentified contact, not a friendly IFF response. TIGER 01:

> Now I know all three of us have it. I'm not sure if it's road traffic or not, but I'm going to lock this contact because I'm responsible for the low altitude. I start to descend out of my altitude . . . again I interrogate Mode I, Mode IV. Each interrogation is about 5 to 6 seconds long, and all of them are negative. (Andrus, 1994: TAB V-029, 21)

Descending quickly through 10,000 feet you look out through your heads up display (HUD). The computer automatically positions the locked target into a transparent target designator (TD) box in your HUD. The bogey is ten miles out and once again sitting right on top of a road. TIGER 01:

> So, one more time, I think it's on road traffic. I say something to number two, basically in plain English, "My box is on a road." I'm trying to tell him again it still might be road traffic. At about seven nautical miles, the TD box comes off the road, and this is the first positive indication I have that I'm not locked to road traffic, because I didn't think there would be a car going off the road this fast. I'm pretty sure now that there's an actual aircraft out there. (Andrus, 1994: TAB V-029, 21)

Even from a distance of seven miles, you can't make out an aircraft. At five miles, you finally see it right there in the TD box; it's a helicopter. You make the call:

"TIGER 01 is tally, one helicopter, standby VID" (Andrus, 1994: TAB V-029, 21).

Having already confirmed electronically that he was not friendly, according to the rules of engagement, you still had to prove hostile. To do this, you needed to visually identify the helicopter. You needed to get as close as possible to this low, slow-moving target without getting shot by it, or running into it or the ground. TIGER 01:

> By this time the environment is very low to the ground, something that I'm not used to doing. I'm in a valley with the mountains on both sides higher than me, and the valley is actually getting skinnier. It's not a very wide valley; it's more like a ravine. So, as I pull up over top of this helicopter . . . now my total attention switches to climbing up over top of the mountains, which are right off my nose . . . because if I hit the mountains, I wouldn't be able to continue, but there was a lot of concern for low altitude environment, something we never ever fly in. (Andrus, 1994: TAB V-29, 23, 41)

The adrenaline is really pumping now. Pulling up hard to avoid the mountains looming in your face, you still aren't quite certain what the proper designation is:

> I had no doubt it was a Hind. My only question was did I mix up the wording between Hind and Hip? So I checked my book to make sure. But basically, with the sponsons and the tail section of the aircraft, I was definite, it was a Hind. (Andrus, 1994: TAB V-29, 23)

TIGER 01 was confident; he had no doubt; he was convinced; it was a Hind. He was also wrong.

Given the general mission context, sequence of events during flight, and interaction with the AWACS and your wingman, what reality would you have constructed? What did you believe was out there? What did you expect to see as you looked down through the canopy of your F-15? How many gaps would you have had to fill in as you flashed by?[13] How would you have filled them in?

TIGER 02 made the wrong call; but the VID wasn't over yet.

Social Interaction

In addition to the general context and sequence of validating mission events, a series of social interactions also contributed to the fighters' misidentification. We have already seen several examples of how TIGER 01 turned to

---

[13] To gain a sense of how difficult a task this high-speed VID was for TIGER 01, imagine trying to tell the difference between a Chrysler Caravan and a Ford Aerostar minivan as one of them passed by you going the other direction on an interstate highway, *and* each of you were driving in excess of 150 miles per hour, *and* your two lanes were separated by at least three football fields, *and* the only view you had of the vans was from above and behind, *and* the vans were painted with appropriate camouflage paint, *and* you suspected that the passengers in the van might be armed with the intent of shooting at you after you passed by them, *and* you had a mountain staring you in the face, *and* you had to make this call while your boss observed your performance from another car driving behind you.

others as he attempted to make sense of a vague stimulus—a green blip on his radar screen. Several additional interactions influenced how TIGER 01 constructed a Hind out of a Black Hawk in his mind's eye.

Reality is, in part, socially constructed. From the two pilots' joint gaming of the mission during the tactical brief; to MAD DOG and DUKE's responses of "negative words" when TIGER 01 called for additional information; to COUGAR's "non-picture call" as the F-15s entered the TAOR; to COUGAR's response of "hits there," versus "paint"; to TIGER 02's reply of "300 feet" indicating non-road traffic; the helicopter that TIGER 01 saw when he looked out his canopy was a social construction, a joint effort. It was just as Weick described, "people making do with whatever they have, comparing notes, often imitating one another directly or indirectly, and then operating as if they had some sense of what was up, at least for the time being" (1995a: 133).[14]

The VID didn't end with TIGER 01's misidentification. The process of social construction continued as TIGER 01 once again turned to his wingman for validation:

"TIGER 02, confirm Hinds."

TIGER 02 made his pass and replied with the call:

"Tally two."

Slip back into the cockpit of the lead F-15 for a minute. How would you interpret this response? Does "tally two" mean "tally *two*" as in one, two . . . I count two? Or does "tally two" mean "*tally* two" as in "tally ho" . . . we're off to the hunt? TIGER 02's response was a nonstandard radio call; it was ambiguous.[15] Each pilot interpreted "Tally two" in different ways. Here's how TIGER 01 remembers it:

> I say on the radio, "TIGER 02, confirm Hinds." I don't remember if that was on the main or aux [auxiliary] radio. His initial response is, "standby"—because he, by this point, just as we briefed, was in three to five nautical mile trail and he has not

[14] In this case, "the time being" lasted almost five hours. We've all heard about CNN wars, how Navy SEALs were met by cameras and news crews in the sand, as they stormed the beaches of Somalia. The first time that the F-15 pilots had any inkling of a mistake—that their "sense of what was up" in the TAOR was faulty—was not until around three o'clock in the afternoon. TIGER 02's "first indication . . . that it wasn't perfect was the CNN report" that he just happened to hear as he sat in his Operations Group commander's office later that afternoon (Andrus, 1994. V-028, 28).

[15] In his work on "Organizational Cultures as a Source of High Reliability," Weick emphasized the delicate interplay between expectations and understanding during short radio calls: "Unless pilots and controllers each anticipate what the other is going to say, the clipped phraseology they use would never work. Their communiqués usually ratify expectations rather than inform . . ." (1987: 121). In his later work on sensemaking, Weick warns that expectations "can be a source of inaccuracy in sensemaking, because expectations filter inputs" (1995a: 146). Keep these cautions in mind as you read the following interpretations of the "Tally two" radio call. TIGER 01 is looking to "ratify his expectations rather than inform"; his expectations were a "source of inaccuracy" because of the way that they "filtered input."

gotten close to the helicopters yet. Then soon after that there's a call that says, "affirmative." I don't know if it was, "affirmative Hind, affirmative VID"—but the gist of it was, yes, they're Hinds. That was from TIGER 02. (Andrus, 1994: TAB V-029, 23)

TIGER 01 interpreted the call "Tally two" as a positive confirmation by his wingman of his initial VID. TIGER 02, on the other hand, remembers it quite differently:

I never came out and said that they—positively ID'd as Hinds. I came in on that ID pass—I saw the high engines, the sloping wings, the camouflaged body, no fin flashes or markings, I pulled off left, I called, "Tally two." I did not identify them as hostile—I did not identify them as friendly. I *expected* to see Hinds on the call my flight leader had made. I didn't see anything that disputed that. I've played that particular sequence over in my mind a couple of hundred times. I don't believe I ever came off and called, "Tally Hind." I called, "Tally two," at that point and the ID was based on what my flight leader called. (emphasis added) (Andrus, 1994: TAB V-028, 28)

Remember, TIGER 02 is TIGER 01's squadron commander. In every role relationship except this particular lead-wing combination, TIGER 02 outranks TIGER 01, and can technically command him to do almost anything within the broad limits of "legal command authority." However, as discussed in chapter 2, in a two-ship flight such as this, what the lead says goes. The junior Captain leads; the senior Lieutenant Colonel follows.

This is a rare example of an inverted hierarchy in action. Since such power inversions are infrequent situations, we know little about how they actually work. However, we can speculate. Imagine once again that you are the flight lead; but this time flying on your wing is your roommate, a peer and drinking buddy of yours, and *not* your squadron commander. As you make your high-speed VID pass, the visual stimulus is equally vague (remember the van analogy) and you are indeed unsure of what you actually *see* through your canopy. Instead of confidently calling "VID Hind—no Hip," because you know that decisiveness is an absolutely essential trait of a successful fighter pilot, especially during a combat engagement with your senior rater flying on your wing—you call, "Tally two helicopters," indicating that you were able to count two rotary-wing aircraft, but were unable to make a positive identification of friend or foe. Your wingman responds, as did your squadron commander, with, "Tally two." Might two peers construct reality differently than two pilots operating in a steeply inverted pyramid? Without stretching too hard, you could at least imagine them making another pass before engaging.

Perversely, the inverted pyramid may have worked double deadly duty during the actual intercept. In addition to subtly encouraging TIGER 01 to be more decisive than he otherwise might have been, the inversion may also have encouraged him to be less risk averse, to take a greater chance with his call, confident that if his call was indeed wrong, surely his more experienced squadron commander would catch any mistake. In the unlikely event that TIGER 01 misidentified the helicopters, there is no way that such an error would slip by his boss. Remember, TIGER 02 was "famous" for being credited with the only confirmed kill of an Iraqi Hind during the Gulf War.

Ironically, we find TIGER 02 similarly seduced into a dangerous mindset. However, instead of inspiring inappropriate overconfidence and risk aversity, the expectations built into the situation by the unique dyadic relationship with his junior lead induced a surprisingly high degree of mindlessness and conformity. Langer describes mindlessness as:

> a state of reduced attention. It is expressed in behavior that is rigid and rule-governed rather than rule-guided. The individual becomes mindlessly trapped by categories that were previously created when in a mindful mode. . . . This mindlessness holds the world still and prevents an awareness that things could be otherwise . . . mindlessness may be severely limiting. (1989: 137, 138)

The category that "traps" TIGER 02 is that of "wingman."

Once again, we can speculate about this curiously submissive behavior on the part of a senior officer based on what we know about fundamental human behavior. One explanation expands on the strong cultural legitimacy attached to the role of flight lead. Apparently this is such a strong norm in the Air Force that, without too much difficulty, we can imagine the wingman, even though he is senior in rank, easily slipping into the role of an obedient subordinate. One only has to recall Zimbardo's prison experiment (1972, 1973) and Milgram's conformity experiments (1963) to understand how easily we can slip into dominant and obedient roles, and how strong our compliance to authority figures can be. According to TIGER 02:

> If I'm flying with a wingman, sir, and I'm leading a flight, if I identify those people as hostile, I expect the wingman to treat those people as hostile and, you know, in our business it's the same. If you're working with a Forward Air Controller, if he rolls in and says, "Hit my smoke," you roll in and hit his smoke, and if he has managed to put the smoke on the wrong spot, that's—terrible—that's tragic, but that goes with the business that we're in. (Andrus, 1994: TAB V-028, 30)

TIGER 02 went on to elaborate even further about a less mechanical and perhaps more rational reason why he didn't question his junior lead's call:

> My flight leader had called out the two helicopters as hostile and thus I expected them to be just that. On this point, it's important to note that I had and still have a tremendous amount of confidence in my flight leader. He's a highly experienced four-ship flight leader and is going to be the next flight commander in our squadron. He has had a previous tour as a forward air controller and this brought him

into daily contact with the U.S. Army. Additionally, he was a participant in Operation Deny Flight over Bosnia and as part of that, his unit intercepted more helicopters than any other unit in the coalition. Because of all these things, when lead said that he saw enemy aircraft, I believed him. . . . I'm simply trying to describe my mental frame of reference when we performed our visual identification pass on the helicopters. (Andrus, 1994: TAB V-028, 11)

Whatever the complex mechanisms operating between the lead and his wingman, clearly this was a powerful and important dyadic relationship that significantly influenced their "mental frames of reference."

In sum, the preflight context, reinforced by a series of mission events, set the stage for ensuing dialogues among various task force members—all trying to make sense out of an emergent set of ambiguous stimuli. Individuals turn to others to collectively construct a shared sense of reality. Social interaction serves to refine and reinforce our growing confidence in what is going on around us. Together, TIGERS 01 and 02 made use of what limited information they had available. Together, they worked hard to make sense of sketchy input. Together, the two of them, supported by a large cast of peripheral players, unwittingly colluded in complex ways to socially construct two enemy Hind helicopters. Once constructed, there was nothing left to do but shoot them down. And so they did. But why so fast?

One of the strongest criticisms leveled by Monday-morning quarterbacks of this tragedy is that the F-15 pilots acted too hastily. Two slow helicopters could never have escaped or harmed two jet fighters in the relatively open terrain of northern Iraq. Why didn't they make another pass? Why didn't they take more time to further develop the situation?

Bruner applies the concept of perceptual "thresholds" to explain how powerfully constrained we are when time also becomes a factor:

Thresholds, the amount of time and input necessary for seeing or recognizing an object or event, are closely governed by expectancy. The more expected an event, the more easily it is seen or heard. (1986: 46)

One reading of Bruner implies that TIGER 01 must have had an extremely strong expectation to "see" a Hind. He didn't require a second pass because his threshold—"the amount of time necessary for seeing or recognizing" the aircraft—was so low; his low ID threshold was met or exceeded by the first pass. A second interpretation of Bruner applies this same principle in reverse. Assuming that he entered the scenario believing that he only had one pass to make the VID—you generally don't live to make second passes in the fighter business—then he only had a split second to receive input. The threshold for identifying his Hind was a constant, and a small one at that. Therefore, the powerful grip of expectancy ruled with an even stronger hand than it otherwise might have, had he had more time to make the call. But he didn't. He expected a Hind, and as Bruner reminds us, "The more expected an event, the more easily it is seen or heard." For retrospective armchair quarterbacks, it seems incredible that TIGER 01 could "see" a Hind, because we know what was there. For TIGER 01 it wasn't incredible at all. He expected to see a Hind; therefore his threshold was low—matching the very real constraint of the high-speed pass; therefore, the Hind was "more easily seen."

Numerous studies of the effects of stress and arousal on human perceptions and performance also inform our understanding of the almost reflexive nature of this shootdown.[16] There is little doubt that executing this low-altitude combat intercept, of an unexpected enemy aircraft, in the "unfriendly skies" over northern Iraq, heightened both pilots' levels of arousal. And we know that high levels of arousal increase the likelihood of an individual exhibiting the dominant response (Spence, 1956).[17] We also know that "extended practice produces automatic rather than consciously controlled processes" (Weick, 1985: 40). At least implicitly, all combat training is based on this principle. Therefore in peacetime, we drill endlessly, especially on those skills central to survival. This training philosophy is based on the theory that, under the high-stress conditions of combat, well-drilled soldiers will respond instinctively, without thinking.

When performing in high states of arousal, people tend to exhibit the overlearned, overtrained, dominant response (English and English, 1958; Eysenck, 1982). Therefore, drill seems like a promising solution to combating the high levels of arousal expected in combat. However, this solution is a two-edged sword. As Weick warns, "overlearning is purchased at the expense of flexibility" (1985, 40). He also warns that

> skills trained just to the point of sufficiency may be potentially the most dangerous, since trainees, trainers and commanders alike assume that the skill is available. In reality, that skill will be one of the first to disappear under pressure. It will be replaced by a much more primitive action that has been practiced for a much longer time. (Weick, 1985: 40)

Based on what we know about the limited helicopter visual recognition training received by the F-15 pilots—as Weick says, "just to the point of sufficiency"—we shouldn't be surprised that this was "one of the first skills

[16] For a thoughtful treatment of how stress affects soldiers, see Weick's chapter, "A Stress Analysis of Future Battlefields" (32–46), in Hunt and Blair's edited book, *Leadership on the Future Battlefield* (1985).

[17] We also know that people tend to "focus on fewer cues when highly aroused" (Weick, 1995a: 141). This further reinforces our understanding of the increasingly mindless state that our two pilots entered as the stressful intercept proceeded—thus, removing a little more of the mystery surrounding the misidentification. By his own account, TIGER 01 was "highly aroused" during the VID, a further explanation for the F-15 lead to only "see" those aspects of the Black Hawks that looked like Hinds.

to disappear" under the pressure of the intercept. We also shouldn't be surprised that it was replaced by "a much more primitive action that had been practiced for a much longer time." In this case, the overlearned, more primitive action—the dominant response—was to engage these helicopters as they would a hostile fast mover, a skill that had "been practiced for a much longer time."

The key here is understanding how our pilots encoded the situation. In their article analyzing the benefits and liabilities of habitual routines in groups, Gersick and Hackman (1990) warn that while routines can be efficient and often quite useful when executed at the appropriate time, they can also cause trouble when situations are miscoded and the right routine is executed at the wrong time. Performance can slip if the group miscodes the situation. F-15 pilots are overtrained to engage hostile fighters; they are not trained to intercept helicopters. Intercepting helicopters looked too much like engaging another fighter. Therefore, performance "slipped" as they miscoded the situation.

TIGERS 01 and 02 were well trained and highly skilled in "dog fighting"— aerial combat against other jet fighters. They were not trained to intercept helicopters. Hence, they coded the helicopter intercept to match up with the next closest thing—air-to-air-combat—a task they understood all too well. Once they were convinced that their targets were enemy, they *mis*coded the helicopter intercept as a fighter intercept, and years of training kicked in. They executed an overlearned sequence of actions to shoot them down. The first pilot to make the correct call and engage, wins. The other one dies. Weick summarizes:

> The costs of being indecisive frequently outweigh the costs of being wrong. This means that sensemaking will tend to be schema-driven rather than evidence-driven, which is what happens when people resolve speed-accuracy trade-offs in favor of speed. Time pressure encourages people to seek confirmation of expectancies, to cling to their initial hypotheses. (1985: 153)

Therefore, we shouldn't be all that surprised by the speed with which the fighters engaged after making their VID. The dominant response for the situation encoded as air-to-air combat was to "engage." And so they did— quickly, mindlessly, professionally, and successfully—just the way they were taught.

Desire: What Did They Want to See?

When the stimulus is ambiguous, not only do we see what we expect to see, we also have more freedom to see what we *want* to see. When sportsmen go hunting, they want to see game. Dozens of hunters are accidentally shot each year by over-eager fellow sportsmen, as are hikers, cows, horses, and even dogs. So great is the desire of some hunters to bag a trophy, to see a deer, to test their skills against their prey, that given the right conditions, almost anything in the woods can be *mis*-taken as the object of their desire. We often see what we want to see. Personal motivations can have a powerful systemic influence on our perceptions.[18]

Warriors spend their entire professional lives preparing to do something that most hope they'll never be called upon to do. And yet when called, there springs forth a deep-rooted desire to demonstrate a lifetime's worth of training and preparation. Combat is the ultimate test for a professional warrior. The no fly zone over northern Iraq was officially designated as a "combat zone." Even though it hadn't been significantly challenged in years, it was still one of the few skies in the world where U.S. fighter pilots had a chance (no matter how remote) to test their mettle against a real enemy. By the time the F-15 pilots made their visual pass, not only did they expect to see the enemy, there was a part of them that no doubt wanted to see the enemy.

> When asked by investigators how he felt after downing the helicopter, TIGER 02 explained: Again, I thought it was a hostile helicopter and I was—pretty excited about having done that . . . that—that's the air-to-air business, that's part of what we do is—is to go out and project air superiority and we had done that and I was—I was pretty excited about having done that. (Andrus, 1994: TAB V-028, 36)

TIGER 02 was "excited" to have done what he was trained to do. He was proud to have had the opportunity to accomplish his mission, to deny the UN-designated airspace to enemy aircraft, to have tested his mettle against a real enemy and won.

Similarly, TIGER 01 responded to the same question in this way:

> It was a—I don't know how to explain it. It was a good, but bad feeling at the same time. Something I had never done before. My adrenaline was high. I was excited that the missile worked and hit and I did everything right. But, at the same time it wasn't what I expected. It was still an aircraft blown up. (Andrus, 1994: TAB V-29, 62)

Even though "it wasn't what he expected," he too was "excited" that he had "done everything right." Like TIGER 02, he too felt "good" about having passed the ultimate test, a combat engagement against a real enemy.

---

[18] There are many other everyday examples where our desires help influence what we see. This happens quite often in sporting events. In baseball, batters see pitches as balls, while pitchers and catchers tend to see them as strikes—not necessarily because either party has an objectively skewed view of the stimulus, but rather because both have a strong desire to see the world in line with their interests. When the stimulus is equivocal, we tend to see what we want to see.

In addition to a personal desire to test one's professional competence, a subsequent General Accounting Office (GAO) investigation uncovered additional evidence suggesting that a rivalry between F-15 and F-16 pilots may have contributed to the F-15's "urgency to engage hostile aircraft" (U.S. General Accounting Office, 1997: 32):

> The Combined Task Force Commander and other Operation Provide Comfort officials acknowledged that a rivalry existed between F-15 and F-16 communities, including those in Operation Provide Comfort detachments. Operation Provide Comfort officials told us [GAO investigators] that while such rivalry was normally perceived as healthy and leading to positive professional competition, at the time of the shootdown the rivalry had become more pronounced and intense. The Combined Task Force Commander attributed this atmosphere to the F-16 community's having executed the only fighter shootdown in Operation Provide Comfort and all the [F-16-credited] shootdowns in Bosnia. In the opinion of the Combined Task Force Commander, the shootdown pilots' haste was due in part to the planned entry of two F-16s into the TAOR 10 to 15 minutes after the F-15s. He said that if the F-15 pilots had involved the chain of command, the pace would have slowed down, ruining the pilots' chances for a shootdown. (U.S. General Accounting Office, 1997: 33)

Note the Commander's choice of words: ". . . the pace would have slowed down, *ruining the pilots' chances* for a shootdown" (emphasis added). This clearly implies that the F-15s wanted an opportunity for a kill; one that they didn't want "ruined" by the F-16s on their tail.[19] F-16s are better trained and equipped to intercept low-flying helicopters. The F-15s knew that F-16s would follow them into the TAOR that day. Any hesitation on the part of the F-15s in either making the call or engaging the helicopters might have resulted in the F-16s getting another kill—additional incentive for the F-15s to see what they wanted to see the first time around.

Summary: Why They Saw What They Saw

Why did the F-15 pilots misidentify the Black Hawks? For me the answer lies at the intersection of an ambiguous stimulus, a powerful set of expectations, and a strong desire to see what they wanted to see (see Figure 3.2). By the time that TIGER 01 finally picked up the helicopter in his target designator box, by the time that he actually peered through his heads up display and saw what he saw, he couldn't help but see an enemy Hind.

---

[19] Everyone's opinions are colored by their perspectives. It is important to note that the Combined Task Force Commander offering this explanation for the F-15s' hasty engagement was himself an F-16 pilot.

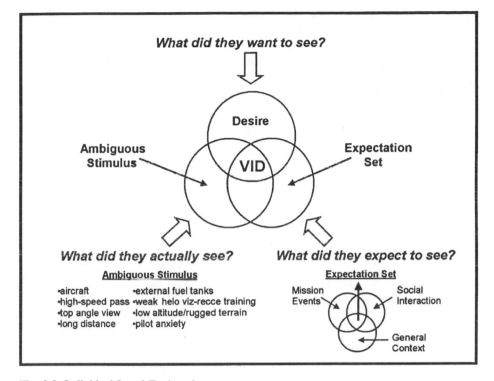

Fig. 3.2. Individual-Level Explanation

Speed, distance, camouflage, and other psychophysiological factors rendered the objective stimulus ambiguous. When presented with an unclear stimulus, we make sense of what we are seeing by placing the inputs into context and by consulting with others.[20] To fill in the gaps, our two F-15

[20] Several classic social psychological experiments have demonstrated these phenomena. As early as 1935, Sherif used the autokinetic effect—a visual illusion in which a stationary pinpoint of light presented in a darkened room appears to move—to demonstrate how individual ranges of judgment converge to a group range. When presented with an ambiguous stimulus, individuals turn to others to create a consensually agreed upon sense of reality, just as TIGER 01 turned to the AWACS and his wingman when presented with the ambiguous stimulus of an unidentified contact. More recently, Zucker (1991) studied the effect of institutionalization on cultural persistence by using the same autokinetic stimulus. In one of her manipulations—"the office condition"—she found that simply by labeling a subject with a position or title, that individual gained a significant amount of legitimacy. Other subjects' perceptions about the range of light movement were more strongly influenced by someone with even the apparently trivial title of "light operator," than they were by non-office-holding members. We shouldn't be all that surprised at the impact that the flight lead's judgment had over his wingman when making the identification of an ambiguously presented helicopter—especially given what we know about the institutionalized strength and hierarchical nature of these two roles.

pilots created a strong set of expectations from what they knew about the general context of their mission, specific key events during their flight, and limited social interactions along the way. Out of this expectation set, a strong desire to engage the enemy, and a relatively ambiguous stimulus, they constructed their own sense of reality. They created the two Hinds; then they shot them down.

4

Group-Level Account: Why Did the AWACS Crew Fail to Intervene?

In an interview with ABC's Sam Donaldson, the AWACS's Mission Crew Commander (MCC) did his best to field this thorny question:

MCC: I know my guys didn't do anything wrong. We didn't pull the trigger. We didn't order them. We didn't direct. We didn't detect. We did nothing wrong.[1] We could have done—when I say "we," I mean me and my crew—we could have done more—possibly. We could have told the F-15s that there were UH-60s down there when they first checked in.

Donaldson: Why didn't you?

MCC: I don't know. And, that's something that we're going to live with for quite a while. (Phillips, 1985)

One of the most nagging questions surrounding this tragedy concerns the inaction of the AWACS crew. After reviewing the data tapes, accident investigators simply could not understand why someone in the AWACS did not question the intercept as it developed. In the following passage, extracted from an interview with the AWACS Senior Director (SD), you can sense the investigator's frustration with this mystery:

Investigator: Based upon what you just told me . . . the mission crew commander is looking at the situation; DUKE is looking at the situation; you're looking at the situation; and the AOR controller is looking at the situation. And none of these four individuals were able to see this continuous intermittent IFF coming and going and sometimes staying for maybe a sweep or two then going away for a whole four—basically, it lasted from 1023 up until 1028. And at that point, I couldn't determine which target was which because the F-15s were—the lawyer is telling me I'm talking too much. My question is basically, what was going on during this time? Why was there not a track on that aircraft until 1027?

SD: I don't know. (Andrus, 1994: TAB V-014, 36)

---

[1] The MCC wasn't the only one on board the AWACS who felt this way. The following comment by the communications technician typifies the crew's sense of detachment from the incident: "Most everybody on the AWACS crew didn't think *they* had done anything wrong. *They* weren't sure if the F-15s had done something wrong. Obviously something was done wrong. I say that because *we* killed twenty-six UN people" (emphasis added) (Andrus, 1994: TAB V-011, 2).

Why was the investigator so outraged? Why was he so frustrated? By taking the Airborne Operational Recording Tapes (AORTAs) generated by the AWACS onboard computer on the day of the shootdown and replaying them through a simulator, investigators were able to re-create the sensor data available to operators during the incident. They were able to see exactly what was displayed on controllers' radar scopes during those fateful minutes just prior to the shootdown.[2] According to this "digital replay," the following sequence of events transpired during the final seventy-five minutes of Eagle Flight. This is what the AWACS mission crew knew, did, and did not do as a major (non)player in this tragedy:

0913   Surveillance section notices unidentified radar returns (reflected off the Black Hawks) and assigns a "friendly general" track symbology and track designator "TY06" to them. Senior Director requests a track tabular display (TD) on track "TY06." This TD included IFF Mode II and III codes.

0916   A green "H"—symbol for friendly helicopter—is programmed to appear at the Black Hawk's location on the Senior Director's scope whenever any IFF Mode I, Code 42 reply (squawk) is detected by the AWACS.

0921   Eagle Flight "checks in" with AWACS on the enroute UHF radio frequency to report its entry into the TAOR at Gate 1. The enroute controller acknowledges this report, observes their Mode I and Mode II IFF codes at the gate, and changes the "friendly general" symbology—track designator "TY06"—to a "friendly helicopter" symbology—track designator "EE01"—to match call sign EAGLE 01.

0924   Helicopters' IFF returns fade as Black Hawks land at Zakhu. Enroute controller "suspends" helicopter symbology—a switch action that temporarily "parks" the symbology in the vicinity of Zakhu, since it no longer has an active signal to lock onto.

0954   Black Hawks depart Zakhu with VIPs and report that they are enroute from WHISKEY to LIMA (code words for Zakhu and Irbil, respectively). The enroute controller acknowledges the call, reintiates the "EE01" track designator, but is personally unaware of the location of LIMA. He has the code list available to him, but does not look it up.[3]

---

[2] AORTAs are magnetic tapes used by the E-3 onboard computer system onto which radar and IFF data received by the E-3 and switch actions taken by the crew are recorded. Through a process called "data reduction," information can be gleaned from the AORTAs using various computer programs. During the court-martial, defense counsel challenged the accuracy of this data reduction process in an attempt to dispute the damaging information that was reportedly available to his client during the shootdown. The Court concluded, however, that while there are some technical difficulties involved with this type of interpretation, by combining what appears on these replays and what appears on the videotape recorded by the commercial camcorder trained on a vacant scope with what multiple witnesses recall seeing, a reasonably accurate reconstruction of the information available to the crew can be determined.

[3] "The enroute controller was responsible for controlling OPC aircraft in Turkish airspace

0955–1011   Green "H" displayed continuously on Senior Director's radar scope.

1012   Black Hawks drop down into mountainous valley; AWACS radar loses line of sight; radar and IFF contacts fade. "H" drops off SD's scope. "No AWACS controller suspended [stopped at one location] the helicopter's track symbology. As a result, the AWACS computer continued to move the symbology based on the last available heading and airspeed information from the helicopters. The enroute controller, who had not transferred control of the Black Hawk flight to the TAOR controller, did not note the heading and speed the helicopters were flying to point LIMA, nor did he identify the flight path the helicopters reported they would follow." (Andrus, 1994, vol. 2, 16)

1013   Air Surveillance Officer (ASO) places an "attention arrow" (used to point out an area of interest) on the Senior Director's scope at the point of the Black Hawks' last known location. This large arrow is accompanied by a blinking alert light on the SD's console. The SD does not acknowledge the arrow and after sixty seconds, both the arrow and light are automatically dropped.

1015   Air Surveillance Officer (ASO) adjusts the AWACS's radar to low-velocity detection settings to improve the radar's ability to detect slow-moving targets. F-15s check in with DUKE and receive, "negative words"—indicating no relevant changes from previously briefed information.

1020   F-15s report their arrival at Gate 1 to the TAOR controller on the HAVE QUICK II TAOR radio frequency. The TAOR controller acknowledges the call, but does not provide the F-15s with a "picture call" (situation update reporting air activity in the area). At this point, the mission crew does not have radar or IFF contact with the helicopters; however, the track symbology continues to appear on their scopes moving along a computer-generated southeasterly path. "As the fighters entered the TAOR to 'sanitize' the area, no one on board the AWACS informed the F-15 pilots of the friendly Black Hawk helicopters in the TAOR, their last known position, or their route of flight." (Andrus, 1994: vol. 2, 17)

1021   The enroute controller finally "drops" (completely removes) the "EE01" symbology for the helicopters—the only remaining visual reminder that there are helicopters inside the TAOR.[4]

---

west of Gate 1. The TAOR controller was responsible for controlling aircraft inside the TAOR, east of Gate 1. Neither the enroute controller nor the senior director instructed the Black Hawk helicopters to change from the enroute radio frequency to the TAOR clear frequency that was being monitored by the TAOR controller. The Black Hawks were also squawking the wrong Mode I code [they never changed over to the different one for inside the TAOR; they continued to squawk the Mode I code for Turkish airspace, the only one they were aware of]. There is no evidence that either the enroute controller or the Senior Director told the helicopters that they were still squawking the Mode I code for outside the TAOR" (Andrus, 1994: vol. 2, 16).

   [4] During the court-martial, the prosecution wanted to know why the helicopter symbology was dropped. According to the SD's testimony, the symbology was dropped for two reasons. First, since it was no longer "attached" to an active signal, they assumed that the helicopter had

1022   F-15 lead reports a radar contact to the TAOR controller, who checks the reported location, sees no radar or IFF returns in that vicinity, and responds with, "clean there." Neither the Mission Crew Commander nor the Senior Director take any action at this point to direct either the weapons or surveillance sections to locate or identify the fighters' reported contact.

1023   AWACS receives intermittent IFF signals from the helicopters in the vicinity of the F-15s' reported contact. The "H" character also reappears on the Senior Director's scope at this time. Intermittent returns increase in frequency until 1026, when they became continuous and remain on display until 1028.

1025   F-15 lead reports "contact" for a second time. This time, the TAOR controller responds with, "hits there"—indicating unidentified radar returns at the location reported by the fighters. However, data reduction analysis clearly shows "IFF paints" at that location—including a reply.

1026   Black Hawk IFF returns are clearly visible on AWACS radar scopes, as are intermittent radar returns—both at the location identified by the F-15 lead. No one on the AWACS advises the F-15s of the presence of IFF data in the target area.

1027   Enroute controller initiates an "unknown, pending, unevaluated" track symbology in the area of the helicopters' radar and IFF returns and attempts an IFF identification. The "H" character is still present on the Senior Director's radar scope.

1028   F-15 lead makes his visual identification pass and calls, "Two Hinds." The TAOR controller responds with, "Copy, Hinds." The track symbology for the F-15s and the helicopters' radar and IFF data are now too close together to distinguish between the two. The F-15 lead calls, "Engaged."

1030   F-15 lead calls, "Splash two Hinds." "There is no indication that the AWACS Senior Director, the Mission Crew Commander, and/or the DUKE made any radio calls throughout the intercept, or that they issued any guidance to either the AWACS crew or the F-15 pilots." (Andrus, 1994: vol. 2, 18)

Subsequent investigation into this sequence of events revealed a considerable amount of confusion within the AWACS mission crew regarding tracking responsibilities for helicopters (Andrus, 1994: vol. 2, 18). What is clear

---

landed somewhere. Second, because the symbology displayed on their scopes was being relayed in real time through a JTIDS (Joint Tactical Information Data System) downlink to commanders on the ground, they were very concerned about not sending out an inaccurate air picture of the AOR. "Even if we suspended it, it wouldn't be an accurate picture, because we wouldn't know for sure if that is where he landed. Or if he landed several minutes earlier, and where that would be. So, the most accurate thing for us to do at that time, was to drop the symbology" (Headquarters, 8th Air Force, 1995: 40.10, 2405–07).

from the evidence, however, is that multiple members of the mission crew had a significant amount of both visual and audio information available to them regarding the presence and location of the helicopters as the intercept developed. What is not clear, what is so frustrating in retrospect, is why more wasn't done—both *within* the AWACS crew to better monitor the helicopters and *between* the AWACS and the fighters to advise the F-15s of the helicopters' presence.

As discussed in the previous chapter, this "non-event"[5]—AWACS inaction—significantly contributed to the F-15 pilots' expectations, misidentification, and ultimate destruction of the Black Hawks. Not surprisingly, such an obvious target also drew a bullet from the Secretary of Defense. In the following indictment, lifted directly from an internal Department of Defense Memorandum, Secretary Perry summarizes multiple "failures to act":

- Although the Black Hawks checked in with the AWACS twice, no one effectively *monitored* the flight while in the "no fly zone" or *told* the F-15 pilots that there were Black Hawks in the area. Then, even though the AWACS's Identification-Friend-or-Foe system indicated that friendly aircraft were in the vicinity of the F-15s' engagement, no one *advised* the F-15 pilots, *warned* the Black Hawks or otherwise *tried to stop* the engagement. (emphasis added) (Perry, 1994:1)

Note how these multiple failures to act fall into two conceptually distinct categories: First, inaction *within* the AWACS crew—failure to effectively monitor the helicopters, and second, inaction *between* the AWACS and other groups—failure to advise and warn the F-15s and the Black Hawks.

In chapter 3, we tried to make sense of the F-15 pilots' misidentification. We tried to understand the actions of individual actors. Here it is "*in*action" that needs explaining—collective crimes of omission, rather than individual sins of commission. Paraphrasing Secretary Perry: The AWACS crew didn't monitor, tell, advise, warn, or stop. In the Mission Crew Commander's own words: "My guys *didn't do anything* wrong. We *didn't* pull the trigger. We *didn't* order them. We *didn't* direct. We *didn't* detect. We *did nothing* wrong." Perry points to AWACS inaction as a contributing cause of the tragedy. The mission's commander points to his crew's inaction to deflect blame. Either

---

[5] The causal significance of nonevents has a rich history in both science and literature. The following exchange between Sherlock Holmes and Inspector Gregory is often cited as a prominent example:

Inspector Gregory: Is there any point to which you would wish to draw my attention?
Sherlock Holmes: To the curious incident of the dog in the night-time.
Inspector Gregory: The dog *did nothing* in the night-time.
Sherlock Holmes: That was the curious incident. (Doyle, 1905: 349)

The dog was significant to Holmes precisely because it "did nothing"—a "curious incident"; just as the AWACS crew is conspicuous by its inaction—an equally curious nonevent.

way, there is a lot of nothing going on here—a lot of nothing that needs explaining.

A Weak Team: Overmatched

A focus on AWACS inaction suggests a group level analysis. After all, "it is the team, not the aircraft or the individual pilots, that is at the root of most accidents and incidents" (Hackman, 1993: 49). Shifting attention away from individual pilots to the AWACS crew requires adopting an entirely different analytical perspective—one based on the central premise that groups are important; and should, therefore, be taken seriously (Leavitt, 1975). This chapter takes groups seriously. By tracing the path of our AWACS crew from its formation to its fateful flight, we'll apply what we know about groups in complex organizations to help us address the question: Why didn't the AWACS crew intervene?

The short answer is that the AWACS crew of record flying on 14 April was weak and underdeveloped. It was weak in both an internal, absolute sense and also in an external, relative sense. In an absolute sense, our AWACS mission crew never grew strong enough as a true team to perform beyond a minimum level of proficiency. As long as mission demands re- mained relatively simple and routine, even our young[6] crew would have performed just fine. Unfortunately, this crew was no match for the unusually demanding set of circumstances they faced on their very first flight together in-country. A weak crew failed to accurately track Eagle Flight helicopters and turned out to be no match for questioning a rapidly developing combat engagement by two fighter pilots.

Ultimately, the AWACS crew's ineffective monitoring of Eagle Flight and failure to intervene can be traced back to a fundamental leadership failure. In short, our AWACS crew experienced a very poor launch. Key leaders failed at the critical task of crew formation. An overreliance on organizationally defined positions, standard operating procedures, and interaction rules led to the unquestioned adoption of a priori scripts as shallow functional substitutes for more deeply shared norms.[7] This is not all that surprising, given the Air Force's historical emphasis on *individual* training and qualification. Air Force personnel systems are primarily designed to select, train, and qualify

---

[6] In this sense, I use the word "young" to refer to the collective age or "mission experience age" of the crew. Individual crew members may have been quite experienced; however, as a team, our AWACS crew was still young in the sense that they had not shared any significant work experiences *together* yet as a team.

[7] Bettenhausen and Murnighan (1985) also found that "deliberate groups," whose members invested time up front to negotiate and fine-tune expected norms, performed better when subse- quent difficulties emerged than did "impetuous groups," who proceeded quickly and confidently, assuming similar a priori scripts.

individual crew members, not intact teams. For example, after the shootdown, a great deal of time was spent trying to determine if the Mission Crew
Commander was technically "mission ready" in accordance with Air Force
Regulations. No emphasis was placed on the relative "mission readiness" of
the ultimate performing unit—the crew as a real team. As a collection of
individuals, they may have been "technically qualified"; as a team, they remained "collectively weak"—weak in an internal, absolute sense. An ad hoc
group of individuals thrown together for this particular rotation never really
gained a true sense of mutual responsibility and accountability for collective
outcomes. In short, the mission crew had not yet developed into a "real
team."

Comparing them to other mission groups—in an external, relative sense—
this failure to develop into a strong team virtually guaranteed AWACS's
subordinate position within the larger OPC supra-system, a position that significantly detracted from their ability to control OPC mission aircraft. All
complex organizations develop informal status hierarchies. The Air Force is
no exception. First, there are two types of people in the Air Force: those that
wear wings and those that don't—pilots and all lesser mortals. Second, there
is a further distinction among pilots. There are fighter pilots—those steely
eyed warriors who fly "fast movers"; and then there are "bus drivers"—
lesser beings who drive slow-moving cargo and tanker aircraft. If you aspire
to the highest position in the Air Force, if you want to be Chief of Staff,
you'd better be a fighter pilot. If fighter pilots sit at the top of the status
pyramid, you can imagine where a nonrated (no wings-wearing) air traffic
controller sits. Given the structurally privileged position of fighter pilots,
even a strong mission crew would have been stretched to intervene in a
fighter intercept based on sketchy information. Hence, it follows that a weak
crew—something less than a "real team"—operating from a relatively low
position within the established social hierarchy, would be doubly hand-
icapped. Under such conditions, crew inaction becomes less mysterious.

Katzenbach and Smith (1993) differentiate between "real teams" and other
levels of performing groups. They also suggest significant performance implications associated with various degrees of team effectiveness. See Figure
4.1 for a diagram of their "team performance curve" and some useful definitions of notional points along this theoretical continuum.

On the morning of 14 April, for a number of reasons that I address below,
our AWACS mission crew fell somewhere down in the performance base-
ment between "working groups" and "potential teams." Though they considered themselves a team, their combined effectiveness was actually worse
than what you would predict by simply aggregating individual capabilities.
In the language of Katzenbach and Smith (1993: 91), they were a *pseudo-
team*—"the weakest of all groups in terms of performance impact. They
almost always contribute less to company performance needs than *working*

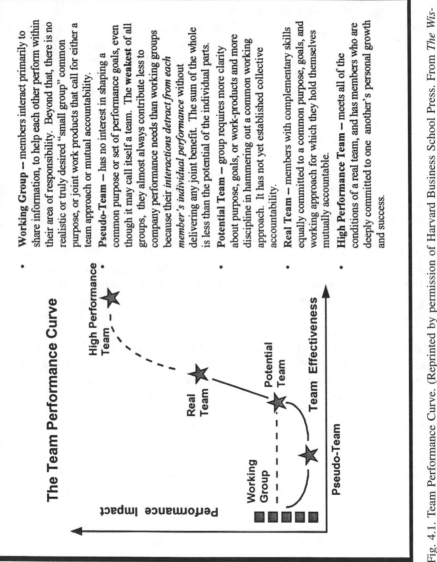

The Team Performance Curve

- **Working Group** – members interact primarily to share information, to help each other perform within their area of responsibility. Beyond that, there is no realistic or truly desired "small group" common purpose, or joint work products that call for either a team approach or mutual accountability.

- **Pseudo-Team** – has no interest in shaping a common purpose or set of performance goals, even though it may call itself a team. The **weakest** of all groups, they almost always contribute less to company performance needs than working groups because *their interactions detract from each member's individual performance* without delivering any joint benefit. The sum of the whole is less than the potential of the individual parts.

- **Potential Team** – group requires more clarity about purpose, goals, or work-products and more discipline in hammering out a common working approach. It has not yet established collective accountability.

- **Real Team** – members with complementary skills equally committed to a common purpose, goals, and working approach for which they hold themselves mutually accountable.

- **High Performance Team** – meets all of the conditions of a real team, and has members who are deeply committed to one another's personal growth and success.

Fig. 4.1. Team Performance Curve. (Reprinted by permission of Harvard Business School Press. From *The Wisdom of Teams* by J. R. Katzenbach and Douglas K. Smith. Boston, MA, 1993, pp. 84, 91–92. Copyright © 1993 by the President and Fellows of Harvard College; all rights reserved.)

groups because their interactions detract from each member's individual performance without delivering any joint benefit. In pseudo-teams, the sum of the whole is less than the potential of the individual parts." In the next section, we will explore the notion of "diffuse responsibility" as a mechanism to help explain how interactions can "detract from each member's individual performance."

But why only a pseudo-team? Why not the real thing? To answer this question we have to trace the history of our particular AWACS crew from its initial formation at Tinker Air Force Base through its fateful performance in the skies over northern Iraq.

AWACS Command Climate

Our AWACS crew didn't form in a vacuum; members were drawn from a larger organizational context, one that came complete with its own unique operational history and command climate. Prior to deploying to Turkey, AWACS crew members lived and worked at Tinker Air Force Base in Oklahoma—the "home of the AWACS"—where all system crews are trained and based. However, increased demand coupled with decreasing numbers of operational airframes and qualified crews forced them to spend most of their time "on the road"—deployed to various regional hot spots and major training exercises around the world.

A brief glance at the upper half of the Causal Map (see Figure 1.3) reveals a troubling combination of environmental forces at work. Beginning with the fall of the Soviet Union, cries for "peace dividends" led to shrinking defense budgets, base closings, and dramatic cuts in the size of the military. However, at the same time that the Pentagon was downsizing, a changing world order demanded significant U.S. military involvement in a series of challenging operations. For example, major cuts had to be temporarily halted and quickly reversed to meet the demands of the Gulf War. Immediately following this massive deployment, a series of smaller "operations other than war" flared up. These missions kept all three services humming at higher sustained operational tempos (OPTEMPOs) than almost anything they had experienced during the Cold War. By the spring of 1993, this combination of decreasing resources and increasing OPTEMPO was beginning to take its toll on both military personnel and equipment.

AWACS crews were not immune; they were in demand everywhere. Increased operational deployments, budget cuts, aging airframes, personnel turbulence, early retirements, force-outs, slowed promotions, deferred maintenance, and delayed fielding of new equipment all contributed to a rapidly deteriorating command climate within the AWACS community. The following comments are extracted from an internal "quality of life survey" conducted in the AWACS's parent Wing just prior to deployment (Anonymous, 1994):

> Our senior leaders are not interested in communicating with the troops, let alone listening to their concerns. To quote a Chief I have interviewed: *"It will take a serious tragedy*, an airplane and crew lost due to their [senior leadership's] indifference, before they in their ivory tower wake up to the realities of AWACS today." Hopefully, we will wake up to the fact that our aircraft are getting older much faster and our troops are getting younger every day, a potentially deadly combination. The -1 [maintenance summary] has enough warnings in it already. We don't need to add a few more just to prove that old airplanes break more often.

> ------------

> The people are tired and the aircraft are in just as bad condition. At the present rate *it will take a major accident before anything is done*. At that point, it may be too late for some of us. The average crew member feels like a piece of meat. When in truth, the meat is treated better than us.

> ------------

> *The wing is on the fast track to a Class A—with fatalities* if things don't slow down. Stress causes mistakes and the law of averages is against us!

> ------------

> If the wing doesn't slow down commitments or buy new aircraft, then *we're going to either kill people or have the good people leave*! The planes are broke, dangerous, and in need of maintenance very badly. Morale is poor.

> ------------

> *This wing is a pile of dynamite waiting to explode*! This wing has been operating at a wartime tasking for four years and people have bent over backwards and sacrificed a lot to make a success out of the operation. The wing leadership has utterly failed to take care of people's needs.

> ------------

> The mission is important, but grinding people to the bone by sending them TDY 120–200 days out of the year to complete the mission can't continue without bad consequences. *I don't think it will be too long before there is an accident* that brings this to light. The jets and people in this wing are tired (emphases added).

Seen through 20/20 hindsight, these predictions are strikingly eerie.

Context is important. It was out of this unhealthy organizational soup that our AWACS crew was drawn. The supra-system within which work groups are embedded strongly influences attitudes, beliefs, and behaviors (Alderfer, 1983). Given this assertion, then the organizational cards were stacked heavily against our crew from the start. Based on the information contained in this climate survey, our AWACS crew was formed out of a rapidly deteriorating supra-system—an unfortunate situation that no doubt added to the challenges of an already difficult crew launch process.

Organizational Shells

When it comes to crew formation, military and civilian aircrews face some unique challenges (Ginnett, 1987; 1990).[8] Particularly important for our analysis is the fact that such teams are often required to form and perform on little or no notice. Personnel turnover is high; hence, crew members must be interchangeable. Drawing from large personnel pools of technically trained and qualified specialists, such crews continuously form, perform, dissolve, and reform. Under these conditions, traditional phase-based notions of group development seem wanting. Uncovered in leaderless minimal groups, linear steps such as forming, storming, norming, and performing (Tuckman, 1965) simply don't fit the empirical reality of aircrews. How then, are such groups able to form over and over again, so quickly? How then, are such groups able to perform relatively effectively under normal conditions? It was while grappling with this "aircrew formation" puzzle that Ginnett and Hackman developed the concept of "organizational shells" (Ginnett, 1993: 91–97).

In both commercial and military aircrews, organizational shells provide a "predefined or expected set of interactions between various elements of the system which permits simpler and more efficient interactions. All individuals coming together to form the crew bring with them the knowledge, skill, and training necessary to perform the group's work. All these crew members were highly qualified in the task requirements of a role that was designed to enable the group to work" (Ginnett, 1993: 92, 93).

When they initially gathered for their rotation to OPC, each AWACS crew member arrived virtually ready to go. Most of the task, norms, and authority information necessary to conduct their mission was already provided; it came prepackaged, drawn from standard, organizationally orchestrated shells. In a complex organization where personnel turnover is the norm, where mission crews form and dissolve overnight, where individual crew members swap in and out at a moment's notice, such overlapping shells stock organizational shelves with "prefabricated" crews, ready for rapid assembly and operation. While groups' organizational shells "will not guarantee that every component for its formation will be established," they do "suggest that somewhere within the bounds of the shell, one might expect to find certain behaviors, roles, norms, or dynamics occurring" (Ginnett, 1993: 92).

Figure 4.2 illustrates how redundant layers of "organizational shells" pro-

[8] Robert Ginnett, a former Air Force officer and Yale-trained organizational behaviorist, studied how commercial and military aircrews formed and performed. As a result, much of his work applies directly to the question of AWACS crew inaction.

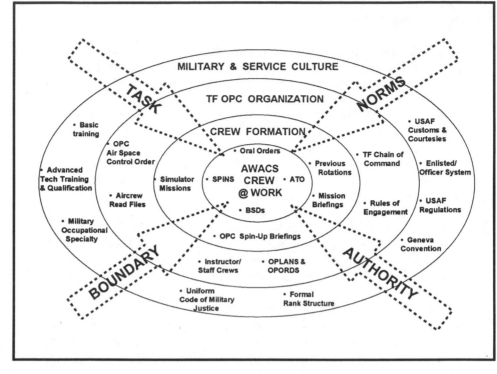

Fig. 4.2. Organizational Shells

vide overlapping sheaths of information that ultimately allow such turbulent teams to accomplish most collective missions on virtually no notice.[9]

In the outermost shell, basic military training in Air Force customs and courtesies provides a broad common base of information concerning fundamental authority and norms. Inside this shell, overlapping layers of organizational training and regulations increasingly fill in the details of role and task requirements. Team boundaries form and dissolve as individual members are selected for various operational crews. Actual composition and member selection is simplified by maintaining a standardized system of personnel training and qualification. Each crew position demands a unique combination of organizationally validated training and experience. Therefore, by the time our AWACS specialists came together to form this particular crew, each of them, as individuals, already possessed sufficient organizational knowledge and technical skills to function in their respective roles—at least to some minimally acceptable level.

The organizational system had trained and validated their *individual*

[9] This figure is adapted from Ginnett's generic conception of organizational shells (1993: 92).

"readiness" to conduct generic missions. However, how do you take a "generic" crew, what Katzenbach and Smith call a "working group" (1993: 91)—each member technically qualified to perform his or her specific task—and form them into a real team?[10] More to the point, why did the system in place at the time fail to meet this challenge for our particular AWACS crew? These questions direct our attention to those activities found in the "Crew Formation" shell (see Figure 4.2).

Good Captain/Bad Captain

When it comes to the task of crew formation, thick organizational shells do most of the work. However, the mere presence of such thick shells can be misleading. Precisely because they provide such a rich base of norms, task, and authority information, their effectiveness tends to seduce crews and leaders both into believing that all of the work of crew formation is done—prebaked by the system—when in fact it isn't. Even the best designed organizational shells require a leader to "breathe life" into them during the critical crew formation process (Ginnett, 1993: 95). However, organizational hubris and time pressures breed a tendency to overestimate the comprehensiveness of such shells. To those immersed in it, such systems appear both omnipresent and omnipotent. As a result, leaders of fast-forming groups often don't invest the necessary time and effort to vigorously develop their organizationally hatched "pseudo-groups" into "real teams."

In his study of airline captains, Ginnett found that paying attention to this requirement was a significant factor distinguishing highly effective captains. Prior to flight, good captains consciously search out and fill in critical gaps in organizationally provided shells. They do this in a variety of situationally dependent ways by "elaborating and expanding" on issues of task, norms, boundaries, and authority as necessary. On the other hand, bad captains either totally "abdicate" (neither confirm nor deny) or even "undermine" (actively negate) preexisting, imported shells. Our Mission Crew Commander (MCC) and Senior Director (SD) had an opportunity to "elaborate and expand" during their pre-mission briefing. In Ginnett's words, they had the opportunity to be "good captains" and "breathe life" into generic organizational shells. However, according to the following testimony of the enroute controller, when the crew prepared to launch on the morning of the fourteenth, both the MCC and SD appear to have "abdicated" instead:

[10] For a detailed theoretical discussion of this question, see "Chapter 6. Moving up the Performance Curve: From Individual to Team Performance," in Katzenbach and Smith (1993: 109–29).

Q: Referring to the pre-mission briefing, you said you felt you had a clear under-
    standing of your responsibilities for the flight. What was the source of your
    understanding?

A: Well, Sir, we were told what our duties would be by the SD.

Q: And do you recall how the Senior Director described your duties?

A: Well, he just said that I would be the enroute controller.

Q: Did he similarly describe other people's duties?

A: Yes, Sir, he specifically said what each controller was going to be doing that
    day.

Q: Did he do that by task description or did he *amplify* [emphasis added]?

A: Merely by task description. (Andrus, 1994: TAB V-016A, 7–8)

The following exchange between an investigator and the AWACS Senior
Director clearly reveals AWACS leaders' tendency to over-rely on thick organizational shells when launching new teams:

Q: On the morning of 14 April, who conducted the pre-mission briefing?

A: The pre-mission briefing before the flight was conducted by the Mission Crew
    Commander.

Q: Do you recall what items were covered in that briefing?

A: The basic items that are usually covered, emergency procedures and basic
    familiarization.

Q: Were crew positions covered at that time?

A: No, they were assigned prior to that.

Q: Were there any briefing items that covered specific duties of any of the crew
    positions?

A: No, not—not at the morning brief prior to the flight.

Q: Would you consider the lack of those briefed items to be unusual or standard?

A: It's standard.

Q: And the reason that they would be considered standard?

A: The reason being [*sic*] is most crew positions are pretty self-explanatory; each
    person has their own area of responsibility which is pretty much dictated by
    their job. The radio operator would perform the jobs of the radio operator and
    such. (Andrus, 1994: TAB V-014A, 2)

This is a powerful illustration of the seductive nature of organizational shells
at work.

The reassuring presence of thick shells works to inhibit critical action on
the part of leaders. Kerr and Jermier have suggested that "certain individual,
task, and organizational variables act as 'substitutes for leadership,' negating
the hierarchical superior's ability to exert either positive or negative influence over subordinate attitudes and effectiveness" (1978: 375). Strong organizational shells fit this description of leader substitutes. Therefore, if such
shells effectively neutralize leaders' influence attempts around such impor-

tant issues as task, boundaries, and authority, over time we might expect leaders to begin to ignore these areas, relying instead on the shells as functional substitutes. This works fine as long as such substitutes continue to effectively fulfill those essential group requirements abdicated by leaders. For most AWACS crews, in most situations, thick organizational shells adequately prepared them to meet routine mission demands. Unfortunately for our crew, the demands were not routine and significant portions of the shells had weakened. In particular, one segment of the crew formation shell—spin-up training—had thinned considerably.

Spin-Up Training

After almost three years of operations, Task Force Provide Comfort had generated numerous mechanisms to help shape and mold periodically rotating, generic aircrews into custom-designed, fully functional OPC teams—at least in theory. Unfortunately, in practice, this process often broke down. For example, due to a last-minute tasking, our crew only received one stateside simulator session. The plan calls for each crew to complete two, full, three-hour OPC sessions *together* in the simulator prior to deploying. The one simulation they did receive was less than effective, partly because the computer tape produced by Boeing used to drive the exercise was based on a much more restrictive set of rules of engagement than those currently in force in OPC. Also, and perhaps most important, several key members of the mission crew were unable to attend. Missing were the Air Surveillance Officer (ASO), the Airborne Command Element (DUKE), and the Mission Crew Commander (MCC)—three out of the four leaders in an AWACS mission crew.[11]

During the court-martial, some witnesses testified to the strength of organizationally provided shells. Others emphasized the importance of training together to fill them out:

> Q: I want to talk a little about crew coordination. We had a couple of witnesses that have testified already that, essentially, doing sims [simulation training]

[11] I have presented this case study to numerous audiences of senior executives around the world. When I reach this point in the story and reveal that several crew members didn't show up for the mandatory spin-up training, I ask them, "Who do you think didn't show up? In your experience, who doesn't normally show up for mandatory training events?" The response is invariably quick and unanimous: "The leaders!" I then ask them why. "Why don't we [leaders] show up for such important training events?" Anxious to defend themselves, I get the following three reasons/excuses: Leaders don't show up for such mandatory training events because: (1) We already know that stuff; that's why we're the leaders! (2) We're busy attending to other important issues! and (3) Because we can; we don't show up to such training events because we can. We're the boss, and so it's up to us whether or not we attend; many times we don't (see excuses 1 and 2 above).

with a complete crew is not that important, that you learn crew coordination in school. First of all, do you think that's true? Do you learn crew coordination in school?

ASO: No, I don't think that's true because every person on the airplane does things different, especially the MCC, the ASO, and the SD; [they] need to have time to learn how—to learn how the other one does business. They all do it differently. Every MCC is different. They all want things done differently and it's the same thing with SDs and ASOs in how are you [sic] going to coordinate. (Headquarters, 8th Air Force, 1995: vol. 10, 97.a11)

Organizational researchers have also found training with a full crew to be important. Hackman explains:

> Constant changes in cockpit crew composition deprive members of the time and experience they need to build themselves into a good team. . . . Scheduling and rostering instabilities constrain a crew's ability to settle in and develop performance strategies and routines that are uniquely suited to the particular demands and opportunities of a given day's work. (1993: 54)

The ASO originally designated and trained to deploy with our crew was instead shipped off to a career school at the last minute. To fill his slot, wing leadership tasked another ASO who was just completing a rotation in Turkey. Instead of returning home with her crew, the new ASO was ordered to stay behind in Turkey for an additional unexpected 30-day rotation to fly with an incoming crew of strangers.

In sum, the crew formation and formal "spin-up" process was not implemented very effectively, resulting in less than robust inner shells. Sworn testimony by the Mission Crew Commander (MCC) supports this assessment:

> We were scheduled for two sim missions where we go out—we go into the simulator and it's a lot of—usually about anywhere from a two to three hour simulator session. We—I did one. *I don't recall who I did it with, but I'm pretty— I'm pretty positive it was not with this crew. It was not with everybody that was a member of our crew during the incident* [emphasis added]. The second sim session that was scheduled was supposed to be a little bit more of the crew that was going to fly in Turkey. That was canceled because of a Wing exercise . . .
>
> The information in the simulator was not current. The maps were out of date. It had old information. The text or the spin-up that they give us—it has—it lists the friendly participants. UH-60s aren't listed as friendly participants. The UH-60s are on the ATO [Air Tasking Order], but again there are inconsistencies. There are no Mode I's listed or anything like that, similar to the way it is in Operation Provide Comfort . . .
>
> We got one spin-up briefing. It was pretty general in nature and again, at no time were UH-60s ever discussed. . . . For mission planning, they gave us only two

copies of the ACO [Airspace Control Order] and the various materials that we needed to review; so you had to, basically, read it fairly quickly—skim it and then pass it on to the next person and they hack off on it. That was also true of the MORF [Mission Operational Read File], and the ARF [Aircrew Read File]. (Headquarters, 8th Air Force, 1995: T-40.10, 2307–08)

Apparently, such lax preparation and less than realistic training is not uncommon in the air traffic control business. While studying high-reliability organizations, Weick found that "training is often used to prevent errors, but in fact can create them. . . . Training settings themselves often have modest validity, as is shown by the widespread agreement that much that is learned during training for air traffic control has to be unlearned once the controller starts to work traffic" (1987: 113).[12] Once again, OPC developed an additional socialization mechanism to address this very possibility, to help incoming AWACS controllers "unlearn" much of what they had learned in their outdated simulation training.

Shadow Crew

OPC leadership recognized the potential for some distance to develop between stateside spin-up training and continuously evolving practice in-country. To help address this challenge, they turned to the experts. For a number of reasons, OPC maintained an AWACS crew permanently stationed at Incirlik Air Force Base in Turkey. In addition to flying operational missions, this unit was also charged with helping rotating crews transition into OPC. They accomplished this by having permanent party "staff or instructor" personnel fly with each new AWACS crew on their maiden flight in Turkey. Therefore, on the fourteenth of April, a "shadow crew" of experts[13] was onboard to answer any questions that our new or "cherry crew" might have about local procedures, to alert them as to how things were *really* done in OPC.

During the court-martial of the AWACS Senior Director, the Mission Crew Commander revealed just how important he felt such first flight "shadow crews" were to his team's transition in-country:

Q: Although you said that you felt rushed, did you feel more comfortable because you knew two staff members would be on the flight?

A: You bet! (Headquarters, 8th Air Force: T40.10, 2348)

Unfortunately, the presence of such "experts" may have done more harm than good. Knowing that they were there and assuming that they would

[12] This apparent disconnect between formal training and operational practice, noticed by Weick in his studies, plays a central role in chapter 6 as I develop a theory of practical drift.

[13] On this particular maiden flight, the "shadow crew" consisted of two key leaders: a staff mission crew Weapons Director (WD) and a staff Mission Crew Commander (MCC).

intervene if any mistakes were made, may have further contributed to a growing sense of confused authority relationships and diffused responsibility within the crew—an argument I develop in the next section.

Pointed cross-examination by defense counsel reveals how such confidence in local staff experts may have been misplaced. By his own admission, at the time of the shootdown, the staff MCC was in the galley "taking a break." The staff Weapons Director went "back to the crew rest seats, read a book, and took a nap" (Headquarters, 8th Air Force, 1995: T40.9, 2248). One member of the court-martial board was so disturbed by this revelation that he interrupted the trial and asked the local Weapons Director, "Can you explain to me how you performed your staff instructor duties asleep in the back of the aircraft?" (Headquarters, 8th Air Force, 1995: T40.10, 2253).

On the surface it appears that there were a lot of well-trained eyes on the scopes. As it turns out, more than a few of them were either busy elsewhere or closed at the time when help was most needed.[14] Under oath, the Advanced Air Surveillance Technician (AAST), who was responsible for directly supervising the three ASTs, admitted, "I was taking a break, and I happened to be monitoring the radios with my eyes closed" at the time of the intercept (Andrus, 1994: TAB V-019, 2). The Airborne Radar Operator admitted that "between the hours of 0630 and 0735 Zulu I was in the back asleep, on break" (Andrus, 1994: TAB V-025, 1). The Airborne Radar Technician told investigators, "I read a lot when I fly. . . . I was reading a book during the time I was sitting on the scope" (Andrus, 1994: TAB V-024, 2). The instructor Computer and Display Maintenance Technician confessed, "I tend to sit there and read books more than anything and kind of ignore the net chatter" (Andrus, 1994: TAB V-023, 2). Therefore, the mere presence of "spin-up" training programs and a large mission crew—complete with shadow experts—may have encouraged an unwarranted level of confidence within the AWACS on its first flight—especially when compared to the questionable benefits actually gained from this training and expert presence as ultimately experienced in practice.

Bad Luck

Practical experience largely reinforces such misplaced confidence. Weak crews fly every day without incident. Most flights led by "bad captains" take

---

[14] Allegations of chronic AWACS crew grogginess peppered the Senior Director's trial. Entered into evidence was a Student Non-Progression (SNP) report charging that on 12 August 1992, while the SD was in school training to be a weapons director, he committed the inexcusable offense of falling asleep while fighters were under his control. Apparently, watching blips on green radar scopes in the back of a modified Boeing 737 for hours on end tends to induce sleep. The MCC was aware of this tendency and had worked out his own solution with the flight engineer: "I like to—I like it to be cold in the back. I like to hang meat in the back. It's cold" (Headquarters, 8th Air Force, 1995: T40.10, 2310).

off and land without notice. According to Ginnett, "The shells for airline crews provide sufficient structure to allow them to perform at some minimal level in spite of ineffective leader behavior" (1993: 94). AWACS's organizational shells performed in this manner. However, Ginnett goes on to warn that "this type of minimally acceptable behavior may well be less than necessary in demanding situations where crew resource management is essential" (1993: 94).

Unfortunately, a series of unpredictable events conspired to make the first flight of our AWACS crew particularly demanding—challenging enough so that "performance at some minimal level" was not good enough. Not only was it unlikely that the F-15s and UH-60s would cross paths at precisely the point where the helicopters were popping in and out of AWACS's radar line of sight, but a second unforeseeable, and at the time apparently benign event also contributed to the confusion by disrupting normal communication patterns on board the AWACS. During their "wake-up orbit," AWACS technicians determined that one of the radar consoles was inoperative. This was not an uncommon failure and certainly not one that generated a great deal of concern. The design solution for anticipated technical breakdowns is to build systems with redundant components. Consoles are going to malfunction and break. Therefore, the AWACS was designed with extra crew position seats. When the enroute controller realized that his assigned console wasn't working properly, he simply moved from his normal position—between the TAOR and tanker controllers—to a spare seat directly behind the Senior Director (SD) (see Figure 2.5).

What seemed like a minor inconvenience at the time, not only removed the enroute controller from the view of his supervisor, but it also effectively removed him from physical contact with the TAOR controller. This second fact is particularly important, because the enroute controller physically "passes" control of all friendly aircraft to the TAOR controller as each flight enters the no fly zone. According to the staff Mission Crew Commander who flew on the fateful mission: "The seating arrangement is very purposeful . . . [key people are] all within earshot of each other, basically. There is noise on the aircraft. You have to speak loud if you have to yell at somebody, but it's possible so they're—they're close" (Andrus, 1994: TAB V-013A, 40). On this morning, as luck would have it (due to a not uncommon, but random event), the two people who really needed to sit close to each other, did not.

In the end, Eagle Flight was never properly passed from the enroute to the TAOR controller.[15] However, the F-15s were. Even though the helicopters

---

[15] Much speculation still exists about this failure to pass the helicopters. Some investigators pointed to inadequate "hand-off procedures." In the words of the Senior Director: "We really don't have a—a set standard that the controllers have to go by. There are several ways they can do it" (Andrus, 1994: TAB V-014A, 3). Among the techniques available for passing aircraft from one controller to another are: sending a computer message (tedious and time consuming to do by email); talking on intercom voice Net Four (sometimes difficult because controllers are

were flying inside the TAOR, they were still talking to the enroute controller on the enroute frequency. The F-15s were talking to the TAOR controller on the HAVE QUICK tactical AOR frequency. The two flights were operating in the same airspace, talking on different radio frequencies, under the control of two different controllers—two controllers physically separated due to a minor electrical problem in a radar console. Systems theorists alert us to how such small beginnings can lead to large outcomes (Maruyama, 1963; Senge, 1990: 80–83). "A small initial deviation that is highly probable . . . [a console failure] may develop into a deviation that is very improbable [friendly fire]" (Weick, 1979: 81).

In sum, group formation is a critical time. "How well or poorly the crew performs is, in large part, established in the course of the first meeting" (Ginnett, 1993: 95). Our AWACS crew was drawn from an unhealthy organizational climate, rapidly deteriorating under the stress of a changing world order. Political and environmental conditions well beyond the control of the immediate organization placed a great deal of strain on its systems. Once solid organizational shells began to weaken and crack under the pressure. Key leaders could have reinforced thinning interior shells with last-minute supplements, but failed to recognize the danger signs in time. A weak team was sent into the fray. As a result of a poor launch and the unfortunate sequence of events encountered on its first flight, our AWACS crew never had the luxury of spending time "at work" to develop into a real team.[16]

As a general set of conditions, understanding the AWACS crew as a weak team is an important piece of the puzzle. But this alone doesn't fully explain inaction. It is certainly possible that even a pseudo-team could have effectively monitored helicopters, if one of its members felt clearly and singularly responsible for this duty. However, this was not the case. It is certainly possible that even a less than fully developed AWACS crew could have

---

simultaneously monitoring several different nets); and finally, physically nudging the other controller and pointing (a method impossible to use with the scrambled seating arrangement). Others maintain that, because the helicopters rarely flew beyond Zakhu—just inside the gate— they "liked to stay on the enroute frequency" (Andrus, 1994: TAB V-014A, 3) and so that's what usually happened.

[16] There is a phenomenon in the airline safety business know as "first flight." Hackman explains: "Even when members of a team have abundant technical and interpersonal skills, it takes time for them to develop into a superb performing unit" (1993: 53). He goes on to illustrate this point by recounting a revealing study conducted by Foushee, Lauber, Baetge, and Acomb (1986) that was designed to assess the impact of fatigue on crew performance. Expecting to find that tired crews perform worse than fresh ones, they compared the performance of numerous air crews coming in off the line to that of fully rested ones by evaluating them in a simulator. "The surprising finding was that the fatigued crews, as crews, made significantly fewer errors than did crews composed of rested pilots who had not yet flown together. Having experience flying together more than overcame the debilitating effects of individual fatigue" (Hackman, 1993: 53).

intervened during the intercept, if it was clear among all players involved that it was their responsibility to do so. However, this was not the case. Without a strongly felt obligation to track the helicopters or intervene in the intercept, neither action took place. One outcome (or symptom) of the AWACS crew's weakness is that responsibility and accountability for these two actions was ambiguous and confused—diffused across various individuals, subgroups, and major players.

Diffuse Responsibility: When Everyone's Responsible, No One Is

Critical mission responsibilities were diffused to the point where no one in the AWACS crew felt responsible enough to track the helicopters or stop the engagement. In the absence of clear lines of authority, the law of social impact explains how obligations to track helicopters and intervene were so diffuse that they failed to generate appropriate responses. Hence, no one in the AWACS positively tracked Eagle Flight or intervened in the shootdown. In addition to being indirect outcomes of a poor launch and a weak crew, these critical failures to act developed as a direct result of two interrelated processes: non-integration at the organizational level and diffuse responsibility at the group level.

First, Army helicopters were not well integrated into the overall operations of an Air Force–dominated Task Force; they just weren't considered very important. During the court-martial, the enroute controller was asked, "What was your understanding as to the priority to be given to helicopters?" He replied, "Unfortunately, we just gave them a low priority; a lot of times we couldn't see them; we couldn't talk to them; we didn't know where they were going; so on the totem pole, they didn't get high priority" (Headquarters, 8th Air Force, 1995: 40.10, 2293). Before addressing this broader organizational level failure in detail (in the next chapter), we will first examine a powerful group level phenomenon that adversely affected our AWACS crew's disposition to monitor and intervene—diffuse responsibility.

The following witness testimony illustrates a puzzling situation, a situation in which no one in particular was responsible, and yet everyone was:

Investigator: Who's responsible on the AWACS aircraft for going through the procedures that the General [Major General Andrus] just described in trying to, in layman's terms, identify the hits there?
MCC: *Everybody is.*
Investigator: Who has primary responsibility?
MCC: *I would have everybody looking at it.* (emphasis added) (Andrus, 1994: TAB V-013, 49–50)

Investigator: Would they [the weapons section] have any responsibility for the
        detection or electronic identification or monitoring of aircraft other than
        fighters—other friendly fighters operating in that area?
MCC: It's possible. . . . As you know, it's—*it's a team effort.* The weapons con-
        troller would—would assist in any way possible, of course. *It is a team effort.*
        (Andrus, 1994: TAB V-103, 13)
Investigator: In the tactical area of operation on board the AWACS, who has
        command, control, and execution responsibilities for ATO tasked missions?
MCC: That's a—that's a very general question. The answer would be *everybody
        on position on the AWACS crew.* (emphasis added) (Andrus, 1994: TAB
        V-013, 19)

*   *   *   *   *   *

Investigator: Who is responsible for tracking north of the 36th parallel inside the
        No Fly Zone?
SD: Weapons tracks Zone Fighters. Surveillance tracks, they track unknown and
        hostile aircraft to the point where we commit on it. Once we commit on an
        unknown or hostile then we'll [weapons section] track it or *it will be a joint
        tracking* then.
Investigator: If the unknown track popped up inside the AOR, north of the 36th
        parallel . . . whose responsibility would it be at that point to observe, detect
        the track and then . . .
SD: To initiate, *it would be the responsibility of the entire crew.* I mean, *everyone
        is responsible* for hitting up unknowns. (emphasis added) (Andrus, 1994: TAB
        V-014, 24)

Key responsibilities were diffused within the AWACS crew. According to
AWACS leaders, everyone was supposed to be responsible for many critical
mission tasks. How can it be then that if everyone was responsible, no one
was? With so many people watching their radar screens and listening to both
the F-15s and the helicopters on their radios, how is it then that no one felt
responsible enough to act?

This is the puzzle that lies at the heart of a theory that social psychologists
call "diffusion of responsibility" (Latané and Darley, 1970; Brown, 1986:
71–73)—a theory developed to explain inaction in groups. Brown captures
the essence of the argument: "Because two or more onlookers together create the social force called 'diffusion of responsibility,' the effective individual probability of helping in a group is lower than the probability that an
individual alone will help" (1986: 73). "Two or more onlookers [individual
members of the AWACS mission crew] together create[d] the social force
called 'diffusion of responsibility,' " and sure enough, the "effective individual probability" of monitoring helicopters was lowered enough to preclude

effective action. Not only was accountability for helicopters diffused within the AWACS, but overall responsibility for controlling the actual intercept was also scattered and confused among the major players. Once again, "two or more onlookers [the ACE, MCC, SD, and ASO] together create[d] the social force called 'diffusion of responsibility,'" and sure enough, the "effective individual probability" of intervening was lowered enough to preclude decisive action.

Latané and Darley's "diffusion of responsibility" theory comes out of a rich stream of research on "unresponsive bystanders" (1970). Conducting a series of experiments that simulated realistic emergencies, these two researchers studied the factors that influence whether or not witnesses to such events will get involved and help apparent victims. In addition to confirming their suspicion that few witnesses choose to help, Latané and Darley also found a surprising relationship between the number of onlookers and the probability that any one of them will help. "The larger the number of onlookers, the smaller the individual probability of helping . . . " (Brown, 1986: 72). Research also shows that the largest impact of increasing the number of onlookers occurs when the numbers go from one to two and from two to three (Morgan, 1978). This is just the range of numbers that come into play in the AWACS. There are three major players involved in the shootdown: the AWACS, the F-15s, and Eagle Flight. There are three sections in the mission crew: the technicians, surveillance, and weapons sections. There are three or four individuals in each of these sections. There are three or four formal leaders organic to the mission crew: the AAST, the ASO, the SD, and the MCC. There are three or four leaders operating at the next level within the AWACS: the MCC, the staff MCC, the DUKE, and the aircraft commander (pilot). Therefore, theory predicts that the effects of responsibility diffusion operated with maximum impact at several levels during the shootdown.

For the most part, unresponsive bystander experiments were designed to study witness responses in situations where there was little or no formal social structure in place. Our shootdown however, took place in an organizational context, a context in which we would expect roles and hierarchy to significantly influence onlookers' dispositions to act. The next section applies "social impact" theory to explain how diffuse responsibility worked to defeat our AWACS crew assuming a largely inert social structure. Following that, I directly address the issue of hierarchy and roles and argue that key authority relationships central to the shootdown were at best ambiguous and at worst contentious. Both within the AWACS and between the AWACS, helicopters, and fighters, so confusing were authority relationships that, instead of solving the bystander inaction problem, they actually contributed to the general diffusion of responsibility and inaction that investigators found so puzzling.

Social Impact Theory

In 1964, around three in the morning, in the solid neighborhood of Kew Gardens in New York City, a vicious murder took place. Catherine (Kitty) Genovese was attacked and savagely murdered while dozens of neighbors watched from their windows in horror and silence. While witnessing a gruesome murder that took over thirty minutes to complete, none of Kitty's neighbors felt responsible enough for the situation they observed to even pick up the phone and call the police. The public reacted in horror, not so much to the vicious death of an innocent victim, but rather to the puzzling inaction of such a large group of bystanders. How could thirty-eight neighbors stand by and watch such a brutal act without ever lifting a finger to help? (How could nineteen members of an AWACS crew stand by and watch two F-15s shoot down friendly helicopters without intervening?)

Apparently the disturbing phenomenon uncovered in the Genovese case turned out to be not all that uncommon. Shocking stories of bystander inaction sprang up in newspapers across the country. Public outcry touched off heated debates about the decaying nature of our society. Fortunately it also stimulated Latané and Darley to conduct their "unresponsive bystander" experiments (1970). Drawing analogies from the physical sciences, Latané (1981) eventually proposed a Law of Social Impact to explain this puzzling phenomenon. According to his theory, we all operate in fields of social forces. Similar to magnetic and gravitational fields, the intensity of these forces impacts on us as a function of three factors: the strength, immediacy, and number of sources. Therefore, the stronger, the closer, and the greater the number of social forces acting on us, the greater the intensity of social impact.[17] Similarly, he derived a "principle of divided impact" to explain how the influence of a single source is diffused or divided among multiple targets. It is this principle that helps explain the disturbing finding consistently present in all unresponsive bystander studies. When applied to emergency situations, the principle of divided impact states that the probability that you will help in an emergency is consistently *higher* if you are *alone* than if you think you are with others. The emergency is the source that emits a social obligation, the intensity of which becomes divided and increasingly diffuse as the number of bystanders increases.

Figure 4.3 illustrates Latané's division of impact as applied to AWACS inaction. The social source is either the obligation to track Eagle Flight or the obligation to intervene in the shootdown. In both cases, the social impact

---

[17] Actually, Latané predicted that, similar to the economic law of diminishing returns, each additional source increases the intensity of impact at a decreasing rate. The second social source provides a much greater kick to the target than the hundred and first.

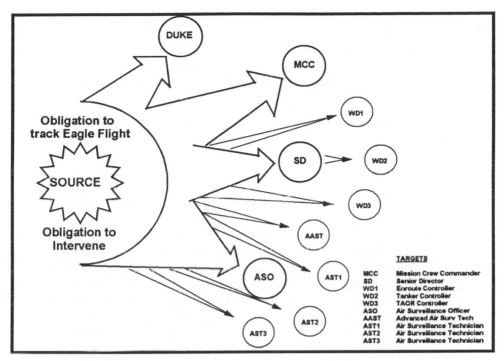

Fig. 4.3. Principle of Divided Impact

is divided among numerous targets. As the number of targets increases, the effective influence of either source on any single actor is reduced.

Drawing from the physical sciences through analogical reasoning, this principle paints a rather clear picture of why we should expect to see increasing probabilities of inaction as the number of social targets increases. However, simply positing a law, by itself—no matter how mathematically appealing and elegant—is not completely satisfying. Fortunately, Latané and Darley didn't stop there. As Brown suggests, "The mediating mental processes supplied by the work of Latané and Darley (1970) are what make the division of intensity really convincing as an explanation" (1986: 32). Two mental processes, "social definition" and "diffusion of responsibility," mediate the impact between the single source and multiple targets so as to decrease the chance of a response:

1. Social Definition—If an individual sees others not responding, that fact helps to define the situation as not really an emergency, not really a situation to which anyone need respond.

2. Diffusion of Responsibility—When one person alone is attendant at

an emergency, then it is clear that the responsibility to help is his; there is no one else. When others are present, it is possible for each to think that someone else must bear the greater responsibility by virtue of ability to help, proximity to the victim, prior relationship to the victim, or some other consideration. Responsibility is diffused; it is ambiguous rather than well defined. (Brown, 1986: 32)

Applying each of these processes to the AWACS crew inaction puzzle helps explain why no one in the crew effectively responded to either obligation.

This was the maiden flight for our AWACS crew. Staff crew members from the permanent party stationed at Incirlik shadowed them precisely to help them adjust to local conditions. There were no explicit or written procedures regarding the control of helicopters.[18] The situation was ripe for social definition. As the Black Hawks faded in and out of radar coverage, and as the fighter intercept progressed, no one on board the AWACS responded. The very fact that no one was responding helped socially define the situation within the crew as "not really an emergency, not really a situation to which anyone need respond." Knowing that the staff crew was monitoring their debut performance, our new crew could only assume that they were (in)acting appropriately. Surely the local experts riding shotgun would intervene if the new crew was misreading the situation. The mental process of social definition mediated the impact between the source and multiple targets in such a way so as to decrease the likelihood of action. The situation was socially constructed as one that required no response.

We have already offered the second mediating process, diffusion of re-

---

[18] During subsequent testimony, the DUKE—the airborne command element (ACE) on the AWACS—commented on his perception of Eagle Flight's importance: "The way I understand it, only as a courtesy does the AWACS track Eagle Flight" (Andrus, 1994: TAB V-026, 10, 24). Similarly, the staff Mission Crew Commander was asked, "To your knowledge, is anybody specifically assigned responsibility for monitoring helicopter traffic in the No Fly Zone?" His answer was simple: "No, Sir" (Andrus, 1994: TAB V-013, 13). Similarly, the enroute controller was questioned about procedures for handling helicopters:

Q: As aircraft arrive at Gate 1, for example, they have been previously identified, according to your testimony, as OPC participating aircraft. Your position as the enroute controller would be to monitor those aircraft prior to that point. Is that correct?
A: Yes, Sir.
Q: Would that also apply to helicopter traffic departing Diyarbakir enroute to Gate 1 to enter the AOR?
A: Sir, on our hand-off procedures—[they] only applied to fighters. We generally have no set procedures for any of the helicopters.
Q: No set procedures refers to written guidance?
A: That's correct.
Q: Were you aware of any verbal guidance or training that you received prior to 14 April regarding helicopters?
A: No, Sir. We never had any guidance at all on helicopters. (Andrus, 1994: TAB V-016A, 3)

sponsibility, as the primary culprit in the AWACS mystery. Social impact theory provides the framework within which this mechanism operates to induce inaction. Diffusion of responsibility powerfully mediated the impact between our crew's obligation to track helicopters and intervene (the source[s]) and the multiple social targets potentially responsible for executing such duties. And, it did this in such a way so as to significantly weaken any one actor's impulse act.

Consistent with Brown's definition, responsibility for tracking the helicopters was indeed "ambiguous rather than well defined." Witness the following summary drawn by a frustrated Major General Andrus, the President of the Aircraft Accident Investigation Board:

> The *AWACS crew* had some confusion regarding tracking responsibilities of unknown aircraft in the TAOR. The *air surveillance technicians* believed their responsibility was south of the 36th parallel and the *weapons section* was responsible for tracking all aircraft north of the 36th parallel. In contrast, the *weapons section* believed the *surveillance section* was responsible for tracking and identifying all unknown aircraft, regardless of location. The applicable Air Force regulations state the surveillance section had tracking responsibility for unknown and unidentified tracks throughout the TAOR.
>
> The *Mission Crew Commander* is tasked with coordinating and directing the activities of both the surveillance and the weapons sections. The Black Hawk helicopters were initially identified and tracked by the *enroute controller*, a member of the weapons section. At approximately 0924, *a member of the surveillance section* asked the identity of the Eagle Flight track, and the *Senior Director* said it was Eagle Flight; *a member of the weapons section* said they were tracking it. (emphasis added) (1994: vol. 2, 18)

At any given time, there were multiple hands in the helicopter pie. Multiple fingers touched bits and pieces of information regarding their presence. However, no one seemed to own them—at least not enough to effectively monitor their status.

General Andrus wasn't the only one confused. Note the embarrassed sense of defeat in the following passage between investigators and the supposed expert, the staff Mission Crew Commander:

> Q: We are attempting to determine who had the responsibility for tracking Eagle Flight.
>
> A: And—and—and I—I don't know. I wish I—I can't say. I—I honestly cannot say whether it was WD1 [weapons director 1 is the enroute controller] or AST1 [air surveillance technician 1]. I—I cannot tell you that. I honestly don't know.
>
> Q: Why is that a difficult question to answer?
>
> A: Because that—that—that's very dynamic. That—that could even change dur-

ing the mission. It was an eleven-hour sortie. They—the—they—the surveillance team could have coordinated with the weapons team halfway through the sortie and said, "Okay, weapons, now we want you to track helicopters in this area." (Andrus, 19994: TAB V-013, 28)

They "could have"; unfortunately, they didn't. The Senior Director (SD) was equally confused. Witness this remarkable exchange between an investigator and the supervisor of the weapons section, the SD:

Q: Who is responsible for tracking helicopters that are tasked, according to the ATO, Air Tasking Order?
A: *No one is responsible*, for a number of reasons. (emphasis added)
Q: Okay. So prior to the mission, neither the surveillance section nor the weapons section is responsible for tracking helicopters for that mission?
A: That's correct. The surveillance section would definitely not be responsible because they don't track anything within our area of responsibility, Iraq north of the 36th line.
Q: So who is responsible for tracking helicopters? Well, if the surveillance section is not responsible, then it must be the weapons section.
A: Except that helicopters, we can neither see nor hear them for the majority of the time they're in the AOR. So we can't track anything we can't see or can't hear. (Andrus, 1994: TAB V-017, 10)

However, both the data reduction tape and the VHS tape—recorded by a commercial camcorder directed at a vacant screen inside the AWACS—clearly indicate that, at least for significant periods of time just prior to the shootdown, the AWACS both "saw and heard" Eagle Flight. Questioning of the Senior Director continues:

Q: What are your procedures to follow if you lose contact, radio contact, between the AWACS and the helicopter? What procedures do you follow?
A: *Absolutely nothing.* It happens all the time. (emphasis added) (Andrus, 1994: TAB V-017, 16)

Once again, there is a lot of nothing going on here—much of which we can explain by applying the subcomponents of Brown's definition of diffuse responsibility.

Because there were so many crew members "present," and each one of them had the necessary information and means available to act, then "it was possible"—indeed likely, given the confused status of helicopters in OPC flight operations—for each of them "to think that someone else must bear the greater responsibility by virtue of their:

- ability to help,
- proximity to the victim,
- prior relationship to the victim, or
- some other consideration" (Brown, 1986: 32).

I will briefly address how each excuse supports inaction—starting with the first one: "ability to help."

Consider the leader-to-led ratio in the mission crew. I count seven leaders and only six subordinates. There were more people looking over shoulders, than there were shoulders to be looked over. There are seven members of the mission crew that, in various ways supervise subordinates: MCC, staff MCC, DUKE, SD, staff Weapons Director, ASO, and the AAST. They are all senior in rank to the six primary worker bees: enroute, tanker, and TAOR controllers, and ASTs one, two, and three. The controllers were all lieutenants, the most junior of which was the TAOR controller, flying on his first operational mission ever. Surely, someone, anyone else on the plane, was better qualified to act than he.[19] The other two controllers each had several missions under their belt, but clearly their immediate boss, the SD (a captain), or his boss the MCC (a major), were both better qualified to act before them—especially when it came to clarifying the ambiguity surrounding Army helicopters or stopping a fighter intercept—two actions apparently well beyond their pay grade.

Even the DUKE, arguably the highest ranking person on the plane, pleaded ignorance as an excuse for inaction. When questioned about his knowledge of AWACS radar symbology he replied, "Sir, my area of expertise doesn't lie there. I'm like a pig looking at a watch. I have no idea what those little blips mean" (Andrus, 1994: TAB V-026, 16). Later, he revealed just how relatively under-equipped he felt, especially when compared to the apparently impressive abilities of the F-15 lead:

Q: When the F-15s called a visual identification on two Hind helicopters, what was your action in the chain of events?

A: My initial reaction was—I said—*Wow, this guy is good*—he knows his aircraft, because not only did he say Hip, but he very shortly thereafter corrected it to Hind helicopters and that meant to me—Well, my initial vis ID may have been a mistake; now I've got them. . . . My reaction was to see what was going to develop. *I did nothing.* (emphases added) (Andrus, 1994: TAB V-026, 18)

This is an example of Brown's first factor in diffuse responsibility. The DUKE clearly felt that "someone else"—in this case an apparently sharp F-15 lead—bore a "greater responsibility by virtue of [his superior] ability to help."[20] Therefore, DUKE "did nothing."

---

[19] Schwarz and Clausen (1970) manipulated the "qualification" variable in a bystander inaction experiment. They simulated a medical emergency—someone having a seizure—when it was known that there was a premed student with experience working in an emergency room among the witnesses. Not surprisingly, results consistently showed that action was more likely left up to the expert.

[20] In the following anecdote, Ginnett reveals this same action-inhibiting dynamic at work in airline cockpits: "One captain with whom I flew made a particularly poor approach which

Turning the tables, both the SD and the MCC lean on the second excuse for not acting. According to the "logic of proximity," these leaders felt less responsible for tracking the helicopters, because they were further removed from the action. Rarely did either the SD or the MCC talk directly to another aircraft; instead, they exercised their influence by working through the appropriate controller. According to the SD, "The controller is the link between the pilot and command and control" (Andrus, 1994: TAB V-014, 15). Hence, neither the SD or the MCC felt *as* "responsible" for physically tracking Eagle Flight. Proximity rules.

It also ruled when the AWACS deferred responsibility for the intercept. Because the fighters were right there, looking at the target, who was AWACS to question the fighters' VID call? The officer in charge of DUKES and MAD DOGS clearly conveys the message that, by virtue of the fighters' "proximity to the victim," they possessed an apparently superior ability to help. Therefore, it was not appropriate for the AWACS to intervene:

> Q: So you are saying if you have a visual ID that *you rely upon the pilot's ability* at that point? (emphasis added)
>
> A: That is our last—in our decision tree as to what we do, when, you know in the identification process . . . our last, our bottom line is the visual identification.
>
> Q: Not only the bottom line, but it would be the apex also in a hierarchy. Nothing comes higher than a visual ID?
>
> A: That is right. (Headquarters, 8th Air Force, 1995: vol. 10, 93.a13)

Apparently, when it comes to combat engagements, the "eyes have it"; proximity rules.

The third excuse, "prior relationship with the victim," speaks directly to horizontal diffusion of responsibility between the enroute and TAOR controller. It also speaks to the diffusion of responsibility between weapons and surveillance sections. When questioned about his failure to assume responsibility for the helicopters from the enroute controller as they passed into his area, the TAOR controller deflected criticism by arguing that he had never talked to the Black Hawks. Following their two check-ins with the enroute controller, Eagle Flight remained on the enroute frequency, even as they flew inside Iraq. From the perspective of the TAOR controller, his section mate, the enroute controller, had established a "prior relationship with the victim,"

---

resulted in an excessive dive on short final, thus setting off numerous alarms. In reviewing the *crew members' inactions* afterward, the young second officer (who literally said nothing during the final approach) admitted that he had never seen an approach quite like that, but figured 'the captain must know what he's doing'" (1993: 89). The tanker controller testified that this same principle is formalized in Air Force Regulation 55–79 which states that "if the fighter pilot feels threatened or *has more knowledge* than someone else, then *he alone is responsible* for what he is doing at that point" (Andrus, 1994: TAB V-018, 8).

and hence, in accordance with the logic of this excuse, the enroute controller bore greater responsibility for them. The ASO defended her section's inaction in much the same way: "Since I've been here, we have never tracked helicopters in surveillance. The weapons team talks to them, so they are responsible for tracking" (Andrus, 1994: TAB V-018, 4). Once again, if another onlooker is deemed to have established a prior relationship to the victim, that effectively relieves those who have not from the responsibility to act.

In addition to ability, proximity, and prior relationship, there is one more obvious factor that should have influenced the diffusion of responsibility in our AWACS crew. Unlike most bystander studies conducted by Latané and his colleagues,[21] our troublesome inaction took place in an organizational context. Therefore, we would expect roles and hierarchy to powerfully influence individual crew members' obligation to act. In situations where responsibility for a specific duty is organizationally defined, either by a witness's job description or hierarchical position of authority, then accountability for action is formally fixed. When roles are clear and the troublesome inaction falls within the boundaries defined by someone's duty position, then fixing accountability is a relatively trivial task. However, as we have seen, many witnesses testified to the significant role ambiguity surrounding the handling of helicopters.[22] Recall earlier testimony provided by the Mission Crew Commander and Senior Director in which they described tracking helicopters as a "team effort," work that was "the responsibility of the entire crew" (Andrus, 1994: TAB V-103, 13; TAB V-014, 24). Apparently responsibility to track helicopters did not fall within any single crew member's formally assigned role.

That still leaves us with hierarchical position as a potentially strong determinant of witnesses' sense of responsibility. Unclear or free-floating responsibilities should migrate upward and roost on the broad shoulders of the first responsible leader. A clear chain of command should resolve most ambiguities by fiat. Unfortunately, authority relationships both within the AWACS, and between the AWACS and the fighters and helicopters, were not very clear.

---

[21] Latané contrived all sorts of "emergencies" to test the effects of numbers on bystander response, including: "a woman in the next room falls and sprains her ankle; smoke begins to pour under a door suggesting fire; someone down the hall is apparently having an epileptic seizure; and a briefly unattended cash register is robbed" (Brown, 1986: 29). Notice however, that none of these experimental situations tested bystander response within a strong organizational context where we would expect issues of hierarchy and roles to play a big part.

[22] During the court-martial, the enroute controller testified to the ambiguous, nonstandard nature of the relationship between helicopters and the AWACS:

Q: Nobody had the responsibility for tracking or flight following helicopters, is that correct?
A: It wasn't standard that we would track the helicopters. (Headquarters, 8th Air Force, 1995: vol. 40.5, 1083)

Roles overlapped vertically, confusing authority relationships and further diluting leaders' normally strong sense of responsibility and impulse to act.

Authority Relationships

The formal organizational chart as depicted in Figure 2.6 for the AWACS mission crew is relatively simple and appears to map out clean lines of internal authority. However, in practice, the overall hierarchical situation in the back of the plane was much more complex and much less clear. ASTs, controllers, and equipment technicians all knew whom they reported to, as did their intermediate supervisors, the AAST, ASO, and SD. However, at the level of the Mission Crew Commander, the authority waters muddy considerably.

Multi-Command Regulation 55-33 states that "the MCC is responsible for the management, supervision, and training of the mission crew. He is responsible for the E-3 mission and performs all applicable duties to support the assigned task" (U.S. Air Force, 1993: 21). However, the MCC is not alone in discharging these duties. He shares responsibility for the E-3 and its mission with several others. First, the aircraft commander (pilot) is overall responsible for the safe operation and flight of the plane. Second, acting in his capacity as the Airborne Command Element (ACE), the DUKE has delegated authority (from the CFACC) to ensure that the larger mission is accomplished in accordance with command guidance and policies. Third, in compliance with political agreements, a Turkish air controller flew along on every AWACS mission. Technically, the Turks retained all air traffic control authority over their sovereign airspace. Fourth, as already mentioned, a staff Mission Crew Commander and staff Weapons Director accompanied our crew on their maiden flight.[23] Finally, the F-15 pilots and Black Hawk pilots

---

[23] The relative authority relationship between these staff crew members and the "crew of record" is not very clear, as the following conversation between the military judge and the MCC of record reveals:

MJ: Did your supervisory responsibilities include the staff MCC and staff WD?

MCC: I was the MCC of record on board the E-3. The other MCC was flying along in a staff position as was the staff WD. Our understanding of why they flew with us was to make sure that we knew the procedures, that we didn't do anything wrong.

MJ: The question is, with them on board, are you supervisory—are you responsible for them or do they supervise you on that flight? What is their role there? Are they just advisors in case you need them or what?

MCC: They are there basically as advisors. As far as their responsibilities, they are technically responsible to me as the MCC.

MJ: Okay, so as the MCC, if you needed them to do something, you could direct them to do something?

MCC: Correct. Major Saylor outranked me, but if I asked him to do—I mean there you get into a little bit of diplomacy.

all worked for separate squadron and detachment commanders. In theory, unity of command is one of the military's most sacred principles of war. In practice however, at least in the back of this E-3, the authority bus was overloaded at the top. Everyone was in charge; hence, no one was.

In the following testimony presented at the court-martial, a former officer in charge of DUKES and MAD DOGS for OPC explains just how contentious and confusing these multiple crosscutting lines of authority had become:

> The situation out there, *there were no real clear lines of authority or responsibility* in this situation. There were sensitivities concerning what the actual role of the DUKE was and the role of the AWACS crews were, because of the multinational forces concern. As a result of that, we were put in the situation that *we weren't really ACEs* (airborne command elements) on board the AWACS. And the AWACS crews were not really in control of anything. . . . It [the acronym AWACS] is probably a misnomer in that AWACS probably did not control anybody in the area of operation and neither did the DUKE, unless it directly applied to the ROE or a safety flight issue. So the aircraft operated out there pretty much on their own.
>
> Under Turkish law and under air traffic control law, *the AWACS crew had no authority at all* to give anybody any vectors or to change their altitude. Their only purview was advisory. As a result of that, in the area of operation, when they got over Iraq, the squadrons that were there basically wanted autonomous operations. They did not want to have close control, in other words, have AWACS controllers be in complete control of the intercepts or any of that stuff. They wanted basically to work on their own. We ran into this situation time and time again at different DETCO (detachment commander) meetings where the squadrons felt that AWACS controllers and the DUKEs were trying to control the situation out in the AOR more than was to their liking.[24]
>
> We hammered it almost continually about the DUKE's word is final in the area of operations. And the reason we did that is because the squadrons were always whining about the authority of the DUKE and that is where I was talking about *we were an ACE, but we really weren't an ACE*, because who was in the aircraft [as DUKES] were majors and lieutenant colonels and until I got there, there were very few pilots in that position. Mostly they were backseaters, F-4 backseaters or F-111 rightseaters.[25]

MJ: Yes, but that's what you were getting at, right, we were trying to figure out whose role was whose?

[24] Interestingly, while the DUKE testified that fighters felt overcontrolled by AWACS controllers and the DUKEs, the tanker controller testified that the DUKE's presence in the back of the AWACS disrupted the normal command structure of the mission crew *as a crew*: "[the DUKE] kind of ties our hands, I think, when we fly in this AOR, because we fly with this DUKE, and he takes over kind of control of the operation, and where *we are trained as a crew* and go and fight in these wars or, you know, to go *as a crew* and do something, we get this DUKE guy who comes on board and he kind of takes over the head honcho role" (Andrus, 1994: TAB V-017, 30).

[25] The backseater in an F-4 and the rightseater in an F-111 are nonrated officers, they are not

There is a sensitivity between pilots and backseaters and rightseaters and navigators that basically that—an F-111 rightseater does not necessarily know the mission of an F-15 or of an F-16 or of any aircraft that he is not assigned to. So, *there
is a point of contention there about whether they had the authority to tell the pilots*
what to do and how to do their mission. In understanding that sensitivity there, we
[DUKES] were always at odds with the squadrons, because many times, almost at
least once a day, they [fighter pilots] would come back and question a decision that
we had made in the DETCO meeting.[26]

As for the helicopters, we had almost no control of them. They did not necessarily maintain their flight plan route in the Air Tasking Order. In fact, they almost
never did. And they almost never talked. Sometimes they would squawk the right
codes; sometimes they wouldn't. As much as we tried to tell them to comply with
the airspace control order, they didn't seem to want to do that. . . . The feeling was
one of—you know, we really had no authority to tell the Army to—*me as a
Lieutenant Colonel in the command post had no authority to tell them or make
them do anything.* . . . So we never really did get a good grip on those guys as far
as exactly what they were doing and when they wanted to do it.

As far as the DUKE on that particular mission, I had to tell him that it was not his
fault. That was not the reaction that he was to expect from the F-15 pilots. That
was the exact opposite reaction that he should have expected. What he was expecting was to be queried as to what they should do, what their course of action should
be. He related to me that he did not really know what "engaged" meant, so when
they said, "engaged," he didn't really understand that they were going to go kill
those guys. And that is why I mentioned before that as a rightseater in a F-111 [the
DUKE'S normal job], it is not his job, nor did the squadrons want him to understand
their job enough, that when they say, "engage" that he would be able to come in
there and say, "no, you are not engaged, this is what you are going to do." (emphases added) (Headquarters, 8th Air Force, 1995: vol. 10, 93.a3–93.a30)

As one witness joked, "Authority relationships were really up in the air."

Notice the highlighted portions of this narrative. Both role conflict and
status incongruence were common dynamics among these groups: "we were

pilots, they are specially qualified navigators and weapons specialists. Recall how the powerful
status hierarchy within the Air Force places pilots (especially fighter pilots) above all others.

[26] According to the General Accounting Office (GAO) report, on 7 April 1994, exactly one
week prior to the shootdown, a significant incident took place that illustrates the contentious
relationship between the Airborne Command Element (ACE or DUKE) and the fighters. "In that
incident, F-15 pilots had initially ignored an Airborne Command Element's request to 'knock
off,' or stop, an engagement with a hostile fighter aircraft they thought was in the no fly zone.
The Airborne Command Element overheard the pilots preparing to engage the aircraft and
contacted them, telling them to stop the engagement because he had determined that the hostile
aircraft was outside the no fly zone and that he was also leery of a 'bait and trap' situation.
After several unsuccessful attempts to call off the engagement during which the F-15 pilots did
not respond to him, he ordered the pilots to return either to their assigned patrol point or the
base" (U.S. General Accounting Office, 1997: 27–28).

an ACE, but we weren't really an ACE"; "AWACS did not control any-body." The DUKE, in his formal role as an ACE (Airborne Command Element) was expected to exercise command authority over all OPC aircraft flying outside a 50-kilometer radius from Incirlik. However, in practice, in his informally subordinated role of advisor to the fighters, any attempts at intervention were resisted.[27] AWACS stands for Airborne Warning and *Control* System; in their formal role, AWACS crew members were expected to *control* aircraft. In practice, "the AWACS crew had no authority at all." In practice, the low status afforded both the DUKE and the AWACS was not congruent with their expected status, that which was required for them to execute their expected duties: "The feeling was one of . . . me as a Lieutenant Colonel in the command post had no authority to tell them or make them do anything"—status incongruence operationalized.

Given the nature and history of flying, perhaps we shouldn't be all that surprised when conflicts over authority issues emerge in organizations with pilots at their center. Over the years, Hackman's studies of airline crews have uncovered three strong influences at work in cockpits: FAA regulatory procedures, cockpit technology, and a factor that he calls "the culture of flying" (Hackman, 1993: 68). The influence of regulations and technology will be examined at length in the next chapter. However, the above narrative by a former pilot, DUKE, and MAD DOG (note the nature of these call signs), clearly illustrates the pervasive influence of the highly individualistic character that lies at the heart of the culture of flying. In flying, this character reveals itself in a number of ways, such as the sanctity of "solo flights" and a deeply held respect for pilots that can "fly by the seat of their pants." In organizations containing pilots, this strongly individualistic orientation raises some serious challenges, especially concerning issues of authority and control.

Not surprisingly then, it seems that everyone wanted autonomy. According to the supervisor of all DUKES: "The squadrons wanted autonomy in the area of operation and they did not want the AWACS crews to be directly controlling them. . . . They wanted, basically, to be left alone" (Headquarters, 8th Air Force, 1995: vol. 10, 93.a3). Apparently, the helicopters also wanted to be left alone. According to the DUKE, "It's kind of an autonomous operation is the way I've always viewed Eagle, above—below and separate of the OPC mission" (Andrus, 1994: TAB V-026, 10, 24). No one wanted to

---

[27] Not only were the DUKE's influence attempts resisted, but the following testimony by the ASO also reveals a hesitancy to tell the helicopters anything: "They [helicopters] are supposed to play by the same set of rules, why do I need to tell them how to fly their airplane? They normally get upset if you do that. And it's verbally over the radio, you can hear them, tell you, yeah I know what I'm doing, leave me alone kind of thing . . . you are verbally reprimanded over the radio for telling them how to do their job" (Headquarters, 8th Air Force, 1995: 40.10, 2255).

be told what to do—especially not a "top gun" fighter pilot by some non-rated "techno-geek."[28] This deep-rooted, highly individualistic culture of flying contributed significantly to the difficult control challenge experienced in the AWACS.

If DUKES found it difficult to control fighters and helicopters, you can imagine how powerless junior controllers felt when faced with the challenge of directing an F-15 pilot. The following revealing discussion between an investigator and the staff MCC illustrates just how little authority AWACS mission crew members felt they had when dealing with fighters:

Q: Missions that are scheduled to go into the ATO, if the MCC wants to make a change, can he do it or will he be overridden by the DUKE?

A: He'll be overridden by the DUKE. The—DUKE is responsible for the fighter flow. He will make the call, "DUKE directs the fighters will—will do something." If we—if we don't say, "DUKE directs," then the fighters normally will not obey the command.

Q: Does that include engagements?

A: If—if we make a call, "DUKE directs, kill this target," I believe the aircraft would kill the target.

Q: If you said, "Kill the target," will the—will the F-15s do it, or whatever aircraft?

A: Possibly.

Q: If one of the controllers gave guidance to one of the fighters to take a certain action, such as terminate the intercept, would the fighter respond?

A: He should terminate.

Q: Would the controller be required to say, "DUKE directs that you terminate the engagement," or would it be sufficient to just say, "Terminate the engagement?"

A: They should comply with the controller's request to terminate. Whether or not they will is your guess as well as mine. If the controller transmitted, "DUKE directs terminate," that would have much more authority than if he said, "Terminate." (Andrus, 1994: TAB V-013, 19–20)

Fighter pilots sit at the top of the authority pyramid, in practice if not in design. DUKES, by virtue of their direct link to the command post and extensive cockpit experience, come in second—but according to witness testimony, it's a rather distant second. Helicopter pilots seem to operate independently of the main Task Force system. This leaves the organic portion of the AWACS mission crew to bring up the rear.

The problem with this powerful informal hierarchy is that it is often at odds with the demands of formal role requirements necessary for the reliable functioning of the system. In the long narrative by the officer in charge of

[28] At a bar in downtown Washington, after a long day of congressional hearings, and also after a few drinks, an F-16 pilot confessed that "techno-geek" is a term of affection used by some "fighter jocks" when referring to the "radar heads" in the AWACS.

DUKEs, you can just sense the frustration that such role conflict and status incongruence breeds. An Airborne *Command* Element (ACE, call sign DUKE) finds it difficult to command without authority. An Airborne Warning and *Control* System (AWACS) crew finds it difficult to control without authority. Therefore, neither commanded or controlled very effectively, further contributing to tragic inaction.

Summary: The Fallacy of Social Redundancy

During the critical period of crew formation, an overreliance on environmentally weakened organizational shells seduced AWACS leaders into abdicating their responsibility to breathe life into their young group. As a result, a weak team was launched into an unfortunate storm of events. But they still had a chance. Even a pseudo-team could have effectively tracked the helicopters and stopped the shootdown if someone would have felt a strong enough obligation to act. Unfortunately, responsibility for these important actions never reached critical thresholds. Instead, they were diffuse—spread so thin by the laws of social impact and confused authority relationships that no one felt compelled to act. Hence, a weak team with diffuse responsibilities contributed to this tragedy by its silence.

In technical systems, engineers rely on redundancy to reduce the likelihood of accidents. "Two engines are better than one; four are better than two . . ." (Perrow, 1984: 128). In his dramatic book recounting the flight of Apollo 13, Henry Cooper explained: "Everyone placed particular faith in the spacecraft's redundancy: there were two or more of almost everything" (1973: 24). After examining the group dynamics at play in the shootdown, I am ready to propose a "fallacy of social redundancy." Two controllers may not be better than one. Four leaders may be worse than two.

In Hackman's book about *Groups That Work (And Those That Don't)*, he suggests that one of the most important features of well-composed teams is that they contain as *few* members as possible—a design feature he calls "optimal undermanning" (1990). Latané's principle of divided impact suggests a group-level mechanism that helps explain Hackman's counterintuitive finding. Perhaps one of the reasons that teams should be slightly smaller than absolutely necessary is because redundancy in social systems can lead to a diffusion of responsibility and a tendency for inaction—a phenomenon known as "social loafing—a decrease in individual effort due to the social presence of other persons" (Latané, Williams, and Harkins, 1979: 823). While we can learn much from engineers who design reliable technical systems, at least one of their tools—redundancy—doesn't always travel well from technical to social systems. Sometimes, when everyone is responsible, no one is.

5

Organizational-Level Account: Why Wasn't Eagle Flight Integrated into Task Force Operations?

> Separate ground, sea and air warfare are gone
> forever. If ever again we should be involved in
> war, we will fight it in all elements with all
> services, as one single concentrated effort.
> Peacetime preparatory and *organization activity*
> *must conform to this fact.* Strategic and tactical
> planning must be completely unified, combat
> forces organized into unified commands, each
> equipped with the most efficient weapons systems
> that science can develop, singly led and prepared
> to fight as one, *regardless of service.* (emphasis
> added)
> *(President Dwight D. Eisenhower [1958])*[1]

"EISENHOWER'S experience on D-Day made him a believer in jointness.[2] It is a sad commentary that 52 years later, some still are not believers." This opinion on the current state of interservice cooperation appeared in an April 1996 editorial in the *Army Times,* titled "Getting it Together." In it the author laments an astonishing lack of progress over the past fifty years in the military's struggle to coordinate joint operations. At the broadest level, understanding this struggle is central to answering the question raised in this chapter: Why wasn't Eagle Flight integrated into Task Force operations?

Unfortunately, the shootdown in northern Iraq is not the first modern tragedy involving coordination failures between services. In 1980, multiple interservice problems doomed President Jimmy Carter's desperate attempt to rescue American hostages held in Iran. Separately trained and equipped Army, Air Force, Navy, and Marine assets were hastily thrown together with tragic results. *Army* operatives flew from Egypt in *Air Force* transport planes to a

---

[1] Based on his personal experience planning D-Day operations, Eisenhower made this statement as he proposed the Department of Defense Reorganization Act of 1958.

[2] In this context, the word "joint" implies military activities, organizations, and doctrine that involve the cooperative efforts of more than one service.

remote location in the Iranian desert. There they linked up with *Navy* helicopters flown by mostly *Marine* crews off of a *Navy* aircraft carrier positioned in the Arabian Sea. At this point, the plan called for the *Army*'s Delta team to transfer from *Air Force* planes onto *Navy* Sea Stallion helicopters for the final flight into Tehran. However, a combination of bad luck, bad weather, poor coordination, and helicopter mechanical problems soon resulted in disaster. As with our shootdown, there is more to it than that. Two of these proximal causes have histories—organizational histories that carried the seeds of future tragedies.

First, the helicopters: Navy mechanics stationed on board the ship that ferried the Sea Stallions to the Gulf failed to adequately maintain them.[3] Not only did they not take care of them, but because the strange helicopters didn't belong to them, they actually used them as "hangar queens"[4]—cannibalizing them for spare parts (Kyle, 1990: 138). As a result, in spite of last-minute monumental efforts to get all eight Sea Stallions launched, only six made it to the rendezvous point in the desert. One was abandoned enroute due to a major mechanical failure and a second one returned to the aircraft carrier with serious flight instrument problems. Ultimately, a failed hydraulic pump on one of the six birds that actually made it to the link-up point dropped the final number of operational aircraft to five—one less than the six required to complete the mission. With insufficient lift, daylight approaching, and their cover blown, the decision was made to abort.

Unfortunately, the tragedy didn't end there. Once again, an apparently remote but deep-seated interservice issue reared its ugly head—separate ser-

---

[3] Two years later, in a British Broadcasting Company (BBC) documentary, the following exchange between the Navy's Admiral Holloway and the Army's Colonel Beckwith (commander of the Delta operatives) demonstrates the interservice disagreements over helicopter maintenance: "As a naval aviator who had examined the helicopter maintenance records, Holloway declared that these eight aircraft were in 'Rolls Royce' condition when they took off from the *Nimitz*. . . . The program then cut to Colonel Beckwith and his BBC interviewer. Speaking in a gravelly drawl, the former Green Beret asserted that the helicopters were not 'exercised enough' (that is, flown under combat conditions). In other words, Beckwith implied, if the pilots had operated the aircraft sufficiently, they would have ironed out the defects that eventually grounded three of the helicopters" (Ryan, 1985: 128). An overzealous concern for operational security kept all but the most senior leaders in the dark about the helicopters' true mission. As a result, the crews charged with maintaining the Sea Stallions had no idea how important their task was.

[4] The label "hangar queen" is military slang for a nonoperational piece of equipment used by local maintenance personnel for parts. Rather than waiting for replacement parts to arrive through the supply system, it often seemed easier to unofficially designate one aircraft, truck, or weapon as hopelessly broken and then periodically raid it for spare parts to keep other equipment operational. While officially discouraged, this practice was fairly common, especially when another unit's equipment was left unattended or when units were deployed and parts were difficult to come by. Both of these conditions applied on the naval ship that carried the strange mission helicopters.

vice procurement systems. Navy, Marine, Air Force, and Army communications systems were largely incompatible.[5] As a result, Marine pilots in Navy helicopters could not talk directly to Air Force transport pilots or combat controllers.[6] In the confusion surrounding their hasty departure, a Navy Sea Stallion helicopter crashed into an Air Force transport plane, engulfing both aircraft in a ball of flames. Eight servicemen died; classified documents and sophisticated military equipment were left behind; the U.S. was embarrassed on the world stage; and the hostages remained in Iran—all largely due to a series of miscues between services.[7]

Three years later, in 1983, similar interservice coordination errors contributed to two additional incidents. According to Allard (1990:1), "organizational and command problems [are] widely believed to have been at the heart of operational failures such as the 1980 Iranian hostage rescue attempt and the 1983 bombing of the Marine barracks in Beirut. Even the successful American invasion of Grenada was included in this criticism, especially when allegations were made that the Army, Navy, Air Force, and Marine contingents deployed to the island had experienced difficulty communicating with one another and coordinating their movements." In a similar analysis of the Beirut bombing, Ryan (1985: 152) notes that "with the best of intentions,

[5] In a frank postscript, Colonel James Kyle, the commander of the Air Force component of the rescue operation, admitted that "neither of us [COL (USAF) Kyle or LTC (USMC) Seiffert] realized the incompatibility of our respective SATCOM [satellite communications] systems—it was years later before this was pointed out to me" (Kyle, 1990: 316). Incredibly, not only were they (Air Force and Marines) unable to talk to each other, but they were in fact unaware that this shortcoming even existed. It wasn't only with SATCOMs that they had problems. Colonel Kyle listed the following as one of the four significant causes of the tragedy: "Helicopter pilots lacked secure modes of communication to receive vital mission information" (1990: 324). Tragically, 14 years later, Eagle Flight suffered from the very same problem. The Black Hawks were not equipped with the new HAVE QUICK frequency-hopping radios used by the Air Force F-15s; therefore, just like in Iran, they could not monitor Air Force communications. Once again, with tragic results.

[6] In addition to incompatible communications equipment, "the imposition of radio silence, a consequence of the heavy emphasis on security, choked off communications during the actual operation. Strict radio silence discouraged the exchange of vital operational reports when the unexpected happened" (Ryan, 1985: 75). The final section in this chapter describes how a similar concern with "radio discipline" contributed to the shootdown in Iraq.

[7] In a later interview with the BBC, Major General Singlaub (USA) summarized the important role that interservice rivalries played in the organization of the failed rescue attempt: "'There were some political considerations. I think that an effort was made to get *all* of the services involved.' . . He went on to say that an operation in which marine pilots flew navy helicopters and carried army troops supported by the air force 'had a nice ring to it, in a public relations sense.' . . Singlaub believed that the rescue failed because it had been hurriedly organized. The Pentagon, he explained, no longer had available men who had trained, planned, and worked together during past years. The rescue did not succeed because, basically, 'we tried to bring disparate units from all over the Armed Forces, from all over the world—and then put them into an ad hoc arrangement to do a very complicated plan'" (Singlaub in Ryan, 1985: 132–33).

the high command had set in motion unlooked-for events likely to bring on a deadly bombing."[8] Only four days after 241 Marines died in Beirut, I learned in a very personal way, just how painful interservice differences can be when I found myself on the receiving end of "friendly fire" from a U.S. Air Force A-7 attack aircraft.

I was a first lieutenant in the Army's 82d Airborne Division celebrating my third wedding anniversary fighting Soviet-supported insurgents on the island of Grenada.[9] On the third day of Operation Urgent Fury, my company ran into stubborn sniper fire just outside the small village of Frequente. Frustrated by our unsuccessful efforts to suppress this deadly nuisance, I climbed a steep knoll behind our perimeter to request artillery support from the 2d Brigade Tactical Operations Center (TOC). The TOC had just relocated from the airfield at Salines to a temporary forward position on top of a ridgeline adjacent to my unit. As I located the Fire Support Officer (FSO), four Air Force A-7 Corsair aircraft screamed by our position, just above eye level. The FSO explained to me that the A-7s were flying close air support for an Army Ranger air assault operation. As we watched, the A-7s completed their first bombing run on Calivigny point—a small peninsula several miles to our east—and circled back around for a second pass. This time, as they made their final approach, one A-7 peeled off and strafed our position with 20mm cannon fire.

[8] Ryan's conclusion aligns with the story told by my Causal Map (see Figure 1.3): "With the best of intentions, the high command [military services] had set in motion [through service separatism] unlooked-for events [lower left-hand half of the Causal Map] likely to bring on a deadly bombing [shootdown]" (1985: 152).

[9] I raise two cautions at this point. First, for reasons of objectivity, I hesitate to include a personal account. However, I have no doubt that this incident has had a significant impact on how I view interservice cooperation. Rather than hiding it, I offer it openly so that you can interpret my analysis in light of my personal experience, rather than in ignorance of it. Second, there is the thorny issue of accuracy. Even though I have since reconciled my version of this event with other witnesses, as well as numerous published accounts, I offer the following wisdom of retired Army Colonel David Hackworth:

War stories present two problems to authors striving for The Truth. First of all, if you live long enough to tell them, and have enough of an audience to practice telling them to through the years, war stories become just that—stories. Just as time distances the storyteller from the events themselves, so do the repeated tellings. Gradually the stories are embellished in places, honed down in others until they are perfect tales, even if they bear little resemblance to what actually happened. Yet the storyteller is completely unaware of how far he may have strayed from the facts. Those countless tellings have made the stories The Truth.

The Second problem with war stories is they have their genesis in the fog of war. In battle, your perception is often only as wide as your battle sights. Five participants in the same action, fighting side by side, will often tell entirely different stories of what happened, even within hours of the fight. The story each man tells might be virtually unrecognizable to the others. But that does not make it any less true. (Hackworth, 1990: 9)

No doubt, I am not immune from the "two problems" raised by Hackworth. With this caution in mind, what follows is "the truth" from where I stand.

Shrapnel from the six-inch-long bullets knocked many of us off the top of the hill. Ironically, the soldier who landed next to me was the Air Naval Gunfire Liaison Company (ANGLICO) officer. ANGLICO team leaders are specially trained and equipped naval officers assigned to Army units specifically to coordinate naval gunfire and fighter support. Since Army and Navy radios were largely incompatible, ANGLICOs packed their own communications gear. I found our ANGLICO with his radio by his side. Blood oozed from small holes in his boots. He complained of sharp pain in his back. The camouflage cover on his flack jacket was torn to shreds. I slipped my hand between the kevlar body armor and his back. No blood. The jacket had saved his life; so far . . .

Incredibly, as the Air Force A-7s flew away, they were replaced by a flight of Navy A-6 Intruders.[10] I watched helplessly as the one person who was supposed to be able to talk to the Navy screamed into his microphone. No reply. He couldn't raise the carrier group. He couldn't raise the fighter pilots. In pain, our ANGLICO frantically worked the controls of his radio. No luck. The A-6 began its attack. I couldn't move. I remember trying to bury my face under a tiny rock. I tried to make myself "small." The jet pulled out of its dive. I was still alive. He hadn't fired his guns. I looked up. There, falling toward the earth, were two bombs (Mk-20s). I felt the heat blast as one exploded several hundred meters away. Friendly fire wounded seventeen; one later died.

In peacetime, we (the Army) rarely trained with the Navy. Why should we have expected such a relationship to work in combat? It didn't in Iran. It didn't in Beirut. It didn't in Grenada. Why then, should we have expected joint service operations to work any better in northern Iraq?

For years, Congress pushed the services to address their differences, to work more closely, to train together, to coordinate better. After each tragic incident, congressional hearings criticized continued shortcomings in the joint arena. Each time, promises were made and specific issues addressed. However, the roots of service separatism had grown long and deep. Congress grew impatient. If the military would not fix itself, then Congress would do it for them.

Due in large part to these tragedies in Iran, Beirut, and Grenada, Congress passed the Goldwater-Nichols DOD Reorganization Act in 1986—perhaps the "most important single defense enactment since the National Security Act of 1947 created a permanent postwar military establishment" (Allard, 1990: 3). This legislation dramatically shifted power from individual services to joint institutions. The commanders in chief (CINCs) and the Chair-

---

[10] Later, I learned that another ANGLICO, supporting a different unit, was "directing" the close air support. Targeting confusion between him and his fighters led to the "friendly" strafing (Adkin, 1989: 285–87).

man of the Joint Chiefs of Staff were given additional authority over the services and joint experience was made a legal prerequisite for promotion to flag or general officer rank. These were powerful structural changes and there have been some bright spots since 1986. Relatively successful joint operations in Panama, Haiti, and the Gulf War indicate progress. However, more recent tragedies such as this one in northern Iraq and the one in Somalia (Allard, 1995) remind us just how deeply ingrained interservice differences really are.

To place this troublesome issue of "joint operations" in context, return to the lower left-hand portion of the Causal Map (see Figure 1.3). The longest arrow leading into the event box labeled "helicopters not integrated into OPC flight operations," snakes its way back to a "long history of interservice rivalry."[11] Out of this organizational sore oozed a causal stream that poisoned cooperative training, organizational designs, equipment interoperability, and even unit location decisions. It is the collective impact of this disease that ultimately infects OPC to create our organizational level variable—"helicopter non-integration."

To get a sense of just how important this "tradition of service separatism" (Allard, 1990: 7) is to the ultimate shootdown, imagine a diagonal bisecting the Causal Map in Figure 1.3 from the upper left- to the lower right-hand corner of the map. Every event beneath this line traces its origins back to the pervasive influence of separate services. The entire lower left-hand half of the map presents the shootdown as an example of interservice rivalry writ small—a story of how deeply rooted service autonomy contributed to the isolation of Army helicopters in an Air Force-dominated task force and how this seclusion ultimately contributed to the tragedy.

However, the path from interservice rivalry to shootdown is long and complex. As a contributing event or condition, "helicopter non-integration" is relatively remote; as a dependent variable, it is conceptually abstract. Therefore, unlike analyses in previous chapters, answering the question at the heart of this one presents two additional challenges.

First, as we move further and further away from the actual shootdown— both in time and physical proximity—the very notion of causality becomes problematic. In contrast to the trivial causal leap from "fighter pilot misidentification" to shootdown, and the rather straightforward connection between "AWACS crew inaction" and the accident, "helicopter non-integration," as

---

[11] For a detailed treatment of the "tension between the joint teamwork demanded by modern combat and the traditions of service autonomy reinforced by competing ideas about land, sea, and air warfare," see Allard's book, *Command, Control, and the Common Defense* (1990). In this book, Allard argues that "the American military establishment embodies a tradition of service separatism, one that has been renewed and reinforced by patterns and paradigms of thought that stress the decisive effect of military force on the land, at sea, or in the air" (Allard, 1990: 7).

an event, occupies a relatively remote position on the causal map. The links between a failure to integrate at the task force level and two pilots mistakenly engaging friendly aircraft are complex and diffuse. Therefore, unlike previous individual and group-level analyses, a complete explanation at the organizational level must somehow account for this significant span of causal distance. In other words: How do you get from non-integration to shootdown?

Second, "non-integration" is not only more distant in terms of causal proximity, but it is also more abstract conceptually. As events, pilot misidentification and crew inaction are relatively concrete occurrences. We can imagine an F-15 lead "seeing" a Hind; we can picture an AWACS crew staring silently at their radarscopes. However, what does "non-integration" look like? Would you know it if you saw it? How was it operationalized in this organization? What concrete evidence is there that Eagle Flight operations were not integrated into the task force?

Once again, Secretary Perry's summary offers some hints:

- The Combined Task Force failed to integrate helicopter operations with other air operations in the "no fly zone." Consequently, on April 14, the F-15 pilots were not made aware of the Black Hawk flight prior to take-off, the Black Hawks were allowed to enter the "no fly zone" before the F-15s, and the aircraft were not all communicating on the same radio frequencies. (Perry, 1994: 1)

In this bullet, Perry offers three analytically distinct empirical examples of non-integration: (1) the F-15 pilots were not informed of Eagle Flight's mission prior to departing from Incirlik; (2) the Black Hawks entered the TAOR prior to the F-15s; and (3) the helicopters and F-15s were on different radio frequencies. Consistent with the logic portrayed in the Causal Map, I add a fourth: (4) Eagle Flight Detachment was unaware that there was a different Mode I IFF code for flying inside the TAOR.[12] All four of these are examples of a particular type of organizational failure—a failure to integrate.

As concrete examples, these four events help us address the two analytical challenges unique to this chapter. First, they help operationalize an abstract concept—"non-integration"—by putting some empirical meat on sparse conceptual bones. Second, by virtue of their logically intermediate position on the Causal Map (see Figure 1.3), they help bridge the significant causal distance between a remote antecedent—non-integration—and the shoot-

[12] I can only speculate as to why this fourth example, as important as it is, did not make it into Secretary Perry's final memorandum. From what I can tell from separate service endorsements to the original accident investigation report and from what I was able to learn from testimony during the congressional hearings, there was a serious and ultimately unresolved disagreement between the services at fairly senior levels about who was to blame for the IFF failures.

down. After a review of the fundamental organizing concepts of differentiation and integration, I frame each of these four events as examples of organizational failures to solve various coordination problems—organizational challenges created by three conceptually different types of interdependence.

Differentiation and Integration: Whatever You Divide, You Have to Put Back Together Again

Pilots misidentified; crews didn't intervene; a task force didn't integrate. Individuals erred; groups under-performed; and organizations failed. At the individual level, to help explain why the F-15 pilots misidentified the Black Hawks, we adopted the general framework of sensemaking. At the group level, to help explain why the AWACS crew failed to intervene, we turned to the literature on teams and bystander inaction studies. At the organizational level, to help explain why Army helicopters never really became a full member of the task force, I will start with the fundamental notions of differentiation and integration.

As analytical tools, the twin concepts of differentiation and integration are extremely powerful. Part of what makes them so conceptually appealing is their elegance. The logic is quite simple: Whatever you divide, you have to put back together again; the more divided, the more effort required to rejoin. How social systems do this is what organizing is all about. Spencer explains:

> A social organism is like an individual organism in these essential traits: that it grows; that while growing it becomes more complex; that while becoming more complex, its parts require increasing mutual interdependence . . . that in both cases there is increasing integration accompanied by increasing heterogeneity. (Spencer, 1904: 56)

To deal with increasingly complex tasks, systems create specialized subunits. Once these subunits are segmented or differentiated, the challenge becomes one of integration or coordination—putting them back together again.

Lawrence and Lorsch (1967) were not the first scholars to apply the concepts of differentiation and integration to organizations.[13] However, they are credited with recognizing the profound cognitive and behavioral implications of fragmenting organizations into subunits. According to Lawrence and Lorsch, earlier writers "did not recognize the systemic properties of organi-

---

[13] Early writers (Fayol, 1949; Gulick and Urwick, 1937) from the classical school of management wrote extensively about how to best divide work within organizations. They offered universalistic prescriptions—"principles of management"—for how to separate tasks and then put them back together again: specialization, line and staff, span of control, unity of command, departmentalization, scalar chains, etc. (Fayol, 1949). According to Gulick, "Division of work and integrated organization are the bootstraps by which mankind lifts itself in the process of civilization" (1937: 4).

zations" and therefore "failed to see that the act of segmenting the organization into departments would influence the behavior of organizational members in several ways" (1967: 9). Differentiation not only means "segmentation and specialized knowledge," but it also implies different attitudes and orientations.

In their classic work, *Organization and Environment*, Lawrence and Lorsch suggest three dimensions along which various subunits might differ in how their members think and work (1967: 9–11). First, they might differ in their *orientations toward goals*. We see this difference between Army aviators (whose primary goal was to satisfy the customers they flew for) and Air Force fixed-wing pilots and planners (who emphasized detailed planning and execution). Ultimately, such divergent goal orientations created conflicting priorities and subsequent coordination problems.

For example, Eagle Flight flew many missions for the MCC commander who worked out of Zakhu. Rarely did helicopter pilots learn the details of their flight until after they landed at Zakhu to pick up their customers. Frequently these flights involved transporting UN representatives to meet with Kurdish leaders deep inside the security zone. It was often impractical to anticipate the length of such meetings. As a result, exact takeoff times and detailed flight plans were virtually impossible to schedule in advance. They were even more difficult to execute with much rigor. In sum, to meet the constantly changing needs of their customer—to help the MCC execute its mission—Eagle Flight pilots prided themselves in their flexibility.[14]

However, such decentralized "flexible" flight plans often clashed with the more centralized linear goals of Air Force planners and their controllers in the AWACS. Unlike Army helicopters, each Air Force fixed-wing aircraft flew as an integral part of a much larger "package"—a virtual symphony of fighters, tankers, electronic jammers, and reconnaissance aircraft. If the daily package was a symphony, then MAD DOG and DUKE were the conductors. Consulting the daily ATO as sheet music, they orchestrated the preplanned "flow" of assets through the AWACS. Air Force pilots flew their missions

---

[14] The following court-martial testimony offered by a senior Army aviator, instructor pilot, and operations officer for Eagle Flight illustrates how helicopter pilots' goal orientations caused coordination challenges for the Air Force:

Army Aviation as a whole supports the ground units. We were doing exactly as we were tasked. We received a mission from the MCC. We planned a mission, and we executed a mission. Where there is a serious command and control issue is that we were not interacted at all with the Air Force flow. We would have gladly interacted and given that information, had we known it was required, but as I testified in my previous testimony, Army helicopter pilots don't deal with things on that level. We're very—we're very mission oriented in supporting the ground commander. We're very flexible. We're very responsive. We provide excellent support in that respect. . . . In the 14 years I've been in the Army, this is the first time I've ever worked with the Air Force in this type of command and control situation, and I was the senior Army aviator there. (Headquarters, 8th Air Force, 1995: vol. 14, 148a.13)

like classically trained musicians, taking pride in executing the detailed schedule to a T.[15] Army aviators, on the other hand, flew more like jazz musicians, guided by a general scheme, but improvising the details—creating their music in real time, in response to the emerging requirements of their customers and the terrain.

In practice, these differing goal orientations caused few problems because, typically, orchestra and jazz combos played different halls. According to the Air Space Control Order, fixed-wing aircraft were required to fly above 1,000 feet, while helicopters had to remain below 400. Occasionally, however, situations arose when simple altitude deconfliction failed to separate the two groups. During such times, marked differences in goal orientations could lead to serious problems. Just such a situation occurred on the day of the shootdown when Eagle Flight departed Zakhu prior to the F-15s completing their sweep of the no fly zone. To meet the needs of their customer— the MCC commander—Eagle Flight picked up their passengers and flew into the no fly zone *before* the F-15s.[16] Consulting their "flow sheet," the F-15s didn't expect anyone to be in the TAOR ahead of them. The ultimate roots of this tragic disconnect can be traced back to divergent goal orientations. The F-15s were following their synchronized flow; the UH-60s were focused on their customers. Tragically, these two goals and four aircraft collided some fifty miles east of Zakhu.

In addition to developing different goals, depending on the nature of their task, differentiated groups often develop different *orientations toward time*. The shootdown dramatically illustrates this point as the fighter pilots—who live and die based on how quickly they react—moved from initial visual identification pass to engagement faster than the crew in the AWACS could even process what was happening. According to the DUKE, "I know I was surprised when the 'splash' call was made" (Andrus, TAB V-026, 22). According to the Enroute Controller, "I think we were all pretty shocked at the speed in which this would happen. . . . They ID'd it as a HIP; then they ID'd

---

[15] The following testimony of the F-15 lead illustrates just how important it was for Air Force pilots to stick to the published schedule:

I'll note here that the times between here and the AOR are pretty accurate because we pride ourselves on making sure that we start on exact time, hit the AOR on exact time. So I looked at my watch and actually count down three, two, one, start engines. . . . We hit Gate 1, which is the actual border between Turkey and Iraq. It's an actual point out there that we're supposed to cross at 0720Z. Again, I know that for a fact because I had been changing my air speeds so that I could talk to COUGAR and enter Iraq at the exact time I was supposed to, because we pride ourselves in doing that. (Andrus, 1994: TAB V-029, 13, 17)

[16] Prior to September 1993, Eagle Flight helicopters flew anytime required, prior to fighter sweeps and without fighter coverage if necessary. After September 1993, helicopter flights were restricted to the security zone if AWACs and fighter coverage were not on station. For the fateful mission, Eagle Flight requested and received permission to execute their flight outside the security zone.

it as two Hinds. Then all of a sudden they were engaged, and we were all surprised at how fast this all happened" (Andrus, 1994: TAB V-016, 25). According to an Air Surveillance Technician, "It was utter confusion. We didn't know—some of us didn't know that anything was happening until after it happened, and the people were worrying about—were kind of in shock that it had happened so fast" (Andrus, 1994: TAB V-021, 11).

While the folks in the AWACS were surprised at the speed, to the pilots in the F-15s the pace seemed normal. According to the wingman, "The engagement was not rushed. That's the other part. I wasn't in a hurry to—to shoot fast. I wasn't in a hurry at all" (Andrus, 1994: TAB V-028: 31).[17] When asked by an investigating officer, "Why did you engage so quickly? In your thought process, did you consider spending more time with COUGAR [AWACS] asking for more information?" the F-15 lead pilot replied, "Not after I positively VID'd them as Hinds. Once I had no doubt that they were Hinds, I had met all the ROE and the next step was to shoot them down" (Headquarters, 8th Air Force, vol. 13: 143a13). And so he did. When you're flying at over 500 knots, the rest of the world seems to move at a different pace.

The third difference identified by Lawrence and Lorsch concerns *interpersonal orientation*—the way members in various subunits deal with their colleagues. Air Force fighter pilots and Army aviators are known for their bravado—a lot of hard work, hard play, and hard talk. In contrast, AWACS crew members are technicians. Interactions are dictated primarily by role specialization; hence, a quiet professionalism reigns. Such markedly different interpersonal orientations reinforced the existing social hierarchy within the task force, contributed to the AWACS's reluctance to intervene with either fighters or helicopters, and served to further differentiate members of these subgroups.[18]

Such differing cognitive and emotional orientations significantly contributed to the organizational challenge of achieving integration—where integration is merely the "state of interdepartmental relations." As a result, how well various departments collaborate and coordinate to achieve unity of ef-

---

[17] Recall (in chapter 3) that at the time the F-15s engaged, two F-16s were already enroute to the no fly zone. A rivalry existed between the two fighter communities and the F-15s were behind. F-16s are better equipped and trained to shoot down helicopters. Therefore, the Combined Task Force Commander concluded that "the shootdown pilots' haste was due in part to the planned entry of two F-16s into the TAOR 10 to 15 minutes after the F-15s" (U.S. General Accounting Office, 1997: 34). Had the F-15s hesitated, there was a good chance that their potential "kill" would have been lost to the F-16s. Remember also, however, that the Combined Task Force Commander was himself an F-16 pilot. There is a second explanation offered for the speed with which the F-15s engaged: Any hesitation on the part of the F-15s might have allowed the helicopters to land and hence preclude the F-15s from scoring a rare kill.

[18] I address the impact of interpersonal relations in greater detail under the section titled *Different Radios & "Min Comm": A Failure to Coordinate by Mutual Adjustment.*

fort depends largely on how differentiated they are in the first place. The greater the differences in cognitive and emotional orientations, the greater the integrative challenge. Therefore, according to Lawrence and Lorsch, successful integration cannot be "accomplished through an entirely rational and mechanical process" (1967: 12). Unlike the mechanical view presented by earlier classical theorists, putting the pieces back together again is not as straightforward and simple as it looks. Organizational designers and leaders both have to be sensitive not only to the rational demands of mechanical interdependence, but also to the deeper challenges presented by differing subunit orientations.

Task Force Provide Comfort was not immune to the integrative challenges identified by Lawrence and Lorsch. The divisive seeds sown by long histories of service separatism were fertilized daily by the practical demands of differentiated work. For the most part, AWACS, fighter, and helicopter communities were physically and socially isolated from one another. They didn't work together and they didn't play together. Their primary tasks demanded different orientations toward goals, time, and interpersonal relations.[19] As a result, clearly divergent cognitive and emotional orientations developed—in particular, between Army aviators and their Air Force hosts.

As the following comments illustrate, Eagle Flight was *not* well integrated into Task Force OPC—at least not from the perspective of the Air Force.

According to the DUKE:

> Only as a courtesy does the AWACS track Eagle Flight. . . . It's kind of an autonomous operation is the way I've always viewed Eagle, above—below and separate of the OPC mission. (Andrus, 1994: TAB V-026, 10, 24)

According to the Assistant Director of Operations:

> Helicopters are generally not considered part of the package. (Headquarters, 8th Air Force, 1995: vol. 13: 144.a8)

According to the Staff Weapons Director:

> I don't know what their [Eagle Flight's] secret squirrel mission is. I don't know what they do. I mean, we weren't really privy to a whole lot of information. Look

---

[19] This finding is consistent with a similar insight uncovered by Hackman while researching *Groups That Work (And Those That Don't)* (1990). "As we carried out the research, we came upon another aspect of the work content. . . . For want of a better term, we refer to it as the *stuff* with which the groups worked. . . . Can there be any doubt that the stuff a team works with significantly affects the character of group life? . . . Surely the content of a group's work significantly shapes both the emotional lives of members and the interactions that take place among them. . . . The team may also develop the collective equivalent of tunnel vision, however, and lose sight of the larger picture into which its work fits" (Hackman, 1990: 487–88). According to Hackman, different orientations develop not only from structural differentiation and isolation, but also from differing work contents.

at the ATO, I mean, it says flying "as required." And they'd show up sometimes; sometimes they'd talk, sometimes they wouldn't. So, I mean—it was a different set of rules for those guys. (Headquarters, 8th Air Force, 1995: T40.1, 2265)

According to the Mission Crew Commander:

Army helicopter operations were, I feel, in retrospect, I guess you look back and say, again hindsight—I guess they were part of OPC, but at the time I never felt the UH-60s were part of OPC. (Headquarters, 8th Air Force, 1995: T40.1, 2315)

According to the Staff Weapons Director:

Helicopters, they're part of the game, but they don't play by the same set of rules. . . . It was just understood that— the general understanding by AWACS crews was that the Army didn't play by the same set of rules we played by. That they were a different organization, and they did different things. . . . It's haphazard, you know, and from my experience, I know that sometimes they talk to you, sometimes they don't. If they do talk to you, sometimes they tell you where they're going and what they're doing, and sometimes they don't. It seemed like they had a higher priority tasking or a higher classification tasking that we just weren't privy to. (Headquarters, 8th Air Force, 1995: T40.1, 2263–2264)

According to the Senior Director, in response to the question: "Do you consider them [Eagle Flight] to be a part of that package for normal control, monitoring, et cetera?"

I'd have to say no. I do not include them with that—in that case. . . . The helicopters operate independent of package—the package being the aircraft that—that fly above the hard deck, the reconnaissance aircraft, the wild weasels, the ECM assets, the E-3 and those aircraft. (Andrus, 1994: TAB V-014, 6)

Apparently Secretary Perry was right. At least from the Air Force side of the Task Force, Eagle Flight was not very well integrated.

But this is only half of the story. After the accident, there was a certain amount of finger-pointing going on. As a former Eagle Flight Operations Officer wrote in a sworn statement to the accident board, "Certain individuals of the CTF [Combined Task Force] staff have accused Eagle Flight Detachment of failing to adhere to certain command and control issues. Army flight crews have no reason to question flight procedures that have been accepted as standard procedure by the CTF staff for over 3 years." (Andrus, 1994: TAB V-50b, 1).

As described earlier, this is not the first time that service separatism has played a role in military tragedies. During congressional hearings following the failed rescue attempt in Iran, Senator Sam Nunn asked the Army's Delta Team commander, "What did you learn from this mission and what can we do to preclude this kind of thing from happening in the future?" Colonel (USA) Beckwith replied:

I learned that Murphy's Law is alive and well. He's in every drawer, under every rock and on top of every hill. . . . What do we need to do in the future? Sir, let me answer you this way. . . . If Coach Bear Bryant at the University of Alabama put his quarterback in Virginia, his backfield in North Carolina, his offensive line in Georgia, and his defense in Texas, and then got Delta Airlines to pick them up and fly them to Birmingham on game day, he wouldn't have his winning record. Coach Bryant's teams, the best he can recruit, practice together, live together, eat together, and play together. He has a team.

In Iran we had an ad hoc affair. We went out, found bits and pieces, people and equipment, brought them together occasionally and then asked them to perform a highly complex mission. The parts all performed, but they didn't necessarily perform as a team. (Beckwith and Knox, 1983: 294–95)

In this short anecdote, Colonel Beckwith captured the essence of why Eagle Flight wasn't integrated into Task Force operations as well as how such a lack of integration can lead to tragedy.

To outfit Task Force Provide Comfort, military planners went out and "found bits and pieces of people and equipment, brought them together occasionally and then asked them to perform a highly complex mission." Serving in sixty-day rotations, Army helicopter detachments rotated down from Giebelstadt, Germany. Every six weeks, a different Air Force fighter wing flew in—also from Germany. And approximately every thirty days, a fresh AWACS crew rotated over from Oklahoma.

Like Colonel Beckwith's *un*successful rescue party, and *un*like coach Bryant's successful football teams, the members of Task Force Provide Comfort did not "practice, live, eat, or play together." And, for the most part, just as in Iran, "the parts all performed, but they didn't necessarily perform as a team." Separate unit preparations appeared seductively adequate in preparing for Iran, but sorely wanting when unforeseen problems forced last-minute changes to the plan. Similarly, in OPC, relatively isolated units operated without incident for some 1,109 days before an unusual confluence of events demanded more than independent actors could provide.

The Task Force didn't practice together. When asked by investigators, "How often do you practice composite sorties to include AWACS when you're at home?" the F-15 wingman replied, "The—rarely. Again, the AWACS that we have over here in the—in this theater [European] are pretty heavily tasked between here [Turkey] and down in Bosnia, so the availability for home station training is—is pretty nil with them. They're—they're on the road a lot" (Andrus, 1994: TAB V-028, 54). Similarly, when asked by investigators, "How often do you practice using a command and control element like DUKE or MAD DOG?" the F-15 wingman replied, "Never" (Andrus, 1994: TAB V-028, 55). In the following court-martial testimony, an Army helicopter instructor pilot from Eagle Detachment reveals mixed feelings about this unique opportunity to work with his Air Force partners. On the one hand:

> We got the impression that we [Eagle Flight] were like the little brother in this whole affair. They [Air Force] tolerated us only because they had to. And they didn't really—they really didn't know what—how to tolerate us.[20] (Headquarters, 8th Air Force, 1995: T 40.6, 1329)

On the other hand:

> For us to operate in this joint environment was a rather unique experience. And we were quite thrilled, to be honest with you, to be part of this entire combined task force operation. And we looked at AWACS as this huge, you know, omnipotent, mysterious, you know, eye in the sky, up there that knew and saw all. (Headquarters, 8th Air Force, 1995: T 40.6, 1336)

But, then again:

> There were many occasions when we were on station, even outside the Security Zone—where we were—the MCC was conducting business on the ground, and when they had completed their business, when they climbed in the aircraft and we took off, AWACS was not on station. Nobody was there. . . . Well, we joked about it among ourselves, that it was time for happy hour at the club and they [AWACS and fighters] were ready to go home.[21] But we always felt like, like the little brother analogy again, that all the big kids had taken their toys and gone home and they left us sitting out there to find our own way back. . . . It didn't sit well with us . . . (Headquarters, 8th Air Force, 1995: T 40.6, 1337)

Not only didn't they practice together, but they didn't live, eat, or play together either. Eagle Flight aviators lived in World War II–vintage Quonset huts in Pirinclik—a remote space tracking station isolated deep in the Turkish countryside (see Figure 1.1). OPC Task Force Headquarters, along with the F-15 Squadron and AWACS crews, all flew out of Incirlik Air Base, over 200 miles west of Pirinclik. Air Force officers lived in modern hotel-style Visiting Officers Quarters (VOQs) and enjoyed most of the com-

---

[20] This perception on the part of the Army seems to square with the DUKE's earlier comment about the relative importance of helicopters: "The way I understand it, only as a courtesy does the AWACS track Eagle flight" (Andrus, 1994: TAB V-026, 10).

[21] This anecdote dramatically illustrates how different goal and time orientations can create serious situations. On the one hand, the Air Force operated on a predictable, well-planned, and tightly executed schedule. Detailed mission packages were organized weeks and months in advance. Rigid schedules were published and executed in rolling cycles of linear, preplanned packages. On the other hand, Army aviators reacted to constantly changing local demands. They worked for customers on the ground who rarely knew from one day, or even one moment, to the next, where they needed to be and when. Not surprisingly, these two dramatically different orientations toward goals and time often resulted in integrative disconnects between the Air Force and the Army.

forts of home on this relatively large "americanized" base. Rarely did Army and Air Force members meet, either formally or informally; and, according to the instructor Mission Crew Commander, there were "no face-to-face briefings between the fighter community and the weapons director (AWACS) community" either (Andrus, 1994: TAB V-013, 10).

Major Young, the commander of Eagle Flight's parent company in Germany, was ultimately responsible for the morale and welfare of his detachment deployed to OPC in Turkey. As a result, he was in a unique position to comment on their relative integration into the Task Force. The following court-martial testimony reveals a series of subtle, but unmistakable signals that constantly reminded Major Young that his helicopter crews wore a different colored uniform than did most other members of the Task Force.

Q: Army personnel assigned to Eagle Flight did not feel like they were a full-fledged member of the OPC team, is that correct?

A: At certain points, yes, it is.

Q: Why?

A: There were a couple of reasons. One had to do with morale support issues and the other dealt more of admin in nature.

Q: Did you have trouble getting joint awards for your people?

A: Yes, I did. The staff at OPC did not feel that we were a part of Operation Provide Comfort, so therefore, they would not approve joint awards for my soldiers that were operating in and around the TAOR.

Q: Were you able to sneak some through?

A: I managed—once the Chief of Staff—I think he went on leave—I immediately processed two platoons' worth of awards through there before he got back. He showed up earlier than I expected. He found out what I was doing and he put a stop to it. So I ended up with two platoons getting joint awards and the last platoon didn't get any. Again, he told me that we were not assigned to Operation Provide Comfort and therefore were not eligible for joint awards.

Q: You also said that you would go down at least once each tour—or once each rotation to check on the quality of life and do what you could to make sure it was acceptable. Did you have any concerns about the quality of life with your troops?

A: That's always been an issue with me as well as any other commander about how soldiers have to live. In my opinion, the conditions that we were living in were substandard. We had officers, aircrew members sleeping two to a room in the old Quonset hut–type billets. Some of the rooms had carpeting that had mildew and mold on them. There were five TVs of which we had to rent from the Air Force so we had a lottery-type deal where we rented the five TVs and as you rotated, if you were lucky enough to get one of the TVs, then you got a TV. So, we resorted to other things like sneaking stuff into the country, al-

though we weren't supposed to have done that. But that was the big issue is
the way we were treated.

We were told that because we were Army personnel that we were not enti-
tled to stay in the billets up in Incirlik as we started to transition a new
platoon in, the aircrews would be forced to spend the night until they could
get everybody down so we would end up spending two or three nights in
Incirlik and they put us out in tents. Now, the same crews that came in with
UH—HH-60s for the Air Force were told that they had to be billeted inside of
the buildings—the hotel-type accommodations because they were aircrews
and we were soldiers so we had to stay in tents.

We got around that by—I started signing all the orders and I wouldn't put
U.S. Army on them. I would just put aircrews and the billeting guy would see
the listing that said aircrews and we would be over to the buildings until we
got sent down to another location. So, we kind of circumvented the system
there also. (Headquarters, 8th Air Force, 1995: T 40.6, 1276–77)

Major Young's creative solutions aside, it's clear that Eagle Flight was not
very well integrated into the overall Task Force. On the one hand, Air Force
personnel viewed Army aviators as Rambo-like rogues, loose cannons off on
some "secret squirrel"–type mission that allowed them to get away with
operating under a different set of rules. On the other hand, Army personnel
felt like neglected stepchildren, misunderstood by their Air Force parents
who merely "tolerated" their presence in the Task Force. While overwhelming testimony clearly establishes the social and organizational distance between Eagle Flight and the rest of the Task Force, how do we go about
explaining it? How does one explain non-integration? I explain it as a failure
to coordinate interdependence.

Interdependence: Multiple Failures to Coordinate

Writing in the same year as Lawrence and Lorsch, Thompson (1967) developed a useful typology that helps frame our problem. According to
Thompson, differentiation creates interdependence among organizational
parts. Interdependence is the extent to which subunit activities are "interrelated so that changes in the state of one element affect the state of the
others" (Scott, 1992: 230). However, not all parts are interrelated in the same
way. To this end, Thompson identified the following three levels of interdependence, in order of increasing complexity: pooled, sequential, and reciprocal.[22]

---

[22] Thompson argues that his three levels of interdependence form a Guttman-type scale. "All
organizations have pooled interdependence; more complicated organizations have sequential as
well as pooled; and the most complex have reciprocal, sequential, and pooled" (1967: 55).

First, work is *pooled* if it is interrelated only in the sense that it contributes to the overall goal of the organization. "Each part renders a discrete contribution to the whole and each is supported by the whole" (Thompson, 1967: 54). For example, the cooks in the mess hall at Pirinclik feed the members of Eagle Flight. Without them, Eagle Flight would not be able to support the MCC; the MCC would not be able to accomplish its task; and the entire OPC Task Force mission would be in jeopardy. Nonetheless, the cooks at Pirinclik probably never interact with the F-15 pilots or AWACS crews at Incirlik; and yet, unless each of these groups performs its task successfully, the overall goal of the organization is threatened. Thompson calls this type of relationship pooled interdependence.

A second, more direct type of relationship develops when some tasks or activities have to be done before others. For instance, AWACS's mission was to provide airborne warning and control for all aircraft flying in support of OPC. To be able to meet this requirement, AWACS had to be the first aircraft in the air each day out of Incirlik. When the relationship between activities is serial in nature, when order is important, such interdependence is termed *sequential*.

Finally, Thompson labels the third and most demanding type of relationship *reciprocal*, because "the distinguishing aspect is the reciprocity of the interdependence, with each unit posing contingency for the other" (Thompson, 1967: 55). This type of interrelationship occurs when work or activities relate to each other as both inputs and outputs. In-flight refueling presents a dramatic example of reciprocal interdependence. The only way to coordinate the mid-air pas de deux required for a KC-135 tanker to successfully refuel an F-15 fighter—while both are flying at 30,000 feet and over 500 knots—is through real-time, two-way communications. Successful refueling requires the movements of each aircraft to be adjusted to those of the other. This requirement for mutual adjustment through two-way, real-time communications distinguishes the integrative challenges of reciprocal interdependence from those of the less demanding sequential and pooled.

"In a situation of interdependence, concerted action comes about through coordination; and if there are different types of interdependence, we would expect to find different devices for achieving coordination" (Thompson, 1967: 55–56). For each type of interdependence, Thompson identified a corresponding form of coordinating mechanism. This relationship is illustrated in the matrix in figure 5.1.

Each type of interdependence in the left column calls for integration by the corresponding mechanism in the right column. Coordination by *standardization* is most appropriate for handling pooled interdependence. Sequential interdependence is best coordinated by *plan*. And coordination by *mutual adjustment* is required to integrate reciprocal interdependence.

In the following three sections, I apply this framework to explain "heli-

TYPE OF INTERDEPENDENCE	COORDINATION MECHANISM
POOLED	STANDARDIZATION
SEQUENTIAL	PLAN
RECIPROCAL	MUTUAL ADJUSTMENT

Fig. 5.1. Thompson's Coordination Matrix

copter non-integration" as multiple failures to coordinate. Each of the four concrete examples of non-integration identified in the beginning of this chapter are explained as organizational failures to coordinate. The Black Hawks' early entry into the no fly zone and the F-15 pilots' ignorance of Eagle Flight's presence are both examples of how sequential interdependence was inadequately coordinated by plan. The fact that fighters and helicopters monitored different radio frequencies while in the TAOR is an example where coordination by mutual adjustment failed to adequately handle reciprocal interdependence. Finally, even pooled interdependence proved too big a challenge for this task force. Relatively simple coordination by standardization broke down as evidenced by Eagle Flight never realizing that there was a different Mode I IFF code for flying inside the TAOR. No one bothered to tell them.

Wrong Mode I: A Failure to Coordinate by Standardization

According to Thompson, standardization involves "the establishment of routines or rules which constrain action of each unit or position into paths consistent with those taken by others in the interdependent relationship" (1967: 56). For example, the Airspace Control Order (ACO) established a rule that constrained the action of fighters into paths consistent with those taken by helicopters. "Deconfliction right now is strictly by altitude. . . . The helicopters are required to fly below 400 feet AGL [Above Ground Level] and fighter traffic in the AOR [Area of Operation] is restricted to 1,000 feet and above . . . so there should be sufficient altitude deconfliction at all times out there" (Andrus, 1994: TAB V-096, 8).

Altitude deconfliction requirements are just one example of how the task force attempted to coordinate pooled interdependence through standardization. The ACO, Air Crew Read File (ARF), Rules of Engagement (ROE), Operation Plans and Orders (OPLANs/OPORDs), and Standard Operating Procedures (SOPs) are chock-full of additional examples of coordination through standardization. These rules and programs "represent agreements about how decisions are made or work is to be processed that *predate* the work performance itself" (Scott, 1992: 231). The design logic here is that whatever decisions can be made ahead of time, should be. If interdependence is of the type that a rule can be written to coordinate it,[23] then it should be coordinated with a rule. This frees up limited human and organizational capacity to handle those unexpected contingencies that arise out of the actual work process itself, those that cannot be accurately predicted and reliably coordinated ahead of time.

Electronic Identification Friend or Foe (IFF) systems are an example of a *technical* fix developed to help solve an important *organizational* problem— integration. Once the military divided itself into separate services, each with its own helicopters and fixed-wing aircraft, the challenge became one of putting them all back together again, on the same battlefield, sharing the same airspace. Increasingly differentiated air assets required novel solutions to integrate operations. While joint doctrine was written to address many of these issues, one particularly stubborn challenge remained. As weapon systems grew more lethal and effective at greater ranges, and the sale of NATO aircraft proliferated around the world, it became increasingly difficult to tell the good guys from the bad guys.[24] Hence, the development of a rather sophisticated electronic IFF system. With sophistication came complexity. With complexity came specialization. And with specialization came increasing organizational demands for integration. Here is how it worked and failed in OPC.

Clearly, IFF codes require coordination. Every aircraft in OPC has to be squawking the correct codes or the system won't work. Interdependence is pooled. Coordination through standardization is appropriate. What went wrong?

The daily Air Tasking Order (ATO) is the definitive coordination document for executing flight operations in OPC. It contains detailed information required by all pilots. Included in the ATO are the day's flight schedule, radio frequencies, IFF codes, and special instructions for the day. All aircrews in OPC are required to have a hard copy of the current ATO with Special Instructions (SPINS) in their possession when they fly.

Somewhere between the CFACC Frag Shop and Eagle Flight operations, communications broke down. But, it did so in a deviously subtle way—so

---

[23] Thompson warns that an "important assumption in coordination by standardization is that the set of rules be internally consistent, and this requires that the situations to which they apply be relatively stable, repetitive, and few enough to permit matching of situations with appropriate rules" (1967: 56).

[24] For a detailed review of these trends and how they impact the incidence of friendly fire in U.S. military operations, see "Who Goes There: Friend or Foe?"—a report written for Congress by the Office of Technology Assessment to "assess the technology and techniques available to reduce such tragic loss of life" (Herdman, 1993: iii).

subtle that no one noticed until after it was too late. Catastrophic collapses in communication systems normally grab our attention. When phone lines go down or radios fail we recognize that important information is not getting through and take appropriate action. Subtle failures are, by definition, much less dramatic; hence, they often fail to grab our attention. Ironically, organizational damage caused by such subtle failures is often much worse than that caused by catastrophes. This is what happened with the transmission of Mode I codes.

About two years prior to the accident, someone in the CFAC staff decided to change the instructions pertaining to IFF modes and codes. No one seems to recall exactly how or why this occurred.[25] However, the change was an important one. Prior to this point, all aircraft squawked a single Mode I code everywhere they flew. Subsequent to the change, all aircraft were required to switch to a different Mode I code while flying in the no fly zone. The change was communicated through the daily ATO. All aircraft on 14 April were to squawk Mode I code 52 while flying inside Northern Iraq. However, the puzzling part of this story is that the Air Force's version of the ATO is not exactly the same as the one received electronically by Eagle Flight.

Incredibly, for at least two years, there existed two versions of the daily ATO: one printed out directly by the Frag Shop and distributed locally by messenger to all units at Incirlik Air Base, and a second one transmitted electronically through an Air Force communications center to Eagle Flight operations at Diyarbakir. The one received by Army aviators was identical in all aspects to the one distributed by the Frag Shop, except for the changed Mode I code information contained in the SPINS. The ATO that Eagle Flight received contained no mention of two Mode I codes.

Exactly how this happened is still a mystery. What is clear is that at some point between day 614 and day 1,103, the Air Force added a second Mode I code to the ATO and this change never reached Eagle Flight. Somewhere somehow there was a disconnect between the Air Force FRAG shop that generates the daily ATO at Incirlik and the Air Force communications center where the Army picked up its message traffic at Pirinclik. As a result of this disconnect, Eagle Flight never knew about the requirement to squawk a different code inside the TAOR. Therefore, at 1021 hours local time, on the morning of the fourteenth, when TIGER 01 keyed his IFF to interrogate an unidentified contact flying low and slow just inside the TAOR, he got no

---

[25] Due to personnel turbulence in OPC, we have been unable to reconstruct the exact circumstances surrounding this important change. U.S. Army Captain Mike Nye replaced Captain Patrick McKenna as the Eagle Flight Detachment Commander immediately following the accident. Captain Nye spent countless hours trying to track down exactly why the changed Mode I codes never reached his unit. The explanation contained here is the best he could come up with. While he was unable to completely verify his story, nothing he or subsequent investigators have uncovered contradicts its main thrust.

response. His interrogator was set to the "CC" position—for "correct code"—in this case, code 52. The helicopters' Mode I transponder was set to 42. The Hawks didn't squawk; interrogators and transponders were set to different codes.[26]

Communications channels break down all the time in complex organizations. However, in situations where differing interpretations do exist, odds are pretty good that over time, if the rule is important enough, such disconnects surface fairly quickly during practice. Part of what makes this particular case so puzzling is that such a serious misinterpretation regarding IFF codes was not discovered until long after it was too late. Prior to the accident, Eagle Flight helicopters flew countless missions inside of the TAOR, all the while squawking the wrong Mode I code. Incredibly, no one ever noticed or said anything until after the shootdown—so great was Eagle Flight's isolation within the Task Force, so secondary was their role.

The following testimony by the Eagle Flight Operations Officer/Flight Instructor addresses this remarkable disconnect:

Q: Would you please tell me about the change in procedure as far as your squawking Mode I, the change after 14 April?

A: Well, prior to that [shootdown on the fourteenth], the Mode I codes that we utilized on the ATO did not differentiate between AOR and TAOR. It just says helicopter, Mode I code. After that, on 19 April, we saw on the ATO, a different code for a TAOR operation and the AOR operation. (Headquarters, 8th Air Force, vol. 14, 148a2)

Consistent with Lawrence and Lorsch (1967: 6–17) and Hackman (1990: 488), members of differentiated subunits develop their own distinct views of the world. This can include speaking in slightly different organizational "dialects." Note the usage of AOR (Area of Responsibility) and TAOR (Tactical Area of Responsibility) acronyms by this Army pilot. Clearly, when he used the term AOR, he was referring to the entire area of responsibility *outside* the no fly zone. He used TAOR to refer to the no fly zone *inside* northern Iraq. To the Army, AOR meant the area outside northern Iraq; to the Air Force, it meant just the opposite. Such differences in acronym usage can develop between isolated units without drawing attention. When the Air

[26] After failing to identify his contact as friendly using Mode I, TIGER 01 then switched his radar to interrogate Mode IV—the second code that all coalition aircraft should be squawking. This is when he received a momentarily "sweet" or positive response, followed by 4 to 5 seconds of "sour." Subsequent attempts by both TIGER 01 and 02 to interrogate using both Modes I and IV also failed. It is now clear why Mode I failed. However, even after extensive equipment teardowns and reenactments with the same F-15s and different Black Hawks, no one has been able to determine "why the F-15 AAIs [air-to-air interrogators] did not receive a Mode IV response from the Black Hawk helicopters' transponders" (Andrus, 1994: vol. 2, 35). In the words of TIGER 01, "All I know is I've seen that before in the aircraft, it's given me false information before . . . the radar can lie to you" (Andrus, 1994: TAB V-029, 19–20).

Force says AOR they mean one thing; when the Army hears AOR they interpret something else. Neither party realizes the subtle disconnect because each hears a familiar acronym and attaches local meaning without discussion.[27] The exchange continues:

Q: You said, prior to 14 April, you used just one code, one mode for both in and out of the AOR?

A: The Mode I, in terms of how we utilize that in the Eagle Flight Detachment which is the Black Hawk company there at Diyarbakir—in every rotation that we've been there, every single instructor pilot, every pilot in command, and every pilot that we have there, reviews the ATO and the SPINS before every flight. This has been going on since my first rotation which was December of 92. We also had one member of Eagle Flight Detachment, Mr. John Garrett, who was in the lead aircraft, who was killed on 14 April, who was a former AWACS crew member. Mr. Garrett was intimately familiar with AWACS procedures and with the ATO and SPINS. Out of all these individuals since December of 92 that I've been operating with in OPC, not a single one of us had determined that there was a separate Mode I code in the TAOR. In other words, we used one Mode I code and we used it enroute and in the TAOR. We've done that on every single mission up until 14 April.

Now, what I don't understand is AWACS has the capability to determine which Mode I code we squawk. In other words, it's not like, from what I understand, the F-15s, they interrogate our Mode I and it's either positive or negative, but they can't tell what number we're squawking, but AWACS has the capability to determine which code number we have set in there.

It's kind of a rhetorical question, but I have to ask the question—If we've been squawking, according to them, the incorrect code for at least a year and a half that I know of and it probably goes back to two years, why didn't they tell us it was the wrong code? If it was the incorrect code, somebody at one point should have raised a flag and said, "Hey, there's something you guys are missing here . . ." You know it would stand to reason that if a procedure has been conducted routinely over a long period of time, that will become common law, so to speak. (Headquarters, 8th Air Force, vol. 14: 148a2–148a4)

Coordination by "standardization" only works when everyone gets the word, when procedures are indeed "standard." For enforcement to be effective, each player must be deemed important enough to the others so that if anyone

---

[27] In accordance with OPC official documents (and also Joint Doctrine), I use TAOR to refer to the area *inside* Northern Iraq. The security zone is a subset of the TAOR; the no fly zone includes all airspace in Northern Iraq north of the 36th parallel; however, the TAOR is a subset of a much broader AOR—a term used to define OPC's entire Area of Responsibility. A much larger area than that encompassed by the TAOR, OPC's AOR included all geographic areas that the Task Force Commander deemed could have an impact on his mission. For OPC this included all of Turkey, most of the surrounding countries, as well as critical sea lanes.

acts out of synch, others will notice and make the effort to correct them. Because Eagle Flight operations were so isolated, an obviously dangerous misinterpretation of a very critical coordinating mechanism went unnoticed for years. It took a tragedy to uncover this deadly failure to integrate.

F-15s Unaware: A Failure to Coordinate by Plan

In chapter 3, I explained the F-15 pilots' misidentification as a consequence of an ambiguous stimulus, a strong set of expectations, and a desire to see what they saw. TIGERS 01 and 02 did not expect any friendly aircraft to be in the TAOR. They did expect to be the first flight of the day into northern Iraq. Therefore, when they picked up two unidentified radar contacts, they presumed them to be enemy.

Two concrete examples of helicopter non-integration played a significant role in creating these errant expectations. First, the F-15 pilots were never informed of Eagle Flight's mission. Second, Eagle Flight entered the TAOR prior to the fighter sweep. Had either of these two events not occurred—had the F-15s been briefed about the helicopters' mission or had Eagle Flight waited until after the TAOR had been sanitized to enter the no fly zone—this tragedy would not have happened.[28]

Both events feed off the same type of logic—a serial logic—the distinguishing feature of sequential interdependence. Certain activities have to occur before others. According to Thompson, sequential interdependence is best coordinated by plan—"the establishment of schedules for the interdependent units by which their actions may then be governed" (1967: 56). Effective integration of a fifty-aircraft package requires a detailed schedule. Order is important. That's why both F-15 pilots flew with a "flow sheet" clipped to their kneeboard. A brief glance at this graphical display of the OPC flight schedule and pilots situated themselves and other aircraft relative to the planned flow.

However, because helicopters were not well integrated into OPC flight operations, they weren't included on the F-15's flow sheet. The F-15s were; they were listed at the very top, as the very first flight of the day. The flow sheet showed all other aircraft following them into the TAOR, thus reinforcing expectations that no one should be out there in front of them, at least no one friendly. Order *does* matter. Based on information received from a series of coordinating mechanisms, including the Airspace Control Order (ACO) that states, "No aircraft will enter the TAOR until the fighters with AI [air interrogation] radars have sanitized the TAOR," the F-15 pilots built a

---

[28] Such conclusions are drawn based on the logic of counterfactual interrogation—a method borrowed from sociological literature about narrative explanations (Abbott, 1990). See Griffin (1993) for a lucid description of this method.

strong set of expectations. They expected to be first in. Unfortunately, they were not.

How could this happen? How could the helicopters enter the no fly zone prior to the sweep? And why weren't the F-15 pilots aware of their presence out there in front of them?

The short answer within Thompson's framework is: Plans failed. Schedules designed to coordinate sequential interdependence between fighters and helicopters failed to effectively integrate these two operations. Eagle Flight went in early and the F-15s were unaware. In the following extracts, our F-15 pilots struggle to make sense of the disconnect between what they expected—based on published rules and plans—and what actually took place:

> TIGER 02:   The source document for our planning is the ATO [Air Tasking Order]
> . . . Where I would really expect to find out, no kidding, what's happening
> with the Black Hawks would be in the ATO. If it's not there, it shouldn't be
> happening. (Andrus, 1994: TAB V-028, 46)

Unfortunately, it wasn't there and it was very much happening.

The only information listed for UH-60s on that day was their call signs, aircraft numbers, type of mission (transport), and general route: from LLTC (identifier for Diyarbakir) to TAOR and back to LLTC. All departure and arrival times were listed "as required." This type of generic entry was standard fare for Eagle Flight. According to General Andrus, "Since the MCC [Military Coordination Center] daily mission requirements were generally based on the events of the previous day, the MCC exercised flexibility in scheduling supporting helicopter flights. A weekly flight schedule was developed and provided to the CTF C3 [operations], but a firm itinerary was usually not available until after the next day's ATO was published. The weekly schedule was briefed in both the C3 and CTF CG [Commanding General] staff meetings on Mondays, Wednesdays, and Fridays; however, the information was neither detailed nor firm enough for effective rotary-wing and fixed-wing coordination and scheduling purposes" (Andrus, 1994: vol. 2, 11).

In the following passage, the F-15 lead echoes General Andrus's conclusion about sparse flight information concerning helicopters. He also goes on to voice concerns about the uneven distribution of flight plans and Eagle Flight's early entry into the AOR:

> TIGER 01:   First, it says in the ACO [Airspace Control Order] that all UN Flights
> will be in the Frag [ATO] with specifics. They [Eagle Flight] were in the Frag
> but no—and it doesn't help to be in the Frag and just put the name—the call
> sign down. Second of all, I have a big question as to why the [helicopter]
> flight plans have been distributed to the F-16 Squadron for a while, but the

F-15 Intel Officer who's been here four months has never seen a flight plan on these flights. The second thing the ACO says, is that AI [air interrogation] radars will always be the first ones to enter the AOR. So, when you go in with that mind set that you're the first one in there, any type of hits out there tend to get your attention [*sic*] quick. (Andrus, 1994: TAB V-029, 66)

There are several important issues here—organizational failures all, failures to integrate sequential interdependence, failures to coordinate by plan: Eagle Flight appeared nowhere on the flow sheet. They appeared only in generic form on the ATO. And, apparently, when they finally did submit their flight plans, it seems that some folks got it and others didn't. Before examining their early appearance in the TAOR, let's follow the path of helicopter flight planning and see where it leads. Let's see why TIGERs 01 and 02 were never briefed about Eagle Flight operations.

Each evening, the MCC (primarily Army) at Zakhu sent a Situation Report (SITREP) to the Joint Operations and Intelligence Center (JOIC)[29] at Incirlik, listing the helicopter flights planned for the next day. Once again, these SITREPS were general in nature and were received too late to be published in the daily ATO.[30] Later, Eagle Flight would call the JOIC to "activate" the ATO line. A duty officer would then send takeoff and gate times to the Turkish C3 (operations) for approval. Meanwhile, a C2 (intelligence) representative in the JOIC consolidated the MCC weekly schedule with the SITREP and used secure intelligence channels to pass this updated information to his counterparts in operational squadrons.

Incredibly, there were no procedures in place to pass this information to the Combined Forces Air Component (CFAC) who exercised ultimate tactical control of the helicopters through the MAD DOG (mission director) and DUKE (airborne command element). The CFAC operated off its own internally generated set of plans and schedules. They dictated to others who would fly when, not the other way around. Hence, information channels were designed primarily for one-way communications—distribution outward and downward. The CFAC was not in the business of soliciting input, especially the troublesome last-minute-type generated by the Army.

While the CFAC and F-15s never received details of Eagle Flight operations, folks flying out of the F-16 squadron did. Why was one squadron informed, while another one, located right across the street, was not?

---

[29] The JOIC was manned around the clock by representatives from both intelligence and operations staffs. The idea was to combine assets from both functions under one roof to create a seamless interface.

[30] This is one more example of how the Air Force and Army developed significantly different orientations toward time. Since the Air Force controlled its own destiny, they were able to plan mission packages far in advance and stick to a regimented system of monthly, weekly, and daily planning schedules. Army aviators worked off of a much tighter planning cycle. Last-minute taskings drove their plans.

As it turns out, the answer is simple and quite consistent with the logic applied in this chapter. Even *within* services, differentiation creates integrative challenges. F-15s are designed primarily for air superiority—high altitude aerial combat missions. F-16s, on the other hand, are all-purpose fighters. Unlike F-15s, which rarely flew low-level missions, it was common for F-16s to fly low. As a result, to avoid low-altitude mid-air collisions, staff officers in F-16 squadrons regularly sought out and briefed details concerning helicopter operations; F-15 planners did not.[31] This disparity between what was being briefed to F-15 and F-16 pilots not only contributed to TIGER Flight's errant expectations on the day of the shootdown, but it also effectively disabled the final control check built into the hierarchy of the Task Force—the commander. I examine this unfortunate connection in detail at the end of this chapter.

In the end, Hackman's insight about "the stuff" of work is most powerful. The specific work content of F-15 pilots—high-altitude aerial combat—significantly shaped their lives. They developed the "collective equivalent of tunnel vision," and lost "sight of the larger picture into which [their] work fit" (Hackman, 1990: 488). Helicopters were a part of that "larger picture"; the F-15s lost sight of them—until they crossed paths in the TAOR during their sweep. However, the "stuff of work" cuts both ways. Just as content-induced tunnel vision in the F-15 squadron blocked fighters' view of helicopters, a similar phenomenon in Eagle Flight Detachment limited their organizational field of vision. The specific work content of UH-60 pilots— ground support—significantly shaped their lives. As a result, they entered the TAOR before it was sanitized.[32]

---

[31] During the court-martial, the F-15 lead was asked why the F-16s were briefed but the F-15s were not. He replied: "I believe the reason it happened was twofold: one is the F-16s, from what I heard, had a fear of having a close pass with a friendly helicopter because they did low-altitude training, something we don't do. They put a request in to get the specific flight plans for the helicopters. I also know from talking to the intelligence officer that he made several requests to get flight plans on any unknown aircraft that were friendly and never got any type of response. His request included helicopters" (Headquarters, 8th Air Force, 1995: vol. 13, 143a.9).

[32] The following testimony illustrates how "the stuff" of Army aviators' "work" powerfully influenced their interpretations of the ACO's restriction on entering the TAOR prior to AWACS or a fighter sweep:

Q: When you discussed in your statement that, to the best of your knowledge before the fourteenth, you did not require fighter coverage or fighters to sanitize the area before you went into the AOR, what was the primary reason for that?

A: I would say it was a combination of things, Sir. Because our primary mission was to support MCC Forward, if, in fact, the requirement to accomplish the mission as a pilot in command—it's the person that I'm supporting—if that ground commander says, "Here's what I need to do to accomplish the mission," and I see no reason to not do it. . . . In this particular case, we saw no reason to believe that it would create problems on the rare occasion that we did go into the AOR before AWACS was on station. (Headquarters, 8th Air Force, 1995: vol. 14, 150a.7)

The Airspace Control Order (ACO) seems clear: "No aircraft will enter the TAOR until the fighters with AI [air interrogation] radars have sanitized the TAOR." However, to Army aviators in Eagle Flight, the word "aircraft" did not include helicopters. Just as Air Force staff planners didn't really consider UH-60s to be "aircraft" for coordination purposes, and AWACS crew members didn't consider them as "aircraft" for control purposes, Army aviators had good reason to believe that this "fighter sweep" restriction did not apply to them.

The ACO also states that no aircraft will fly in the TAOR without AWACS coverage. However, Eagle Flight had an official exception to this policy. Helicopters were allowed in the TAOR without AWACS coverage, as long as they stayed inside the security zone. To aviators, fighter coverage and AWACS coverage were synonymous. AWACS always flew with fighter coverage. Hence, since they were allowed to fly inside the security zone without AWACS coverage, they were also able to fly there without fighters overhead.

This issue came up numerous times during the court-martial. In the following testimony, the senior Army helicopter flight instructor/operations officer for Eagle Flight was questioned about his understanding of this restriction:

Q: You believe that the helicopters did not have to wait for the fighters, let's say in the beginning of a package, you did not have to wait for a fighter to come in and sweep the area clean before you went in?

A: No, we didn't have to wait for that. That was based upon our understanding of the procedures at the time. We did not require AWACS coverage to fly missions within the security zone. Therefore, we didn't require AWACS coverage and we didn't require anyone else to be overhead as well. (Headquarters, 8th Air Force, 1995: vol. 14, 148.a8)

Later, CW4 Menard, the standardization officer responsible for Army aviation policy in the entire European Theater, testified to what he found during his rotation to Eagle Flight, which just happened to be during the time of the accident:

Q: Is it your understanding that all pilots had the responsibility to comply with the ACO?

A: To comply with the ACO, yes, Sir. That would be a true statement. The SOP [Standard Operating Procedure] that we had at Eagle Flight alluded to a couple of things that I would characterize as "different" than the ACO. It clearly was my understanding that there was a negotiated process—for example, we were allowed to be in the TAOR without AWACS coverage, as long as we didn't enter [sic] the security zone. I remember the fact that the ACO referred to AWACS coverage being required for all players and that we were clearly an exception to that by our SOP. I saw nothing wrong with that because we were supporting the MCC Forward guys and also it created no conflict that I was aware of, so it was not something I focused any energy on to attempt to resolve because I didn't think it was—I wasn't trying to fix anything that wasn't broken. (Headquarters, 8th Air Force, 1995: vol. 14, 150.a12)

Notice CW4 Menard's local orientation. Just as the "stuff" of F-15 pilots' work caused them to lose sight of helicopter operations, the "stuff" of UH-60 pilots' work caused them to develop a similar "equivalent of tunnel vision," and lose "sight of the larger picture into which [their] work fit" (Hackman, 1990: 488). The process works in both directions to induce a kind of organizational blindness. The F-15s lost sight of the UH-60s; the UH-60s lost sight of the F-15s. Neither group saw what was coming. CW4 Menard continues:

Q: And it would have also been your assumption that it [coordination] was being done, it had been coordinated with everyone?
A: Yes, Sir. That clearly is, I guess, what I was trying to say. It wouldn't be in the SOP. I assumed it wouldn't be in the SOP if it wasn't acceptable and we routinely operated that way, and when AWACS would, in fact, come on station, we were already downrange in the AOR and no one ever said anything to us about it, any more than no one ever made an issue about our Mode I when we crossed into the gate. No one ever alluded to the fact that it was a problem that we were in the TAOR prior to AWACS coverage anymore than they suggested we should change our Mode I code at the gate and it was during repeated discussions that we had with the operations personnel in that Squadron [AWACS] that the opportunity was given often for that to take place. It never did. (Headquarters, 8th Air Force, 1995: vol. 14, 150.a13)[33]

Daily practice reinforced each party's perception of the world as they saw it. F-15 pilots flew hundreds of successful missions without any specific knowl-

---

[33] During the Article 32 investigation, CW3 Holden testified repeatedly that Eagle Flight routinely flew inside the security zone prior to a sweep and nobody ever told them it was wrong:

Q: When you were flying during those 45 missions in the TAOR, did any AWACS crew ever tell you that you weren't supposed to be in the TAOR prior to the AWACS itself being there or the sweep being done, excuse me?
A: No, I was never informed of that.
Q: Did they ever tell you you couldn't enter the TAOR until the sweep was done?
A: No, they didn't.
Q: If that had been told to you again, would you bring that to the attention of your whole Det [detachment]?
A: Yes, of course . . .
Q: And in your almost two years over there, did anyone ever mention that to the Det, the fact that they were not allowed to enter the TAOR prior to a sweep?
A: No, we were not aware of that. (Headquarters, 8th Air Force, 1995: vol. 14, 148a.23)

edge of Eagle Flight operations. UH-60 pilots frequently entered the TAOR prior to AWACS/fighter support without incident or comment.

The members of each unit developed a form of collective tunnel vision effectively blinding them to the operational realities of others. The following testimony by CW3 Holden reveals how a lack of integration at the organizational level resulted in unawareness at the individual level:

Q: Have you ever flown in the TAOR when the fighters entered for that sweep, that you're aware of ?

A: We were not—in the overall scheme of how we were integrated into the entire system, we were not aware of what was going on with the F-15s and the sweep and the re-fuelers and the recon missions and AWACS. We had no idea who was where and when they were there.

Q: So, Mr. Holden, if you were in the TAOR when the fighters entered for their sweep, you would not be aware that the fighters were entering for their sweep?

A: That's correct. We would not be aware of that. (Headquarters, 8th Air Force, 1995: vol. 14, 148a.24)

Eagle Flight was indeed isolated, largely unaware of the larger scheme of operations going on around them. So great was the differentiation between Army and Air Force flight operations in OPC, that in-place plans and schedules failed to adequately coordinate sequential interdependence between the F-15s and UH-60s. F-15 pilots were unaware of Eagle Flight operations. Helicopters entered the TAOR early. No one sensed the disconnect; no one anticipated the potential danger—including the integrator of last resort, the commander.

Before examining this failure to monitor, one more level of interdependence exists—reciprocal. After standardization efforts fail, after plans and schedules fail, real-time coordination can still be accomplished by mutual adjustment. Even though the UH-60s were squawking the wrong Mode I, even though they entered the TAOR before the fighter sweep, even though the F-15 pilots were unaware of Eagle Flight's presence, the unanticipated reciprocal interdependence between fighters and helicopters still need not have resulted in disaster. All they had to do was talk to each other.

Different Radios and "Min Comm": A Failure to Coordinate by Mutual Adjustment

Unlike pooled and sequential interdependence, reciprocal interdependence cannot be coordinated by agreements that predate work activities. Because each unit poses a real-time contingency for the other, because the exact nature of the interdependence cannot be anticipated in advance of practice, rules and plans cannot be formulated ahead of time. According to Thompson's framework, such last-minute coordination must be accomplished through mutual adjustment—"the transmission of new information during the process of action" (Thompson, 1967: 56). This requires real-time communication. Interdependent parties must exchange information while in the act of performing. In the case of our shootdown, this simply did not happen. Black Hawks and F-15s never talked to each other. AWACS said little to anyone. In sum, coordination through mutual adjustment failed.

But, why? Why weren't helicopter and fighter pilots talking to each other? Why were AWACS controllers so reticent? What limited real-time communications between key players? In short, why was there so little mutual adjustment, so little "transmission of new information during the process of action?"

Secretary Perry tells us that "the aircraft were not all communicating on the same radio frequencies" (1994:1). But this is only part of the problem. The roots of sparse communications during OPC flight operations run much deeper. The dearth of real-time talk between pilots can be traced back to strong norms of radio discipline and service interoperability issues. A Task Force policy called "min comm" restricted radio conversations to short bursts. Separate service procurement systems fielded Air Force fighters and Army helicopters with largely incompatible radios. Mutual adjustment failed to work because of strong normative and technical barriers to real-time communications.

Three technical obstacles stood in the way of direct fighter-helicopter communications: (1) physical line-of-sight restrictions, (2) different radios, and (3) different frequencies. First, most FM radio systems require largely unobstructed line-of-sight between transmitter and receiver for clear communications. Eagle Flight operations officer CW3 Holden explains:

> The maximum altitude for helicopter operations in the TAOR is 400 feet AGL [Above Ground Level]. The steep terrain severely limits our ability to maintain radio contact at these altitudes. As a result, we make our calls in the "blind" when necessary and report our location to Arrow base [MCC Headquarters] over the "TACSAT" [tactical satellite][34] after landing. (Andrus, 1994: TAB V-050b, 1)

Rugged terrain and altitude deconfliction restrictions combined to keep Eagle Flight helicopters incommunicado a great deal of the time while operating inside the TAOR.[35] Outside the TAOR, they were able to fly at higher alti-

---

[34] As a backup to their on board radios, Eagle Flight carried a portable tactical satellite radio with them at all times. While fairly reliable, it was impossible to operate from inside a moving helicopter. Therefore, each time they landed, MCC would set up the antennae and call in a situation report.

[35] Flying at high altitudes, with large antennae, and extremely powerful communications platforms, even the AWACS had difficulty maintaining contact with Army helicopters. According to the Senior Director (SD):

tudes. This provided greater line-of-sight, and hence, more reliable communications with the high-flying AWACS and F-15s. Inside Iraq, however, helicopters hugged the ground. Flying in the tactically sound "contour"[36] terrain flight mode—both to avoid mid-air collisions and to mask their presence from threatening ground-to-air Iraqi radars—Eagle Flight pilots found it almost impossible to maintain continuous radio contact while operating inside Iraq.[37]

Even if line-of-sight had been no problem, a second technical obstacle stood in the way of mutual adjustment. Years of separate service procurement programs resulted in the fielding of Army and Air Force aircraft equipped with different communications systems. Both helicopters and fighters flew with a variety of UHF and VHF radios.[38] However, both F-15s and the AWACS were outfitted with the latest in anti-jamming technology—frequency-hopping, HAVE QUICK II radios. By rapidly changing frequencies many times per second, these radios dramatically complicate enemy jamming efforts. Therefore, the preferred mode of communications for AWACS and F-15s inside the TAOR was "secure HAVE QUICK II." Since Eagle Flight's helicopters were not equipped with HAVE QUICK II technology,[39] they could neither monitor or talk to the F-15s while flying inside the TAOR.

A big problem we have with helicopters is that helicopters like to navigate by roads and by the rivers and stuff. And therefore, they don't like to fly straight over peaks and stuff. They like to fly in the valleys and the low-level areas. It's not uncommon for us to lose radar, to lose IFF, or to lose radios with those helicopters or anybody flying low level for that matter. There's other limitations to our system. But, basically, you know, line-of-sight is our biggest limitation. If an aircraft goes into a valley where there's a mountain peak between us and the helicopter, there's no way we're going to be able to see them. There's no way we're going to be able to talk to them. (Andrus, 1994: TAB V-014, 44)

[36] There are three types of "terrain flight": low level, contour, and nap-of-the-earth or NOE. Aviators select the appropriate mode of flight based on a wide range of tactical and mission-related variables. "Low level" terrain flight is flown when enemy contact is "not likely." "Contour" flying is closer to the ground than low level and is followed when enemy contact is "possible." Nap-of-the-earth or NOE flying is the lowest and slowest form of terrain flight, flown only when enemy contact is "expected." Eagle Flight helicopters flew "contour" most of the time while operating inside northern Iraq.

[37] The following testimony of CW3 Holden is typical of Eagle Flight pilots' descriptions of communications inside the TAOR:

Q: While you're flying in the TAOR, are there any procedures that you must follow if you lose radio contact or radar coverage with AWACS?

A: No, Sir. Our radio coverage with AWACS is very limited, Sir. The terrain is very steep, very mountainous terrain and we fly in a tactical flight envelope, which is normally at 100 feet AGL for us. And then in the terrain that we fly in, we lose radio contact quite often, Sir. The further we move to the east, the south and to the east, we lose . . . the more often we lose radio contact. (Andrus, 1994: TAB V-50A, 10)

[38] AWACS carries an extensive communications platform which gives them the capability to monitor and talk on a wide range of data and voice channels.

[39] The Army was behind the Air Force when it came to fielding the latest in technological innovations such as HAVE QUICK. As a result, not all of the UH-60s supporting Eagle Flight were equipped with the hardware to handle HAVE QUICK. Ironically, both Black Hawks in-

Even though the F-15s preferred to use the more advanced HAVE QUICK technology, they were capable of communicating in a clear, non-HAVE QUICK mode. In fact, under special circumstances, the Airspace Control Order (ACO) directed them to do just that. For example, when Air Force F-1s, who, like the Black Hawks were not HAVE QUICK capable, flew in the TAOR, the ACO directed F-15s to use the "clear UHF TAOR, non-HAVE QUICK frequency." Incredibly, even if the ACO had contained a similar provision to coordinate the radios of F-15s and non-HAVE QUICK capable Black Hawks—which it didn't—operating with technically compatible radios would not have solved the problem. Yet a third technical obstacle stood in the way of direct fighter-helicopter communications—confused frequencies.

The ACO directs that "non–HQ-II [HAVE QUICK II] capable aircraft will use ATO Tactical freqs in the TAOR." Since the Black Hawks were "non-HQ II capable," according to the ACO then, they should have been communicating on the "ATO Tactical freq" while flying inside the TAOR. Unfortunately, they weren't. The following opinion, voiced by CW3 Holden, was widely shared by all Army helicopter pilots and operations personnel in Eagle Flight:

Q: Would you please talk to us a little bit about the frequency that you would talk to COUGAR [AWACS] with throughout the mission? It's my understanding that you primarily stayed on the enroute frequency throughout your conversations with AWACS?

A: Yes, that's correct.

Q: Is that when you were also going into the TAOR?

A: Yes, that's correct. On two occasions, on previous rotations, in the TAOR, COUGAR has asked me to come up on the mission frequency. Within 5 or 10 minutes of coming up on that frequency, AWACS asked me to go back to the enroute frequency, even though I was operating in the TAOR in Northern Iraq. Normal operations in the TAOR were conducted on the enroute frequency. (Headquarters, 8th Air Force, 1995: vol. 14, 148a.6)

Helicopters stayed on the enroute frequency the whole time they flew inside of the TAOR. This breakdown in coordination is similar to their not switching to a different Mode I code for flying inside the TAOR. Just as no one ever told them to switch Mode I codes, no one ever required them to switch to the TAOR frequency.[40] According to the Staff Weapons Director:

---

volved in the accident were equipped with HAVE QUICK capable radios. However, one contained an outdated earlier version called HAVE QUICK I—which was not compatible with HQ-IIs—and the other one did not have the cryptographic support required to synchronize its hardware with other OPC players. Because not all of their helicopters supported HAVE QUICK II, the CFAC staff declined to support Eagle Flight operations with the necessary cryptographic support. (Source: Phone conversation with Captain Michael Nye, 7 June 1996.)

[40] The fact that no one in the AWACS ever corrected Eagle Flight pilots for using the wrong

I don't remember ever telling them specifically to change it. They're supposed to play by the same set of rules, why do I need to tell them how to fly their airplane? They normally get upset if you do that. And, it's verbally over the radio, you can hear them, tell you, yeah I know what I'm doing, leave me alone kind of thing. (Headquarters, 8th Air Force, 1995: T40.1, 2255)

So separate, so insignificant was Eagle Flight's presence in the minds of AWACS controllers, that even though they were well aware of serious disconnects, they never took any action to address them.[41] According to the Tanker Controller:

Q: Did you require them to change their Mode I code upon entering the TAOR?
A: No.
Q: Did you have them change their radio frequency while they were in the TAOR?
A: No, we traditionally didn't.
Q: What frequency did they maintain in the TAOR?
A: It would be the enroute clear frequency. (Headquarters, 8th Air Force, 1995: T40.1, 2290)

As unremarkable as these practices seemed to both helicopter pilots and practicing AWACS controllers, to the Staff Weapons Director such a disconnect was unimaginable if the helicopters were planning to fly beyond Zakhu:

Q: And you wouldn't imagine that [staying on the enroute frequency while inside the TAOR] happening, would you? On any flight?
A: If I was a controller, I would want them on my freq. If I was a TAOR controller, and if I was a helo pilot, I would definitely want to be on that freq [TAOR]. I'd push myself before anybody pushed me.
Q: On all your flights, just your experience as an AWACS controller, you can't imagine that anyone would keep them on the enroute, can you?

---

frequency or squawking the incorrect code is even more puzzling, given controllers' perception of their role as rule enforcers. According to the Staff Weapons Director:

We [AWACS controllers] talk about the procedures because—we're probably the only people who read the procedures. And, that's obvious by some of the comments that I've heard on the radios. There's a lot of guys who don't read it except for the one paragraph that pertains to them. Some guys probably don't care if a F-111 is squawking this squawk, because I'm a F-16 pilot and all I need to worry about is my four-ship. Okay. We're [AWACS] going to live and die by the command and control. . . . If we don't follow that stuff, then we can't be doing our job properly. (Headquarters, 8th Air Force, 1995: T40.1, 2271)

[41] During the Article 32 Investigation, CW3 Menard was asked why no one in the AWACS ever bothered to correct them and why they wanted the helicopters to stay on the enroute frequency. He replied:

The primary reason that we felt—I can't substantiate this in any way—I felt, for them to monitor us, it was more of a bother than it was; in other words, they didn't want to be bothered with us. (Headquarters, 8th Air Force, 1995: vol. 14, 148a.7)

A: If they're going beyond Zakhu, I can't imagine that any controller would do
     that, nor that any pilot would allow them to do that. (Headquarters, 8th Air
     Force, 1995: T40.1, 2277)

This testimony offers a hint as to how such a common practice, so dangerous
in hindsight, might have developed and continued without setting off alarms.
Because many Eagle Flight missions ran from Diyarbakir to Zakhu and
back; and, since Zakhu was located just inside the TAOR, it hardly seemed
worth switching them over to the TAOR frequency for only a few minutes.[42]
Following this practice only became a problem during those occasions when
Eagle Flight flew beyond Zakhu, east deeper into the TAOR, as they did on
the day of the shootdown.

If it wasn't terrain masking, it was radio incompatibility. If it wasn't different radios, it was different frequencies. Compounding and interrelated
technical challenges[43] worked hard to prevent helicopter and fighter pilots
from talking to each other. However, even if no mountains had gotten in the
way, and both aircraft had been equipped with compatible radios, and all
pilots had been monitoring the same frequency, an additional obstacle
blocked any attempts to coordinate by mutual adjustment. As if technical
challenges weren't enough to defeat the real-time communications necessary
to handle last-minute unforeseen contingencies, a strong cultural norm
worked overtime to discourage any movements in this direction. The generic
term for this military norm is "radio discipline"; in OPC, it was called "min
comm."[44]

According to the AWACS Senior Director (SD), "min comm" is an abbre-
viation (appropriate) for a policy of minimal communication:

[42] Court-martial testimony of the Staff Weapons Director develops this hypothesis in greater
detail, as does his testimony in the following paragraph where he applies this same reasoning to
account for AWACS's failure to correct helicopters flying inside the TAOR while squawking the
wrong Mode I code:

> For a helicopter, if he's going to Zakhu, I'm not that concerned about him going beyond that.
> So, I'm not really concerned about having a F-15 needing to identify this guy. If I know he's
> going—if he comes up and tells me he's going beyond Zakhu, then I'm going to make
> certain, especially his AOR controller—that he has got the correct Mode I. (Headquarters,
> 8th Air Force, 1995: T40.1, 2254)

[43] While I have presented these three technical obstacles as separate issues, they are in fact
interrelated. Not only are different radios and different frequencies connected, but the fact that
controllers didn't respond to Eagle Flight squawking a single Mode I code is also related to
keeping them on the enroute frequency. An internally consistent argument tied all of these errant
practices together in such a way that it "made sense" to do what they were doing.

[44] CW3 Holden describes how the "min comm" policy was operationalized by AWACS
controllers:

> The AWACS crews, when they spoke to us over the radios, they were very curt, very abrupt
> in their communication. It's part of the culture of the AWACS community that they were very
> abbreviated in their communications. (Headquarters, 8th Air Force, 1995: vol. 14, 148a.23)

It changes from theater to theater. Usually, it is associated with brevity. Using brevity words, not talking in long lengthy sentences with adjectives and adverbs. Tell them what they need to know, get off the radio. Try to keep all your transmissions down to three or four words. Don't tell them stuff that they already know. Don't tell them stuff that they should know, unless they ask for it such as this is where your tanker is. This is where the AWACS is. (Headquarters, 8th Air Force, 1995: T40.10, 2409)

The Senior Director, the officer responsible for supervising all controllers on the AWACS, interpreted the standing policy of "min comm" to mean, "Don't tell them stuff that they *should* know" (emphasis added). No doubt this policy contributed to AWACS's general reluctance to enforce rules. No doubt "min comm" contributed to AWACS not correcting Eagle Flight's improper Mode I code. No doubt an emphasis on brevity, on not telling pilots "stuff they *should* know," discouraged controllers from pushing helicopter pilots to the TAOR frequency when they entered Iraq. No doubt a policy of "min comm" seriously hampered any attempts to coordinate through mutual adjustment. Once again, the Senior Director explains:

Contrary to how we work in most theaters, in this theater we work more towards minimal communication. What that means to my controllers is that the fighters don't want to hear a lot of chatter on the radios. . . . It's pretty much a big boy principle, you know. Give them a call if it looks like they don't know it, and one call is more than sufficient. If they want the information, they'll ask it from you. (Andrus, 1994: TAB V-014, 26)

The Senior Director's interpretation appears consistent with that of the fighter community, as indicated in the following exchange:

Q: Do some of the fighters believe that the COUGAR Flight [AWACS] was cluttering up the radio with conversation?
A: I didn't, but I'm positive there are some that felt that way, yes.
Q: Did you hear any of your fighter mates who talked about whether they thought COUGAR was cluttering up the radios inside the AOR?
A: Yes, I know there were instances of that. (Headquarters, 8th Air Force, 1995: vol. 13, 143a.10)

Unlike the AWACS, which had a nineteen-member crew to handle its responsibilities, the F-15 (C-model) is a single-seat fighter. Therefore, the pilot not only flies the plane, he is also the navigator, weapons officer, and communications specialist. Even under relatively benign training conditions, fighter pilots are kept extremely busy in the cockpit; their cognitive capabilities are often taxed to the limit. As a result, any unnecessary interruptions on the radio are a significant distraction from important competing demands. Hence, there was a great deal of pressure within the fighter community to minimize talking on the radio. The F-15 lead's testimony continues:

Q: When you talked about communication, you said, usually the breakdown
    comes in the communication part. Do you recall that?

A: Yes, Sir.

Q: Would you please explain that a little bit more to me? What did you mean by
    that?

A: Comm is something we probably work on more than anything in the air-to-air
    community. It's really important because it's one of the major ways you get
    information to other people, but it can become a hindrance if it comes to a
    point where there is too much communications . . .[45] We tend to try to only
    talk on the radio to get new information, not to repeat information that some-
    one else already put on the radio. (Headquarters, 8th Air Force, 1995: vol. 13,
    143a.10)

This tendency to minimize talk frustrated any attempts to coordinate by
mutual adjustment. "Min comm" severely limited fighter pilots' interaction
with the rest of the command and control community. The tendency "to try
to only talk on the radio to get new information, not to repeat information"
discouraged any efforts to check accuracy and understanding. Interpretations
such as "don't tell them stuff they should know" and maxims such as "the
big boy principle" both assume that all is well, that everyone knows what
they should know, that everyone is a "big boy." However, as the facts of this
case bear out, in complex organizations all is rarely well, not everyone does
know what they should know, and not all boys are big boys.

In his study of high-reliability organizations, Weick emphasizes the importance of Thompson's third level of coordination. To Weick, coordination
through mutual adjustment is critical because of the inherent complexity in
such systems. "Accidents occur because the humans who operate and manage complex systems are themselves not sufficiently complex to sense and
anticipate the problems generated by those systems" (1987: 112). He calls
this challenge "the problem of requisite variety." One solution to increasing
requisite variety in the humans who manage such systems is to increase the
richness of information available to them. While he recognizes the same
trade-offs raised by our F-15 flight lead above,[46] Weick concludes that "high-

---

[45] TIGER 01 puts his finger on an important trade-off also uncovered by Turner in his 1976
study of *The Organizational and Interorganizational Development of Disasters*. From his in-
depth study of three disasters, Turner concludes that "the cost of obtaining one piece of information has to be balanced against the cost of obtaining an alternative bit. This state of the
variable disjunction of information cannot be dismissed as a lack of communication. Rather, it
is a situation in which high complexity and continuous change make it necessary to be extremely selective in the use of communications" (Turner, 1976: 383). Multiple competing demands on fighter pilots require a similar selectivity to avoid sensory overload.

[46] Similar to our F-15 lead's intuition above, Weick also maintains that "too much richness
introduces the inefficiencies of overcomplication, too little media richness introduces the inaccuracy of oversimplification" (1987: 115). The policy of "min comm" tips the scales heavily in
favor of oversimplification.

reliability systems need rich, dense talk to maintain complexity" (1987: 115). Min comm is the antithesis of rich, dense talk. CW3 Holden described AWACS communications as "very curt, very—rather abrupt" (Headquarters, 8th Air Force, 1995: T-40.6, 132)—not the kind of exchange likely to convey subtle complexities.[47]

In sum, not only were there some very real technical barriers to communication, but OPC's policy of "min comm" further discouraged the real-time exchange of mission-critical information. Hence, Thompson's third level of coordination through mutual adjustment failed. AWACS controllers were reluctant to say more than absolutely necessary, while UH-60 and F-15 pilots assumed all was well. Unfortunately, it wasn't. Another key player also assumed that all was well—the task force commander.

Fallacy of Centrality: A Failure to Notice Coordination Failures

Jeffrey Pilkington, Brigadier General (BG), U.S. Air Force, co-commanded Task Force Provide Comfort. Ultimately, investigators asked him the central question, "Who is responsible for coordinating fixed-wing and helicopter operations and integrating those operations where appropriate?" He didn't hesitate: "Well, I am responsible for—for integration of the forces as the commander" (Andrus, 1994: TAB V-033, 18). Bureaucratic hierarchical structures such as the military are designed to coordinate by inclusion. Activities at one level are overseen and coordinated by authority at the next-higher level. In accordance with the time-honored traditions of unity of command and the scalar principle, at the top of each military organization sits a single commander. Occupying the structural apex, commanders are the ultimate coordinating device—the mechanism of last resort. By virtue of their position at the top, interrelated actions of subordinate units are coordinated through their office.

Why did General Pilkington fail to notice the serious disconnects in his

---

[47] A similar lack of "rich dense talk" has been suggested as a contributing factor in the 20 December 1995 crash of an American Airlines 757 just outside Cali, Colombia. According to the *Washington Times*:

> The two pilots of American Airlines flight 965 grew increasingly confused about air traffic control instructions and then lost track of their position before the plane crashed into a mountain near Cali, Colombia, killing 160 people. The Cali air traffic controller handling the flight told investigators he realized that the crew's replies to some of his instructions "made no sense" and were "illogical," but he lacked the proficiency in colloquial English to confront the crew. So he merely repeated his instructions, never believing the plane was in danger. (1996: A6)

When investigators later asked the Colombian controller what he would have done differently, if the pilot he was speaking to that fateful night was Spanish-speaking, he said he "would have told them that their request made no sense. . . . but he didn't know how to convey these thoughts to the flight crew of AAL 965 in English" (*Washington Times*, 1996: A6).

Task Force? From his structurally privileged position as Commander, how could Eagle Flight's dangerous isolation have escaped his attention?

It is not uncommon for senior leaders to lose touch with day-to-day operations. Seduced by the trappings of executive privilege and removed from the line by considerable social and structural distance, top office-holders often find themselves insulated from reality in the trenches. Perhaps nowhere do such pressures operate with as much force as they do in the office of General Officers. In many ways, military Flag Officers are the closest thing we have to royalty in this country.[48] As the commander of a combined task force, General Pilkington was not immune. However, all evidence indicates that he was unusually active in his struggle to combat the potentially isolating effects of this hierarchically borne disease.

As a rated F-16 pilot, General Pilkington flew regularly in the AOR. Flying five to six times a month, he logged over sixty-five missions during his ten months in command. As the senior officer in the Task Force, he was also a regular passenger on Eagle Flight helicopters. BG Pilkington explains:

> I have probably had more experience operating with Eagle Flight than anyone except the Colonel Thompson that's—that's at MCC now. And by virtue of the fact that he's not a pilot, I think I have a—a unique perspective on Eagle Flight operations that nobody else has. (Andrus, 1994: TAB V-033, 39)

General Pilkington was no stranger to air operations in his task force. In his role as an active pilot, he was able to obtain a unique inside-out view of his organization as it actually operated—a rare privilege for such a senior officer. As a frequent flier with Eagle Flight, he was also able to periodically observe helicopter operations under actual mission conditions.

If he was such an active participant in air operations, then how could such serious communication breakdowns persist without his knowledge? The following exchange contains a clue:

> Q: Prior to the fourteenth, who knew that Eagle Flight was taking off from Zakhu and going to Irbil? That is, who at Incirlik was aware of that?
>
> A: I don't know. But, *by virtue of my experience* and by virtue of my experience as late as the Tuesday, two days prior [to the accident], that information would have gotten down to as low as the Squadron Operations Center (SOC) to be briefed to the crews, so my assumption would have been that all echelons in between would have been aware of that. (emphasis added)
>
> Q: Because that information apparently did not reach the F-15 squadron, would that indicate to you that there was a break in the communication process?
>
> A: Yes, in that specific instance, so—but, I don't know who else it didn't reach, so if it only didn't reach the F-15 squadron, I would say yes, there was a

[48] For a fascinating account of this enduring phenomenon, see General J.F.C. Fuller's book, *Generalship: Its Diseases and Their Cures* (1933).

break. If it didn't reach many other echelons, then—then I would consider
that there's a—there's an organizational deficiency. (Andrus, 1994: V-033, 28)

Ironically, General Pilkington's ignorance of this "organizational deficiency"
prior to the accident was not due to a *lack* of participation in daily flight
operations, as we might have suspected—given his status and position. In
fact, just the opposite is true. It was precisely *because of* his active participation that he remained in the dark. His perspective, unusual for his rank, as an
active F-16 pilot created an organizational blind spot concerning the dissemination of information on Eagle Flight operations.

Because F-16s periodically flew low-level missions, SOC 2—the squadron operations center supporting F-16s—faithfully briefed planned helicopter activity in the TAOR. General Pilkington was an F-16 pilot who routinely
flew out of SOC 2. Therefore, every time he flew, he was dutifully informed
of all planned helicopter operations prior to flying. Unfortunately, F-15 pilots
were not. SOC 1 that supported the high-flying F-15s never briefed helicopter operations because their aircraft never flew "down in the weeds."

It was General Pilkington's intimate knowledge of OPC flight operations,
from the perspective of an F-16 pilot, and not the more common general
insulation from life in the trenches, that effectively blinded him to the possibility that all pilots might not be receiving the same information:

> I know I was accustomed to that information (takeoff times for Eagle Flight) get-
> ting down as far as the Squadron Operation Centers and being routinely briefed
> at—at—in—at the step brief. So by virtue of that, I made an assumption, since it
> was getting to the lowest echelons, that the other echelons had the same informa-
> tion. (Andrus, 1994: TAB V 033, 13)

The following testimony further illustrates just how strongly the General's
sense of organizational reality was grounded in his unusual experience as an
active F-16 pilot of general officer rank and frequent UH-60 passenger:

Q: By virtue of your experience, in seeing that coordination process take place,
   that is in seeing the end result of that coordination process, would it be correct
   to say that you were confident that people were accomplishing the required
   coordination?

A: Based on my lengthy discussions with Captain McKenna, who was the pilot
   of the lead helicopter on the day of the accident and the detachment commander—who had been the detachment commander basically the same
   amount of time that I have been here as the commander. . . . I was confident
   that—that all forms of coordination between Eagle Flight, MCC operations
   and the JOC were functioning smoothly. Then, by virtue of the fact that—
   that I was normally and routinely given information on Eagle Flight operations in a step brief at Squadron Operations Center Two, before I flew, and
   then based on the fact that I attended Eagle Flight pre-mission briefings at

> Diyarbakir in their operations where they reviewed the ATO, discussed the
> squawks, discussed frequencies, discussed code words, and discussed the rest
> of the—of the ATO and flew, in fact, I know they flew with the ATO in their
> hand. By virtue of the fact that I often listened to them talk to COUGAR imme-
> diately after takeoff, listened to them use the code words, listened to them
> coordinate gate times, I was confident that the coordination was—was hap-
> pening quite smoothly and efficiently. (Andrus, 1994: TAB V-033, 18)

Unlike other senior leaders, who often rely on indirect sources of information such as reports, or artificial scenarios such as inspections, General Pilkington based his assessment of the level of integration within his task force
on intimate personal knowledge. Based on his own experience at multiple
levels in the process, with various players, he was "confident that the coordination was happening quite smoothly and efficiently." Unfortunately, he
was wrong.

His confidence not only applied to F-16s and UH-60s, but also to the
AWACS:

> Q: You mentioned that the AWACS was to provide flight following. Do you
>   know if the AWACS crews were aware of that guidance?
> A: Well, my experience from flying dozens of times on Eagle Flight, which
>   that—for some eleven hundred and nine days prior to this event, that was—
>   that was normal procedures for them to flight follow. So, I don't know that
>   they had something written about it, but I know that it seemed very obvious
>   and clear to me as a passenger on Eagle Flight numerous times that that was
>   occurring. (Andrus, 1994: TAB V-033, 12)

Notice his choice of words, "It seemed very obvious and clear to me . . . that
that was occurring." Once again, from his perspective, coordination appeared
to be happening as planned. Once again, he was wrong.

> Q: If, for instance, the pilot of EAGLE 01 were to call AWACS, call sign COUGAR,
>   and report that he was departing "Whiskey for Lima," would you then have
>   expected COUGAR or AWACS to have provided flight following for the heli-
>   copter as the helicopter proceeded along that route?
> A: Absolutely.
> Q: Would you have been surprised if the AWACS crew had merely noted the
>   radio call and taken no further action to determine the location of the
>   helicopter?
> A: I would be surprised. (Andrus, 1994: TAB V-033, 12)

From the back seat of a UH-60, it sure seemed like AWACS was "flight
following" the helicopters. Unfortunately, they weren't.

I met BG Pilkington following the Congressional Hearings in August of
1995. As a commander, he never shied away from taking personal responsibility. As a professional, he simply couldn't understand how he had failed.

He was a "hands-on" general. Aware of the dangers of being insulated, he had gone out of his way to stay actively involved—and still he failed. He failed to notice that helicopter operations were not effectively integrated into OPC flight operations.

There is a name for this phenomenon. Westrum calls it the "fallacy of centrality" (1982): Because I don't know about it, it must not be happening; or the corollary: It must be happening the way I know about it. Weick explains: "Experts overestimate the likelihood that they would surely know about the phenomenon if it actually were taking place" (1995a: 2).[49] There is a paradox here. Experts are subject to the fallacy of centrality; nonexperts are subject to ignorance of a different kind. By becoming an "expert," by actively involving himself in OPC flight operations, by—in his own words—gaining "a unique perspective on Eagle Flight operations that nobody else has," General Pilkington became susceptible to the fallacy of centrality. Had he chosen the more common route and remained secluded in his office, he would have been accused of being not active enough. BG Pilkington, fully aware of the insulating dangers of senior officer position, but apparently unaware of the fallacious seduction of centrality, chose to become "an expert." Paraphrasing Weick, OPC's commander overestimated the likelihood that he would surely know about non-integration if it were actually taking place (1995: 2).

Summary: How It All Came Apart

Whatever you divide, you have to put back together again. In the end, General Pilkington was simply one more human being with insufficient requisite variety to match the complexity growing in his organization. He was simply one more, highly visible victim of a deeply differentiated, complex organization whose coordinating mechanisms failed to effectively integrate its disparate parts. Long histories of separate services had driven deep wedges between Army and Air Force operations. Reinforced by intimate relationships with the stuff of their work, F-15 pilots, AWACS controllers, and UH-60 pilots all developed dramatically different orientations toward goals, time, and interpersonal relationships. Complexity led to differentiation. Differentiation demanded integration.

---

[49] According to Westrum, "This fallacy is all the more damaging in that it not only discourages curiosity on the part of the person making it, but it also frequently creates in him/her an antagonistic stance toward the events in question" (1982: 393). There is some evidence of this in BG Pilkington's command. There are numerous examples in the accident report and the GAO report (U.S. General Accounting Office, 1997) of various individuals raising concerns about helicopters not following procedures (Headquarters, 8th Air Force, 1995: T40.10, 2263–73) as well as fighters (Headquarters, 8th Air Force, 1995: T40.6, 1279–82). Apparently, little was done to address these concerns.

Consistent with the conclusions of Lawrence and Lorsch (1967), complex collective tasks, such as OPC's, require high degrees of both differentiation and integration. In addition to spawning differing cognitive and emotional orientations, task force mission requirements also created a myriad of complex interdependencies. Pooled, sequential, and reciprocal interdependence abounded. For some 1,109 days, coordination by standardization, plan, and mutual adjustment adequately handled the challenge of integration. On 14 April 1994, these mechanisms failed. Eagle Flight entered the TAOR early; the F-15s were unaware; the Black Hawks squawked the wrong code; and fighters and helicopters couldn't talk to each other. Due to multiple coordination failures, Eagle Flight was not adequately integrated into the task force. In the end, this non-integration, an organizational-level failure, increased the likelihood that something bad was going to happen.

6

Cross-Levels Account:
A Theory of Practical Drift

EACH of the last three chapters explains a separate piece of the puzzle, each at a different level of analysis. Individuals erred; groups floundered; and organizations failed. If the F-15 pilots had not misidentified the Black Hawks; or, if the AWACS crew had effectively monitored the helicopters and intervened; or, if Eagle Flight had been better integrated into the Task Force, then there might have been no shootdown. However compelling each explanation may be in part, however logically the parts fit together as a whole, apart or together, they still don't adequately explain the shootdown in its totality.

While each chapter in some sense explains the accident, something is still missing. While I now understand why two F-15 pilots saw what they saw—given their strong set of expectations when confronted with an ambiguous stimulus—I am even less convinced that this accident was *caused* by individual error. While I now understand why the AWACS crew didn't intervene—given a weak team with diffuse responsibilities—I am less convinced that collective inaction *explains* the shootdown. While I now understand why multiple coordinating mechanisms failed to integrate Eagle Flight—given the long history of separate services and highly differentiated tasks—I am even less sure that this is simply a case of organizational failure.

After explaining each of these critical events, I am more convinced than ever that we cannot fully capture the richness of such complex incidents by limiting ourselves to any one or even a series of isolated, within-level accounts. We must look across levels. We must search for mechanisms that operate across individual, group, and organizational boundaries. We must spin a story of the shootdown that captures the dynamic, integrated nature of organizational reality—one that, while acknowledging the parts, also recognizes the whole.

Explaining complex organizational incidents such as this shootdown requires the successful completion of three conceptually distinct tasks: classical analysis, inductive synthesis, and holistic integration. To Western-trained scientists, the first two come naturally; the third one doesn't.[1] First, complex-

---

[1] In their *Fieldbook*, Senge and colleagues emphasize "the primacy of the whole," in which "wholes are primordial to parts" (1994: 25). They warn that "in the West, we tend to think the

ity must be rendered intelligible through careful reduction. This is the essence of analysis—studying the whole by examining its parts. I did this in two steps. Constructing the Causal Map, I emphasized completeness by trying to include all significant antecedents. Then, guided by expert findings and the logic of counterfactual interrogation, I distilled dense causal clouds into three stories—each at a different level of analysis. Individual, group, and organizational explanations are the end products of the first task.

The second task follows logically from the first. After breaking the whole into parts and explaining each one of them, all parts then had to be examined as they related to each other and to the whole—a process of inductive synthesis. Flowing naturally from the first, this second task was also included in each of the previous three chapters. As I explained individual-, group-, and organizational-level phenomena, I also related each part to the other and to the whole. At the organizational level, helicopter non-integration set the conditions for AWACS crew inaction at the group level; while both organizational and group contexts contributed to individual F-15 pilot misidentification, and ultimately, to the shootdown itself.

Finally, the shootdown must be studied as an organic whole—a unity that is as much process as product—embedded in an evolving social system that is always something more than the sum of its parts.[2] No matter how skillfully we reduce complexity through analysis, no matter how successfully we put the pieces back together again, there are dangers inherent in the very process of analytical induction. "It is one thing to see where we are going and quite another to get there: to build up, piece by piece, a picture of the dynamic unity of a [phenomenon] when, in taking the pieces out of the whole, we may falsify them and it" (Homans, 1950: 9). The very process of analysis "takes the pieces out of the whole." Having examined the parts, how then do we "build up, piece by piece, a picture of the dynamic unity" without "falsifying" either the parts or the whole? How do we recapture that which was lost through analysis?

This isn't a new question. Some of the earliest scholars of behavior in

---

opposite. We tend to assume that parts are primary, existing somehow independent of the wholes within which they are constituted" even though "there is no intrinsic set of categories, no innate way to define elements that is built into the nature of the 'real thing' we are looking at" (Senge et al., 1994: 25). This chapter directly addresses Senge's concern by shifting our attention from the parts to the whole.

[2] In his book, *The Fifth Discipline* (1990), Peter Senge explains the importance of seeing the whole:

There is something in all of us that loves to put together a puzzle, that loves to see the image of the whole emerge. The beauty of a person, or a flower, or a poem lies in seeing all of it. It is interesting that the words "whole" and "health" come from the same root (the Old English *hal*, as in "hale and hearty"). So it should come as no surprise that the unhealthiness of our world today is in direct proportion to our inability to see it as a whole (Senge, 1990: 68).

complex organizations struggled with this very same challenge—the relationship of parts to the whole. In the following excerpt, Homans draws his inspiration from the wisdom of Mary Parker Follett:

> In studying any organized social activity we must study the "total situation." But we must not merely "be sure to get all the factors into our problem."[3] We must examine "not merely the totalness of the situation, but the nature of the totalness. . . . What you have to consider in a situation is not all the factors one by one, but also their relation to one another . . ." (Follett in Homans, 1950: 8)[4]

In the previous three chapters, I was initially concerned with getting "all the factors into our problem." Then, while explaining "all the factors one by one," I also considered "their relation to one another—not merely the totalness of the situation, but the nature of the totalness." Figure 1.3, the Causal Map, is a tangible product of these first two concerns.

Having seen stories at each level and examined how they are interrelated, we must now somehow look across them—see them all at once. Homans continues: "Mary Follett affirmed 'that the whole determines the parts as well as the parts determine the whole'" (Follett in Homans, 1950: 8). The shootdown (the whole) determined the multitude of causal events (the parts), just as the parts (individual, group, and organizational behavior) determined the whole (the shootdown). Homans on Follett:

> She recognized that unity is not a static, finished thing, but an ongoing process: "The same activity determines both parts and whole. . . . We are speaking of a unity which is not the result of an interweaving, but *is* the interweaving. Unity is always a process, not a product. . . . I have been saying that the whole is determined not only by its constituents, but by their relation to one another. I now say that the whole is determined also by the relation of whole and parts. . . . It is the same activity that is making the whole and parts simultaneously." (Follett in Homans, 1950: 8–9)

In the preceding chapters, I explained the whole "by its constituents"; I explained the shootdown by multiple antecedent events. I also explained "their

---

[3] This is not to discount the theoretical importance of being exhaustive, of considering "all the factors." Vaughan emphasizes how it is this "requirement to fully explain the case, which forces us to take into account and integrate all data that bear on the incident or activity in question." It also protects us "against force fitting the data to the theory and generate[s] new theories we would not have predicted in the beginning" (1996: 457). Surely, "getting *all* the factors into our problem" is important; but Follett warns us that being exhaustive at the molecular or atomic level is not sufficient; a molar perspective is also required—a caution that Vaughan heeds with great success in her historical ethnography *The Challenger Launch Decision* (1996).

[4] All Follett quotations are taken from *The Psychology of Control* (1941), in Metcalf and Urwick, eds., *Dynamic Administration: The Collected Papers of Mary Parker Follett*, 183–209. For a more recent treatment of Follett's remarkable work, see *Mary Parker Follett—Prophet of Management: A Celebration of Writings from the 1920s* (Graham, 1995).

relation to one another"—how non-integration contributed to crew inaction, which in turn, contributed to pilot misidentification. While each explanation was revealing in and of itself, and while, when taken together, the three tell a compelling story, Follett reminds us that "the whole is determined also by the relation of whole and parts"—the shootdown is determined also by the relation of the accident and individual, group, and organizational action. "It is the same activity that is making the whole [shootdown] and parts [individual, group, and organizational events] simultaneously."

What is this activity? What interweaving process created the shootdown and its constituent parts?

This chapter addresses this question by considering the shootdown as a dynamic whole, as a unity. Stepping back from the details and integrating central themes from previous chapters, I propose a dynamic, cross-level theory, one that suggests a *mechanism* that operates across time—since "unity is not a static or finished thing"—and also across levels—since "it is the same *activity* that is making the whole and parts." The mechanism I call "practical drift"; the activity is "practical action."

Practical Action: A Core Category

According to Strauss and Corbin (1990: 142), the final step in developing grounded theory involves selective coding. This process is primarily a challenge of narrative integration—"getting the story straight, developing a clear story line, and translating these into an analytical story. Central to these procedures is the selection of a core category." Integrating individual, group, and organizational stories yielded just such a category—practical action.[5] I define practical action as behavior that is locally efficient, acquired through practice, anchored in the logic of the task, and legitimized through unremarkable repetition. Over time, out of multiple journeys between the data, the literature, and the Causal Map, this single broad category of "practical action" emerged for me as a powerful unifying theme.

At the heart of each explanation in the previous three chapters lies an argument based on the compelling logic of practice. No matter whom the actor, no matter what the level of analysis, each explanation tells a similar story: *Globally untoward action is justified by locally acceptable procedure.* For example, most outsiders simply could not fathom how two experienced pilots could misidentify the Black Hawks and shoot them down so quickly—globally untoward action. However, to the F-15 pilots, their actions seemed

[5] See Strauss and Corbin (1990), *Chapter 8: Selective Coding*, for a detailed description of how to go about selecting a core category—"the central phenomenon around which all the other categories are integrated" (116). In my case, informant testimony converged around a common story so that committing to a single core category, "practical action," was surprisingly easy—considering the complexity of the shootdown and multitude of alternative possibilities.

perfectly natural, locally acceptable procedure. Given their training and what they knew at the time, from their perspective, "seeing" two Hinds and quickly shooting them down fell within the bounds of "acceptable procedure." Their actions were practical in the sense that they grew directly out of practice, out of the *logic of the task* at hand. The task, as coded by the pilots, was a high-speed air-to-air engagement. An intimate relationship with this task—in this case, also a highly over-trained one—heavily influenced their action. Fully immersed in the logic of the task, they simply executed a *locally efficient* procedure, exactly as they were trained. When viewed in this context, from the fighters' perspective—which stands in sharp contrast to the orientation of puzzled outsiders—the actions of our two F-15 pilots were very practical indeed.

The story behind AWACS inaction reveals two additional aspects of practical action.[6] First, the standard for monitoring helicopters was *acquired through practice*; there were no formal procedures regarding rotary-wing aircraft.[7] Second, locally developed norms for controlling helicopters were, not surprisingly, *locally efficient*[8]—as was AWACS's reluctance to tell

---

[6] The dependent variable in chapter 4 was AWACS crew inaction. Explaining *in*action poses an interesting conceptual challenge. With a few exceptions (Gilbert, 1988; Seligman et al., 1968), behavioral scientists focus on explaining behavior, not the lack of it. The AWACS crew's failure to effectively monitor helicopters and intervene—their failure to *act* in two specific ways—only became relevant in a post-accident atmosphere. How can we go about explaining a "non-behavior" after the fact? One way is to explain what the crew was in fact doing at the time we expected them (retrospectively) to be doing something else. What they didn't do contributed to the shootdown; what they did do seemed very practical to them at the time.

[7] When AWACS crew members were questioned during the accident investigation, comments such as the following were common regarding the lack of formal procedures for handling helicopters; techniques for monitoring Eagle Flight were learned "on the job":

There—um are no set procedures to track helicopters. (Andrus, 1994: TAB V-016, 10)
There really—ah no set procedures for anyone to track helicopters. If you happen to be wherever and you see them, you apply symbology. (Andrus, 1994: TAB V-016, 11)
Sir, on our hand-off procedures—only applied to fighters. We generally have no set procedures for any of the helicopters. . . . We never had any guidance at all on helicopters. (Andrus, 1994: TAB V-016A, 3)
It is not written down, but understood that weapons is responsible for tracking helicopters. (Andrus, 1994: TAB V-020, 1)

[8] Recall, for example, controllers' testimony about the common practice of ignoring helicopters they lost contact with:

Q: So who is responsible for tracking helicopters? Well, if the surveillance section is not responsible, then it must be the weapons section.
A: Except that helicopters, we can neither see nor hear them for the majority of the time they're in the AOR. So we can't track anything we can't see or can't hear. (Andrus, 1994: TAB V-017, 10)
Q: What are your procedures to follow if you lose contact, radio contact, between the AWACS and the helicopter? What procedures do you follow?
A: Absolutely nothing. It happens all the time. (Andrus, 1994: TAB V-017, 16)

fighter pilots what to do.[9] Given their understanding of what was "standard practice" for controlling helicopters in OPC, it was *im*practical for members of the AWACS crew to closely monitor Eagle Flight and intervene in a fighter-directed engagement; and so they didn't.

Anchored in the logic of the task, locally efficient procedures acquired through practice gain legitimacy through *unremarkable repetition*. If such emergent actions survive long enough without interfering with global interests, and if local procedures are successfully repeated without consequence, they stand a good chance of becoming accepted practice. In the words of Eagle Flight's senior aviator, "You know it would stand to reason that if a procedure [squawking the wrong Mode I code] has been conducted routinely over a long period of time, that will become common law, so to speak" (Headquarters, 8th Air Force, vol. 14: 148a.4). Several examples of coordination failure attained the status of "common law" through just this process. For example, helicopters routinely flew inside the TAOR prior to fighter sweeps. Eagle Flight helicopters flew hundreds of missions inside the TAOR while squawking the wrong Mode I code. Helicopter pilots routinely remained on the enroute frequency, talking to the enroute controller, while flying inside the TAOR. Helicopter operations were never listed on the daily flow sheet and detailed information about Eagle Flight operations was never briefed to F-15 pilots prior to stepping. All of these factors illustrate how locally efficient practices can gain legitimacy through unremarkable repetition.

Given the nature of Army helicopter operations, it simply was not practical— from a local (Air Force) perspective—to fully integrate them into the Task Force. It wasn't practical for Eagle Flight customers to wait for fighter sweeps. It wasn't practical for the AWACS TAOR controller to talk to non–HAVE QUICK–capable helicopters on the TAOR frequency. It wasn't practical for Air Force planners to include late-breaking details of Eagle Flight operations in the ATO or flow sheet. It wasn't practical for F-15 squadron support staff to brief their pilots on low-flying helicopter operations. Since it was often locally impractical (read: inconvenient) to follow many globally sound procedures, without sanctions of some sort, over time, local procedures ruled.

The following testimony of CW4 Menard, helicopter standardization instructor pilot for the European Theater, illustrates just how this tacit approval process worked—how local procedures attained legitimate status through unremarkable repetition:

> We [Eagle Flight] *routinely operated that way* [flew inside TAOR prior to AWACS
> and fighter sweeps], and when AWACS would, in fact, come on station, we were

---

[9] The Senior Director in the AWACS was asked if he was "comfortable with the identification by the fighter flight." He replied, "I can say that it wouldn't have mattered whether I was comfortable or not with the call. It's—it's not my position to—to stop an intercept with the fighters already engaged" (Andrus, 1994: TAB V-014A, 9).

already downrange in the AOR and *no one ever said anything to us about it*, any more than *no one ever made an issue about our Mode I* when we crossed into the gate. *No one ever alluded to the fact that it was a problem* that we were in the TAOR prior to AWACS coverage anymore than they suggested we should change our Mode 1 code at the gate and it was during repeated discussions that we had with the operations personnel in that squadron [AWACS] that the opportunity was given often for that to take place. It never did. (emphases added) (Headquarters, 8th Air Force, 1995: vol. 14, 150a.13)

Eagle Flight instructor pilot CW3 Holden also testified as to how successfully repeated practical actions gained legitimacy in the absence of any critical intervention:

Q: When you were flying during those 45 missions in the TAOR, did any AWACS crew ever tell you that you weren't supposed to be in the TAOR prior to the AWACS itself being there or the sweep being done, excuse me?
A: No, I was never informed of that.
Q: Did they ever tell you you couldn't enter the TAOR until the sweep was done?
A: No, they did not.
Q: And, in your almost two years over there, did anyone ever mention that to the Det [Eagle Flight Detachment], the fact that they were not allowed to enter the TAOR prior to the sweep?
A: No, we were not aware of that. (Headquarters, 8th Air Force, 1995: vol. 14, 148a.23)

Over time, globally designed but locally impractical procedures lose out to practical action when no one complains. Gradually, locally efficient behaviors become accepted practice.

As a core category, practical action has promising conceptual wingspan. It covers all levels of analysis, is central to each critical path in the causal chain of events, and appears in most attempts by informants to make sense of this senseless tragedy. However, a single category does not a theory make. What a category needs is context and process; what practical action needs is a story line. During the court-martial of the AWACS Senior Director—the only service member court-martialed as the result of the shootdown—defense counsel offers a hint:

What we're looking at is not one small dereliction, Your Honor. . . . That shootdown was not the result of anything Captain Wang [the Senior Director] did, but it's the result of a chain that goes back years. . . . *What was this system that was so corroded that this sort of thing could happen?* (emphasis added) (Headquarters, 8th Air Force, 1995: T-40.1, 122)

By placing "practical action" in context, the following section examines how a "corroded system" led to tragedy.

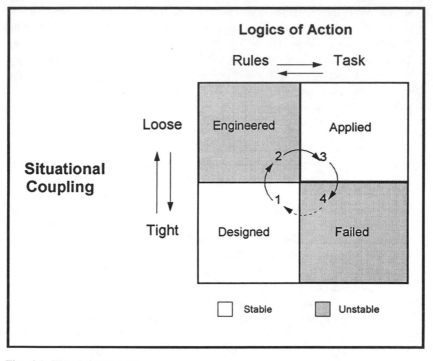

Fig. 6.1. Theoretical Matrix

Practical Drift: A Theory

To help demonstrate how the core category is related to other important parts of the story, I looked for an efficient way to capture both contextual and temporal aspects of the phenomenon. What I needed was a picture, a moving picture, one that tells the dynamic story of practical action. What I constructed was the theoretical matrix in Figure 6.1.

Sutton and Staw argue that "good theory is often representational *and* verbal. The arguments are clear enough that they can be represented in graphical form. But the arguments are also rich enough that processes have to be described with sentences and paragraphs so as to convey the logical nuances behind the causal arrow" (1995: 376). Hoping that my arguments are both "clear enough" and "rich enough," I start by "representing" my theory in "graphical form," and then follow with "sentences and paragraphs."

[10] Once again, for a detailed description of how to use diagrams—"graphical representations or visual images of the relationships between concepts"—to develop grounded theory, see Strauss and Corbin (1990: 197–223).

Also mindful of Sutton and Staw's warning that "diagrams are not theory," I offer this matrix as a "stage prop rather than the performance itself" (1995: 376). I use this figure, like any good prop, to help tell a story or, as Weick suggests in his commentary on Sutton and Staw, I offer the diagram not "in lieu of strong theory," but rather to "inch toward stronger theory" (1995b: 385).

The matrix captures three dimensions: situational coupling, logics of action, and time. First, the vertical axis represents two important states of nature inside the organization. The situation can be either loosely or tightly coupled. In this case, "coupling" refers to the level of interdependence between subunits within the task force.[11] Loose coupling "simply connotes things, 'anythings' [in this case, subunits of OPC] that may be tied together either weakly or infrequently or slowly or with minimal interdependence" (Weick, 1976: 5). When elements are tightly coupled, "there is no slack or buffer or give between two items. What happens in one directly affects what happens in the other" (Perrow, 1984: 90).[12]

In his article on *Educational Systems as Loosely Coupled Systems* (1976), Weick suggests that "it may not be the existence or nonexistence of loose coupling that is a crucial determinant of organizational functioning over time, but rather *the patterning of loose and tight couplings*" (emphasis

[11] Weick informs us that "there is no shortage of potential coupling elements" (1976: 4). Here, I apply his concept to label different states of intraorganizational subunit interdependence— what is either loosely or tightly coupled are major actors within Task Force Provide Comfort.

[12] Normal accident theorists suggest that tight coupling contributes to catastrophic failures by accelerating small ripples from tiny disturbances into tidal waves of disastrous proportions so quickly that operators don't have time to intervene (Perrow, 1984). Task Force officials seem to have appreciated this logic and hence included a rule in the Airspace Control Order that "was specifically designed to slow down a potential engagement to allow CFAC [Combined Forces Air Component] time to check things out" (U.S. General Accounting Office, Office of Special Investigations, 1997: 34). This rule required pilots to "report to the Airborne Command Element in an 'unusual circumstance'" (U.S. General Accounting Office, Office of Special Investigations, 1997: 26). Whether or not the F-15 pilots actually followed this rule is in dispute; the issue was not addressed in the original accident investigation. According to the Board's Senior Legal Advisor, the Board did not specifically address this requirement because it was clear that the Airborne Command Element (DUKE) had monitored the engagement and was aware of the intercept. "Further, the Operation Provide Comfort management, in the Board's opinion, had allowed operations to degrade to such a degree that it 'may not have been common practice' at the time for F-15 pilots to contact the Airborne Command Element. He said that partly because of this degradation, the Board's focus turned to the command and control failures that had created an environment that allowed the incident to occur" (U.S. General Accounting Office, Office of Special Investigations, 1997: 27). The way that operations "degraded" into "common practice" so as to create an "environment that allowed the incident to occur" is the essence of practical drift. In the heat of battle, rules designed specifically to keep situations loosely coupled also fell prey to powerful logics of action. Globally established formal rules lost their grip on the F-15 pilots as they focused on the immediate demands of their work.

added) (1976: 12).[13] Taking the hint, I explore the dynamic nature of subunit coupling in OPC to help explain the shootdown. As the organization shifts from tight to loose and back to tight again, as various subunits vacillate between high and low degrees of interdependence, alternating demands are placed on the system. In this chapter, I explore the impact that this *pattern of coupling* had on behavior inside the Task Force.

The second dimension, "logics of action," is displayed along the horizontal axis. A concept borrowed from the sociological literature of new institutionalism (Friedland and Alford, 1991: 248–53), logics of action are "systems of scripts, norms, and schemas among which people shift" according to context (DiMaggio, 1994: 39). They are context-dependent mind-sets or frames that influence behavior in predictable ways. Weick argues that "the two most commonly discussed coupling mechanisms are the technical core of the organization [task] and the authority of office [rules]" (1976: 4).[14] Since tasks and rules have been repeatedly identified as two of the most powerful mechanisms at work linking action inside organizations, I selected them to capture the primary paradigmatic influences on behavior. My premise is simple: Organizational members shift back and forth between rule- and task-based logics of action depending on the context and these shifts have a predictable impact on the smooth functioning of the organization.

The third dimension is time.[15] Arrows drawn at the center of the matrix suggest a general sequence. The fact that they form a circle implies a cycle.[16] Each quadrant of the matrix represents the organizational system in a different state of the cycle—as determined by the interaction of a unique combi-

[13] Most applications of Weick's notion of "coupling" have focused on how either tightly or loosely coupled systems explain organizational outcomes. I am unaware of any studies that have explicitly used patterns of coupling to explain outcomes.

[14] In-flight refueling is an example of an activity primarily driven by a task-based logic of action. Both tanker and fighter pilots focus on the shared task of refueling. The actual, real-time demands of refueling—the task—dictate the action, not some artificial set of rules. In contrast to a task like refueling, many organizational activities are driven primarily by authoritative rules. For example, periodic curfews were imposed—during which time all OPC personnel were restricted to their base. In this case, it's not the task that dictates the action, but rather an authoritative rule.

[15] Strauss and Corbin emphasize the importance of including time by encouraging researchers to bring "process" into their analysis:

The grounded theory that evolves when process is built into analysis is a dynamic one. Process is a way of giving life to data by taking snapshots of action/interaction and linking them to form a series. To capture process analytically, one must show the evolving nature of events. (1990: 184)

This is just what I did by including time as a third dimension of my model. To "bring life" to my data I suggest a general sequence of events.

[16] Once again, Senge reminds us that "reality is made up of circles, but we see straight lines . . . every influence is both cause and effect. Nothing is ever influenced in just one direction" (1990: 73, 75).

nation of situational coupling and logic of action. However, these two dimensions are more than simply independent variables that suggest interactions; they also represent underlying mechanisms. The twin muscles of behaviorally anchored *logics of action* and stochastically determined *situational coupling* combine to drive the theory. Quadrants 1 and 3 represent relatively stable states of nature; the logic of action "matches" the situation. Hence, movement from quadrants 1 to 2 and 3 to 4 is situationally driven—either by design or by happenstance, respectively. Quadrants 2 and 4 represent inherently unstable states for the organizational system; rule-based logics don't match loose coupling and task-based action is no match for tight coupling. Hence, movement from quadrants 2 to 3 and 4 to 1 is fueled by an imbalance in the system. These twin engines work with alternating strokes in a piston-like fashion to propel action in a clockwise direction from quadrants 1 through 4.

Each quadrant then, represents an artificially inscribed stopping point—a convenient pause in the natural "stream of experience"—each with a label to capture the dominant feature of the organization at that point in time.[17] For example, quadrant 1 represents the organization on the drawing board, where imaginary members of a "designed" organization follow global rules in a tightly coupled world. Quadrant 2 depicts an "engineered" organization, one that is operating as designed. The situation may be loosely coupled, but operators are following the rules. In quadrant 3, the dominant feature is practical application. Local task-based logics rule, as life inside the organization takes on a decidedly pragmatic bent. Finally, in quadrant 4, organizing itself fails. Local task-based logics don't match the global demands of a tightly coupled situation; this is when friendly helicopters get shot down.

Having briefly described the basic conceptual building blocks, I now turn to a more complete rendering of the theory. By stepping through the matrix, quadrant by quadrant, I hope to emphasize the dynamic nature of the model.

---

[17] In the following passage, Weick describes how we retrospectively construct reality by bracketing discrete segments of time, imbue them with meaning, and tag them with labels. This is the process behind my construction of the theoretical matrix and the Causal Map (Figure 1.3):

> Time exists in two distinct forms, as pure duration and as discrete segments. Pure duration can be described using William James' image of a "stream of experience." Note that experience is singular, not plural. To talk about experiences implies distinct, separate episodes, and pure duration does not have this quality. Instead, pure duration is a "coming-to-be and passing-away that has no contours, no boundaries, and no differentiation" (Schutz, 1967: 47). Readers may object that their experience seldom has this quality of continual flow. Instead, experience as we know it exists in the form of distinct events. . . . To cope with pure duration, people create breaks in the stream and impose categories on those portions that are set apart . . . [they] chop moments out of continuous flows and extract cues from those moments. (Weick, 1995: 25, 35)

This is how we create distinct events; this is how I created the four organizational states depicted in the matrix, by artificially freezing the flow of time in order to make sense of the world.

In so doing, I also remain true to Follett's admonition that "unity is always a process, not a product" (Follett in Homans, 1950: 9). The process starts in quadrant 1—a place in time where the organization only exists in the imagination of its designers—hence, the label, "designed."

Quadrant 1: Designed

Starting in the lower left-hand quadrant, imagine yourself as an officer assigned the task of writing the rules to coordinate the actions of various subunits in Operation Provide Comfort (OPC). Planning is a deeply rational activity. Therefore, sitting in your planning cell in the Pentagon, you try to picture the worst possible scenario in terms of interdependence—in engineering terms, your "design criteria." You select the situation when the system is tightly coupled—when the activity in one unit directly affects what happens in another. You also assume that organizational members will be "following the rules" that you write. Hence the "design state" depicted in quadrant 1 is defined by a rule-based logic of action and a tightly coupled situation—a rational fit.

While on the surface, it seems only prudent to design systems and write rules that are capable of handling the most demanding conditions, Weick alerts us to consider the possibility that, contrary to the classical rational model—which depicts organizations as tightly coupled mechanical systems—perhaps we ought to view them instead as *loosely* coupled systems (Glassman, 1973; Weick, 1976). In fact, upon closer inspection, we find that the activities of major subunits in large organizations are loosely coupled *most* of the time. Once again, Weick argues that "the bonds among most subsystems, in most organizations, should be relatively loose. This means that both stability and adaptation are achieved with less interdependence, less consensus, less mutual responsiveness than we usually assume" (Weick, 1976: 110).

If we counted the total number of minutes that the actions of our AWACS, F-15s, and Black Hawks *directly affected what happened to each other*, and divided that sum by the total number of minutes, hours, and days of the operation since its inception, the resulting fraction would be very small indeed. In practice, the actions of the three main actors in our case were rarely tightly coupled; and yet, because the result of a coordination failure among these actors is potentially fatal, as the author responsible for designing coordinating rules, you would want to write them so as to handle just such an occurrence, no matter how unlikely. That is, of course, exactly how Operation Plan 91-7 was written.[18]

---

[18] OPLAN 91-7 was still in force, as the overarching Operations Plan governing Task Force Provide Comfort at the time of the shootdown.

Economists are quick to point out two particularly salient characteristics of the original authors of OPLAN 91-7 that might have encouraged them to overdesign such coordination rules: costs and information.[19] First, as planners—not operators[20]—they were in the somewhat enviable position of having to design a system in which they would never have to work. As a result, they wouldn't have to bear any of the practical costs of overly burdensome rules. However, they *were* exposed to the potentially high costs of writing a set of rules that contained loopholes or too much slack in them. In the unlikely event that a tragedy should occur during future OPC operations, it was certainly possible that blame could be traced back to the planning team for shoddy design. Therefore, if they were going to err along this dimension, they were encouraged to err in favor of overdesign.

This brings us to economists' second point, which has to do with information quality. Because these authors were writing an Operations *Plan* to coordinate the subunits of a future Task Force, they had very limited specific knowledge to draw on. Not only were they planners and not operators, but the organization they were designing was not yet in place. There was no concrete specific knowledge available from the field to build on. As a result, a great deal of uncertainty characterized the rule-writing process. Within this rather broad range of uncertainty, authors enjoyed considerable leeway to write overly burdensome rules. With a strong incentive to avoid unlikely tragedies, and little incentive to avoid the practical headaches of overcontrol, OPLAN 91-7 and its supporting OPORDS were designed to accommodate situations of tight coupling. Similar to an architect or mechanical engineer's tendency to "overdesign" buildings and bridges, the original planners of OPC tended to "overdesign" the rules written to coordinate subunit interdependence.

On 7 April 1991, the United States launched Operation Provide Comfort, immediately transforming our "design organization" from the drawing board into an operational task force. Empty boxes on organizational charts were filled with numbered units and positions within the task force were filled with real people as Combined Task Force Provide Comfort took to the field. This change in situation moves us up from quadrant 1 into quadrant 2. The upper left-hand box of the matrix depicts an "engineered" organization, one that "stands up" as planned, one where novice operators rely on design rules

---

[19] I owe this insight to a colleague of mine, Don Sull, who reminded me that there are only two important variables to economists: Any behavior can be explained in terms of information and costs. I'm not in the habit of automatically turning to economic models to explain behavior; however, planners live in an unusually isolated rational world where many of the assumptions underlying an economic model of behavior fit relatively well.

[20] To the best of my knowledge, none of the original authors of OPLAN 91-7 ever had to work under the rules that they designed. As special staff planners, there was no requirement for them to deploy and serve in the organization that they helped to design.

to guide their action—rules based on the worst-case assumption of tight coupling.

Quadrant 2: Engineered

This quadrant is defined by the interaction of a rule-based logic of action and a loosely coupled situation. As the Task Force stood up, it did so with a plan. The advance party of Task Force OPC deployed with a set of coordinating rules designed to handle the worst-case scenario of a tightly coupled situation, a situation where the actions of any one subunit were assumed to have an immediate and substantial impact on the operations of others. However, in practice, this was not the norm. While designers envisioned tightly coupled scenarios requiring the close coordination of fighters, AWACS, helicopters, and ground units, in reality what happened most days rarely involved such closely linked action. For the most part, operations in OPC were loosely coupled.

Early on, however, operators were unaware of this reality. During the first confusing months of the operation—at least through September of 1991 when most of the ground forces were sent home—most players labored under the same set of conservative assumptions that guided designers. The operation was still "new"; uncertainty was still high; and the potential downside was simply too great to ignore. Not following the rules surely invited reprimand and punishment—at the very least. Worse yet, most assumed there must be a substantive reason for these rules; hence, serious violations were presumed to involve risks of a much greater sort. Until the accumulated experience of daily practice outweighed the risks of breaking the rules, no matter how intrusive they seemed, during the early days of OPC, people generally followed the rules as they were designed. The dominant logic of action was rule-based, even though the actual situation was loosely coupled.

Such a disconnect between the real world constraints of everyday practice and those imposed by artificial, externally dictated logics of action creates an inherently unstable situation. Instability generates pressure for change. While action moved from quadrant 1 to 2 based on a change in situations—from design to implementation—movement from quadrant 2 to 3 is driven by a behaviorally anchored shift in logics of action—a phenomenon I call "practical drift."

Practical Drift

Given that the operational situation during the first three years of OPC was primarily loosely coupled—at least in terms of the interactions among our three primary actors—the "design set of rules," written to meet the worst-case scenario imagined in quadrant 1, were bound to be interpreted as overly controlling and as an unreasonable burden on operators in the field. In contingency language, the rules didn't match the situation *most* of the time.[21]

When the rules don't match, pragmatic individuals adjust their behavior accordingly; they act in ways that better align with their perceptions of current demands. In short, they break the rules.[22] According to General Carleton, the Task Force Commander who took over after General Pilkington was relieved: "Violations of policy and guidance occur minute by minute out there. Some are willful violations, but most are not" (Headquarters, 8th Air Force, 1995: T-40.1, 91). For example, according to the Staff Weapons Director:

> Helicopters played by a different set of rules. . . . It's haphazard you know, and from my experience I know that sometimes they talk to you, sometimes they don't. If they do talk to you, sometimes they tell you where they're going and what they're doing, and sometimes they don't. (Headquarters, 8th Air Force, 1995: T-40.10, 2263, 2264)

To the controller in the AWACS, this might look like a willful violation of Task Force rules. To the helicopter pilot who is flying "contour" to avoid being shot down, this is no rules violation, but rather a very practical action indeed.

Such mismatches between the local demands of the situation and those of global design rules occurred with increasing regularity as operators gained personal experience in the field. As a result, the pervasive demands of day-

---

[21] My theory of practical drift suggests a general sequence of events that occurred in OPC over approximately three years. However, most of my data is cross-sectional in nature—drawn primarily from the immediate events leading up to the accident. Fortunately, on 20 June 1994, the USCINCEUR requested the Aircraft Accident Investigation Board (AAIB) to contact individuals who had served in OPC during tours *prior to* the accident. As a result, investigators located and interviewed sixteen additional individuals who commented on relevant practices within OPC during the three years prior to the shootdown. Based on archival records and these interviews (contained in a special Supplement to the AAIB report dated 23 June 1994), I was able to get a decent sense of how procedures and practice evolved between the time the task force stood up in 1991 and the time of the accident in 1994.

[22] In a telling example of just how accepted a practice "rule bending" was in OPC, the following comment by Captain Mike Nye—Eagle Flight Commander following the accident—illustrates how Commanders would adjust their orders accordingly, anticipating the fact that they would not be followed. "But General Pilkington's point of view, relayed through Colonel Pingel, was if we keep them [fighters] at a thousand feet, they'll probably stay above five hundred" (Andrus, 1994: TAB V-104, 11). This comment referred to an effort being made by the Task Force to de-conflict fighters and helicopters following a near miss outside Zakhu. Notice General Pilkington's assumption: He assumed that fighters would break the rule if the hard deck was set at a thousand feet. Instead of addressing a fundamental discipline problem in the fighter community, a problem that was later confirmed by the General Accounting Office's subsequent review of the accident investigation (U.S. General Accounting Office, 1997: 32–33), the Task Force Commander chose to alter the rule instead, to accommodate expected rule-breaking.

to-day practice inevitably *shifted* the logic of action from one based primarily on formal rules, to one driven more tightly by the task—the ever-present demands of minute-to-minute practice. Over time, the seductive persistence of pragmatic practice loosens the grip of even the most rational and well-designed formal procedures. I call this phenomenon "practical drift"—the slow, steady uncoupling of local practice from written procedure—the muscle behind the movement from quadrant 2 to quadrant 3. After extended periods of time, locally *practical* actions within subgroups gradually *drift* away from originally established procedures—those conservatively written rules designed to handle the worst-case condition when subunits are tightly coupled.

Valid justifications abound for deviating from globally established routine in the names of practicality and common sense. In the following exchange, Colonel O'Brien, the CFAC C3 (Director of Operations, Plans, and Policy) tries to explain to investigators why he didn't aggressively integrate helicopters into OPC flight operations as originally conceived design rules required:

Q: Are you aware of a provision in OPLAN 91-7 that states that the CTF C3 through the CFAC Frag Shop will be the focal point for coordinating Army rotary-wing flying with available fighter assets?

A: No. Well, I'm aware that a lot of things are written down. . . . There are a lot of things that a C3 would normally do that are not done here. . . . I'm only here for four months. There has been a case in the past where the C3s here became too involved in operations according to the CFAC DO [Director of Operations] people. When I first came here and I talked to them, they asked me not to be involved in operations. They said, "You are a staff position." . . . I wanted to write down before I left a delineation of responsibilities between the C3 and the CFAC DO—here is what you do and here is what I do, because *things had evolved so much over the three years. [OPLAN] 91-7 has changed so much, in fact, that thing—if you look at it, it's so very old it doesn't really apply in most respects*; it has to be changed. Nothing was written down that really gave me a true picture of what was happening here about what was coordinated. (emphasis added) (Andrus, 1994: TAB V-097, 16–17)

Practical drift is the slow steady uncoupling of practice from written procedure. Colonel O'Brien saw it creep into OPLAN 91-7. "Things had evolved so much over the three years" that, according to the C3, OPLAN 91-7—the authoritative coordination document in force at the time of the shootdown—didn't "really apply in most respects." Nothing written down gave the Director of Operations and Plans "a true picture of what was happening" and "what was coordinated."

Constant demands for local efficiency dictate the path of the drift. Over time, incremental actions in accordance with the drift meet no resistance, are implicitly reinforced, and hence become institutionally accepted within each subunit. In the following passage, Colonel O'Brien explains how such demands for efficiency combine with the informal socialization of rotating staff to lock-in the trajectory of practical drift:

> We work seven days a week. I'm constantly reshuffling priorities to get the hot one of the day done and to not drop any. And I also have to say that when I arrived and I looked at the great deal of taskings that we had and things to accomplish, *I had to go with what my predecessor in-briefed me with*, what were my responsibilities and my tasks, and that of my—the people that worked in C3. *I had to go with a chief of plans who had been here for four months*, who had gone through a plans review with EUCOM [European Command] before that, during his time.
>
> Yes, a lot of these things were my responsibility, but I was looking at the—the emerging requirements we had throughout my time here, and those that were, what I thought—were *the ones that could get people hurt*. . . . So, the questions like, do I read the JOC (Joint Operations Center) book every day? No, I don't. Should I? In a normal world, yes, I probably should. But the *activity has been so intense and so constant* and again, seven days a week, we're always open in the JOC and I'm in there seven days a week. (Andrus, 1994: TAB V-097A, 21)

Like most of the staff supporting OPC, Colonel O'Brien was deployed to Turkey for only four months. Yes, he had access to a stack of written documents such as OPLAN 91-7. Yes, he could have demanded that his staff follow these old procedures to a T. However, as a practical matter, whom would you listen to: the ghost of some long-forgotten planners in the form of an outdated OPLAN, or your immediate predecessor and current chief of plans? Through such informal socialization procedures, incremental movements away from the originally established base line (see Figure 6.2) get locked in and passed along to succeeding cohorts. As long as the system remains loosely coupled, drift continues to creep along largely unnoticed and unchecked.[23]

Weick anticipates several of these points:

> A loosely coupled system may be a good system for localized adaptation. If all of the elements in a large system are loosely coupled to one another, then any one element can adjust to and modify a *local* unique contingency without affecting the whole system. These *local adaptations* can be swift, relatively economical, and substantial. By definition, the antithesis of localized adaptation is standardization and to the extent that standardization can be shown to be desirable, a loosely coupled system might exhibit fewer of these presumed benefits. (1976: 6–7)

---

[23] Notice how I have taken the original core category of "practical action"—along with each of its central characteristics—and transformed it into "practical drift"—a dynamic version of its former self. Adding process and context to the original core concept, I make the most of the cumulative efforts of grounded theory by extending originally static and isolated categories into burgeoning theory.

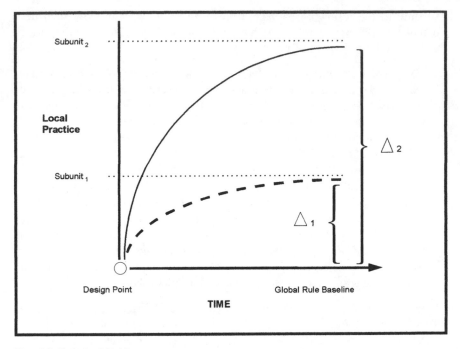

Fig. 6.2. Practical Drift

The organizational challenge arises precisely because, as each uneventful day passes in a loosely coupled world, it becomes increasingly difficult to demonstrate the integrative benefits of global standardization over the practical benefits of local adaptation. Hence, the behavioral balance tips in the direction of local adaptation at the expense of global synchronization.

"Local adaptations can be swift, relatively economical [efficient], and substantial" (Weick, 1976: 6–7). Over time, such drift can result in a dramatic delta or practical gap between global written rules and local practical action. Figure 6.2 graphically illustrates this process as it played out over the first three years of Operation Provide Comfort.

The general phenomenon of *drift* and ensuing chasm between what is formally written and actually done is a common theme in organizational literature: Weick warns that "the current state of any system is the result of continuous change away from some original state, but these changes need not be in the direction of increasing orderliness" (1979: 120). Founding organizational goals can drift dramatically (Selznick, 1949). Theories in practice can differ substantially from those espoused (Argyris and Schon, 1974). Formal and informal structures, driven by the often competing logics of efficiency and sentiments, frequently result in the pursuit of contrary goals (Roethlisberger and Dickson, 1939: 562–64). Individual behaviors mirror the dramaturgical divide between front-stage and backstage performances (Goffman, 1973). Formal structures may be little more than myths when compared to actual practice in institutionalized organizations (Meyer and Rowan, 1977). And finally, local adaptation to specific work requirements in pursuit of expertise obtained through a subjective process of boundary exploration often results in post-hoc attributions of human error (Rasmussen, 1993a).

Quadrant 3: Applied

The net effect of this practical drift is a general loosening of globally defined rationality. Gone is the tightly logical and synchronized rationale that governed system design and rule production at birth. In its place are multiple incrementally emergent sets of procedures, each born out of unique subunit logics grounded in the separate day-to-day pragmatics of loosely coupled worlds (see Δ_1 and Δ_2 in Figure 6.2). Gone is the single rationally designed "engineered world" governed by intricate sets of global rules. In its place is an "applied" world where locally pragmatic responses to the intimate demands of the task dictate action. Such applied solutions to real-world demands steadily drive out what appear to local practitioners as ill-conceived design deficiencies. Over time, the globally engineered, standardized organization is replaced by a series of locally adaptive subunit logics, each justifying their own version of "the rules."

Drift itself is common in organizations. For example, designers originally thought it important to brief all incoming aircrews on the color scheme of enemy aircraft. In the following exchange between an investigator and General Pilkington, this seemingly reasonable requirement appears to have "slipped out" or "drifted" away over the years:

> Q: The Iraqi Hind helicopters are painted in a light tan/brown color scheme. Would the C2 [intelligence officer] be expected to provide that sort of information to the CFAC so the CFAC could, in turn, pass that information to the aircrews?
>
> A: I say yes, but—but I'd have to jump back three years to say that—that that was—would have, in my estimation, would have been something that was important to highlight in April, May, June of 1991. The operation having progressed for over eleven hundred days prior to this incident, where Black Hawks routinely flew almost every day, six days a week, and very often two to three to four days a week in the TAOR, the necessity for highlighting that information may have *slipped out many C2s ago*. (emphasis added) (Headquarters, 8th Air Force, 1995: T-40.1, 060.14)

This apparently trivial task "slipped out" over the years. Unfortunately, it turned out to be not so trivial after all. Gone is the tightly synchronized and logical rationale that governed system design at birth. In its place, internally

consistent sets of subunit behaviors crystallize, become locked-in, and reinforce themselves across levels of analysis. This makes practical drift exceed-
ingly difficult to prevent or eliminate.

But our OPC Task Force is more than simply another doomed frog in a
pot of steadily heating water. While a frog won't notice the increasing water
temperature until it's too late, in our case, it's not the boiling water per se
(the practical drift) that defeats the frog (causes the coordination failure). But
rather, it is the fact that individuals in different subgroups act based on the
assumption that people outside their own unit are behaving in accordance
with the original set of established rules.[24] After all, this is the only—and
arguably the best—assumption that can be made. When we meet a stranger
on the street, we act toward him based on the assumption that he will conform to culturally accepted norms. We naturally, and rightfully, assume that
when we interact, others will conform to standard *rules of engagement*. And,
we do all this knowing full well that *we* ourselves rarely act in accordance
with such formal norms in the absence of others. Problems occur when either party miscodes the situation or fails to act in accordance with shared
rules—either because they are unaware of the others' presence or personally
ignorant of the applicable behavioral rule, such as the case with a foreigner
or a child. This phenomenon applies equally well to individual-group, group-
group, or even group-organization interactions.

Such miscoding problems arise because individual actors cannot simultaneously be members of all groups. By definition, then, they are not privy to
others' subtle drift away from standardized procedures—let alone in what
direction, how fast, or how far that drift may have carried them from our
rule-supported, synchronized design point.[25] Once again, Weick anticipates
my argument:

---

[24] During lengthy questioning about various OPC players not following the rules, an exaspe-
rated Staff Weapons Director revealed his frustration when such expectations are not met:
"They're supposed to play by the same set of rules, why do I need to tell them how to fly their
airplane?" (Headquarters, 8th Air Force, 1995, T-40.10: 2263)

[25] In the following passage, the F-15 wingman provides one explanation as to how such
disconnects may have developed in OPC:

> One of the first things that happens when you walk into a base, whether you're going there
> for a training exercise or whatever it is, you sit down and you have a briefing and it's the
> guys that no kidding are there full time that come in and provide a briefing to you, and they
> say, "This is the way we do things. This is how you can get yourself in trouble. These are the
> square corners that you need to watch out for." In this particular circumstance down here [in
> OPC], instead of having a centralized clearing house that ensures that everybody has the
> same ungarbled word, what we basically have is a "county option," where each squadron has
> their own new guy briefing that they give, each squadron has their own plan on how they spin
> people up to speed and tell them what to expect out there. And I think over the time, what has
> happened is I think it has tended to get watered down. (Andrus, 1994: TAB V-028, 43)

It remains to be seen under what conditions loosely coupled systems are fragile structures because they are shored up by consensual anticipations, retrospections, and understanding that can dissolve and under what conditions they are resilient structures because they contain mutations, localized adaptation, and fewer costs of coordination. (1976: 14)

Loosely coupled systems are both resilient and fragile. They are resilient for the reasons Weick cites, but only as long as the system remains loosely coupled. Likewise, they are also fragile for the reasons he cites, precisely because such systems rarely remain loosely coupled forever—hence, the value of exploring an empirical example where the dynamic *pattern* of coupling enters play.

Quadrant 4: Failed

Then, in one of those rare stochastic fits,[26] the system becomes tightly coupled (driving us from quadrant 3 south into quadrant 4 in the matrix), and we are forced to act based on our assumptions about the behavior of others—interdependence. The best assumption—indeed the only assumption that we can make—is that others will be acting in accordance with originally agreed-upon standard procedures. Remarkably, we *do* act based on this assumption even knowing full well that *we* rarely act in accordance with such established guidelines ourselves. But, what else *can* we do? What else could the F-15 pilots assume on that fateful morning, except that the members of the helicopter unit, the crew in the AWACS, and the entire OPC organization were following the rules?

During situations of tight coupling, it is this disconnect, this delta, this gap between the locally emergent procedures actually being followed in various subgroups from those that engaged actors assume are dictating action, that constitutes a general set of conditions that increases the likelihood of disastrous coordination failures. Imperceptible drift creeps into the system and carries practical action far afield from originally established and agreed-upon procedures. Each subgroup follows its own unique path angling ever further from the baseline. Each uneventful day that passes in a loosely coupled world reinforces a steadily growing false sense of confidence that everything is all right—that I, we, my group must be OK because the way we did

---

[26] Note that the mechanism that moves us from quadrant 3 to 4 is the random error term found everywhere in nature. Hence, I do not completely discount the validity of such comments as, "Hey, it was their day. I mean what were the odds that the two F-15s would pick them [UH-60s] up just as they had disappeared behind a mountain?" The odds were low indeed; but that doesn't mean it couldn't happen. It did. Therefore, while I don't dwell on it, I do include a stochastic element in my theory to recognize the inherent unpredictability of hyper-complex organizational phenomena.

things today resulted in no adverse consequences. Therefore, two F-15s shot down two friendly helicopters as a crew of AWACS controllers looked on. Therefore, after months of political pressure and numerous investigations, there are no obvious scapegoats. A perverse combination of practical drift and tight coupling set the conditions for randomly triggered disaster.

Before retiring our theoretical matrix to the prop room, return to Figure 6.1 for a moment. I want to emphasize an additional insight revealed by the matrix. Notice that quadrants 1 and 3 describe states of quasi-equilibrium. Because there is "a match" between the situation and the dominant logic of action, there is no pressure to move out of either of these two positions. As long as the basic planning assumptions don't change, the "designed" quadrant represents a relatively stable state of affairs. In fact, until they actually are placed into service, many OPLANs sit on the shelf "as written" for indefinite periods of time. A similar match between a task-oriented logic of action and a loosely coupled situation creates stability in quadrant 3. For almost three years, Task Force Provide Comfort operated successfully in an "applied" mode, one dominated by loosely coupled subunits' intimate relationship with their task—the core concept of practical action.

In contrast to the states of quasi-equilibrium found in quadrants 1 and 3, conditions depicted in quadrants 2 and 4 are inherently unstable. Any mismatch between the predominant logic of action and the nature of situational coupling produces instability in the system and pressure for change. The "engineered" state of quadrant 2 is characterized by a mismatch where rule-based logics of action struggle to survive in a loosely coupled world. This combination can't last long. Over time, practical drift gradually transforms the system into a more stable state of affairs, where strong local task-orientations overtake overly burdensome global rules. The most dramatic mismatch occurs in quadrant 4. Numerous subunits, each following their own locally validated task-based logics of action, clash in a stochastically induced fit of tight coupling. Previously obscured coordination gaps, created by practical drifts of various trajectories, are brought into sharp relief under the powerful light of tight coupling. When drifting subunits are wrenched back together and physical interdependence climbs, the mismatch between locally determined task-oriented logics and globally synchronized rule-based action is magnified by the integrative demands of tight coupling.

At a general systems-level, these alternating periods of stability and instability provide the evolutionary energy that fuels change. By definition, disasters are inherently unstable situations. Therefore, we rush in to save our organizations by swiftly snatching them out of the perverse grip that defines quadrant 4. Unfortunately, in our haste to escape immediate danger, in our zeal to make sure that such disconnects never happen again, we often overlook the systemic nature of the tragedy.

Quadrant 1': Redesign

Finally, the dotted arrow leaving quadrant 4 feeds *back* into what was originally quadrant 1—now 1'; after one cycle it has changed—suggesting a cyclical explanation. Due to the inherent lag between "fixes" implemented during "*re-design*" in quadrant 1' and the ultimate impact of their consequences when played out through the system, we tend to over-correct for task-based orientations by overtightening rules (Senge et al. 1994: 119). You can imagine what a disaster of this magnitude (quad 4) had on the "design criteria" (quad 1') the next time around. Within hours, OPC's higher headquarters in Europe dispatched a sweeping set of rules in documents several inches thick to "absolutely guarantee" that whatever caused this tragedy would never happen again.

This is a common pattern noted by systems experts. Labeled "delays"—situations "when the effect of one variable on another takes time"—such lags between action and system response can lead to serious problems. They often result in "overshoot, going further than needed to achieve a desired result" which can "lead to instability and breakdown, especially when they [delays] are long" (Senge, 1990: 89). In our shootdown case, we see long delays between "designed" and "failed" phases of the organization. It took almost three years for the cycle to play out. Not surprisingly, we also see "overshoot" in the guise of a typically bureaucratic overkill response to the incident.

Left unchecked, such organizational knee jerks provide the system with the necessary energy to kick off subsequent cycles of disaster. Extending this logic into the future, the circle at the heart of our theoretical matrix then takes on the image of a downward spiral—a self-fueling spiral. Tighter design criteria increase the likelihood that such rules will be perceived as overly controlling, wholly inappropriate in a primarily loosely coupled world, and clearly unsustainable in the long run. Over time, as new units rotate into the Task Force and the memories of the twenty-six dead fade, so do the lessons learned. The tighter the rules, the greater the potential for sizable practical drift to occur as the inevitable influence of local tasks takes hold. All of this sets the scene for lady luck's next stochastic fit to tighten the coupling of our system and increase the likelihood of another failure as the cycle begins anew.[27]

[27] Based on an extensive historical review of *Military Misfortunes*, Cohen and Gooch concluded that "true military misfortunes are failures of the organization, not of the individual" (1990: 3). In their study, they identified three broad types of failure: (1) a failure to *learn* from the past, (2) a failure to *anticipate* the future, and (3) a failure to *adapt* to the present. Catastrophic failures happen when all three failures occur either simultaneously or consecutively. My theory of practical drift, as depicted in Figure 6.1, complements Cohen and Gooch's findings. Designers failed to anticipate the practical impact of their plans (quad 1); operators failed to effectively adapt global plans to the realities of local day-to-day practice (quads 2, 3); and leaders failed to learn from the incident (quads 4, 1').

7

Conclusions:
There But by the Grace of God . . .

RECALL Secretary Perry's comments to the families of those who died in the shootdown: "This accident should not have happened, but these brave individuals will not have died in vain *if we learn from and correct our mistakes*" (emphasis added) (Office of the Assistant Secretary of Defense for Public Affairs, 1994: 1). A flurry of activity followed the shootdown. We corrected many mistakes; however, what have we learned?

Sifting through mountains of data, no smoking gun emerged. And, I admit this in spite of the fact that the hubris-driven investigative reporter in me never gave up hope. Throughout this study, a part of me always yearned to uncover *the* missing piece of the puzzle. Somewhere, just around the corner, in the next interview perhaps, I hoped to uncover a startling revelation that would blow this case wide open. It simply didn't happen.

Instead, two years of inquiry largely confirmed my original suspicions; my basic assumptions remain intact. There weren't any bad guys; hence, no one to blame. There weren't any catastrophic failures of material or equipment; hence, nothing to fix. No gross negligence or act of God caused this tragedy. The more I looked for traditional culprits, the more I realized that this accident occurred not because something extraordinary had happened, but rather just the opposite. This accident happened because of, or perhaps in spite of, everyone behaving just the way we would expect them to behave, just the way theory would predict—given a clear understanding of the circumstances. Indeed, this accident was "normal," not only in the sense that Perrow suggests—"that it [was] an inherent property of the system" (1984: 8). But rather it was normal because it occurred as the result of normal people behaving in normal ways in normal organizations.

Everywhere I looked, whether it was at the *individual* pilots who misidentified the Black Hawks, or the *group* of AWACS controllers who sat idly by and watched the engagement, or the *organization* that failed to integrate Eagle Flight, I found nothing "out of the ordinary"; that is, I found nothing that I couldn't explain, given what we already know about individual and group behavior in complex organizations. With such an extraordinary outcome to explain, I could find nothing extraordinary occurring at any level of analysis.

This journey played with my emotions. When I first examined the data, I went in puzzled, angry, and disappointed—puzzled at how two highly trained Air Force pilots could make such a deadly mistake; angry at how an entire crew of AWACS controllers could sit by and watch a tragedy develop without taking action; and disappointed at how dysfunctional Task Force OPC must have been to have not better integrated helicopters into its air operations. Each time I went in hot and suspicious. Each time I came out sympathetic and unnerved. Sympathetic because, given what we know about behavior in complex organizations and the specific conditions within the task force at the time, odds are I would have made the same mistake as the F-15 pilots; I no doubt would have sat on my hands as a member of that AWACS crew; and I probably wouldn't have noticed the non-integration had I been a member of the task force staff or leadership. Unnerved because such personal revelations eliminate all of the easy attributions; unnerved because, there but by the grace of God . . .

If no one did anything wrong; if there were no unexplainable surprises at any level of analysis; if nothing was abnormal from a behavioral and organizational perspective; then what *have* we learned?

Perhaps the fundamental lesson is that as basic scientists, we do know quite a bit about individual, group, and organizational behavior. However, as applied theorists, we know much less about how complex untoward events cut across levels of analysis and time; and as practitioners, we seem largely incapable of either identifying or recognizing general sets of conditions that increase the likelihood of failures at all levels. Contemporary behavioral science theories proved surprisingly adequate when it came to explaining each individual, group, and organizational failure identified by Perry's three bullets. Chapters 3, 4, and 5 remove much of the mystery behind the shootdown. However, it's one thing to explain why two or three individual components failed and quite another to explain the whole event—the entire shootdown. When it comes down to answering the fundamental question, "How in the world could this happen?" both traditional theory and method fall well short.

In spite of this shortcoming, at each level of analysis there are some powerful messages—reminders if you will—for both theorists and practitioners.[1] After briefly reviewing these, I'll address some of the more puzzling implications of this study. How should we think about causation when it comes to explaining such complex events? How should the leaders of high-risk organizations respond to such tragic failures? What are the limitations and implications of this study for future research?

---

[1] See Appendix 2 for a list of case-related questions designed to elicit the transfer of shootdown-peculiar lessons to other organizations.

On Theoretical Reminders: Normal Behavior, Abnormal Outcome

While explaining why the F-15 pilots misidentified the Black Hawks, and the AWACS crew didn't intervene, and the organization failed to integrate doesn't fully *explain* the shootdown, within each of these intra-level accounts, there is wisdom to be gleaned. There are lessons here for both research and practice. Since we could largely account for each of these critical antecedent behaviors using generally accepted behavioral science theories, then individual, group, and organizational behavior was "normal" in the sense that it fell within the bounds of established theory. If normal people were behaving normally in normal organizations, then why the initial shock and outrage at misidentification, non-intervention, and non-integration? If nothing abnormal was happening, then why wasn't someone able to see this mishap coming? If each of these behaviors could be adequately explained using generally available and accepted theory, then why couldn't someone predict the outcome *before* it happened?

Part of the answer lies in our inherent limitations as information processors. Part of the answer lies in our linear deterministic approach to causality. And, part of the answer lies in the inherent unpredictability of events in complex organizations. Only in retrospect did these three somewhat arbitrarily defined events grab our attention; only in retrospect was it possible for us to see how they contributed to the shootdown; only in retrospect was I able to dig into our theoretical tool kit and account for each of these events—and then, only one by one.

When it comes to predicting such infrequent outcomes *before* they occur, the enormous complexity of the situation quickly outstrips our cognitive capabilities as bounded information processors. We are severely limited when it comes to our ability to recognize and pay attention to the infinite number of potential accidents waiting to happen (Simon, 1955). However, we can pay attention to some of the more obvious lessons that seem to pop up over and over again. The following three sections summarize some of these lessons within the context of the shootdown. Few if any of them are "new news"; however, I raise them again here as recycled gifts from theory to practice, as practical reminders of lessons learned over and over again—all too often the hard way.

Individual Lessons

Reviewing the story of our two F-15 pilots, I find two basic lessons. First, the fundamental attribution error is alive and well. And second, sensemaking offers significant conceptual leverage when it comes to prying open the behavioral mysteries of seemingly perverse action.

Fundamental attributions. The fundamental attribution error lives. In spite of repeated warnings to the presence of this human frailty, when it comes to accidents such as this shootdown, our desire to blame the "man in the loop" remains overwhelming. Immediately following the engagement, the DUKE— airborne command element onboard the AWACS—remarked that "he hoped we had not shot down our own helicopters and that *he couldn't believe anybody could make that dumb of a mistake*" (emphasis added) (Andrus, 1994: TAB V-008, 2). No matter how often we are reminded of our natural inclination to blame the individual (read: "others"), no matter how often these attributions turn out to be false, the simple fact remains: our first impulse is to point the finger at the nearest person when something goes wrong. When it comes to explaining the cause of accidents, pilot or operator error remains the single most common attribution—by far.

Since we are all well aware of this human tendency, why dwell on it? Why raise it again here as a "lesson learned," when we've heard it all before? First, simply because we've heard it all before and yet continue to hear it again and again is reason enough to dig a little deeper. Our tendency to blame individuals for perverse outcomes of complex incidents continues to be perhaps the most consistent finding across all accident investigations I have reviewed. People do make mistakes. After all, to err is human and if there is a "man in the loop," and if we can't seem to find any other obvious scapegoats, then. . . . Second, the most proximate cause of many of these accidents, the final link in a long chain of events, often does turn out to be an individual action: an operator turns off a safety valve in a nuclear power plant (Perrow, 1984); the skipper of the *Vincennes* believes that an Iranian airliner is an enemy F-14 fighter (Hill, 1989); an Apache helicopter pilot fires a Hellfire missile at a friendly Bradley Fighting Vehicle in southern Iraq (U.S. Congress, Office of Technology Assessment, 1993); and two F-15 pilots shoot down two Black Hawks in Operation Provide Comfort. Even TIGER 02 reminds us: "Human error did occur. We misidentified the helicopters; we engaged them; and we destroyed them. It was a tragic and fatal mistake . . ." However, he also goes on to offer the following insight:

> History has shown it normally isn't an isolated event which causes an accident like what happened on 14 April. Instead, in most cases, as appears to be the case here, there's *a chain of events or circumstances* which come together and lead to a tragic outcome. Remove any one link in the chain and the outcome could be entirely different. I wish to God I could go back and correct my link in this chain—my actions which contributed to this disaster. (emphasis added) (Andrus, 1994: TAB V-028, 12)

While admitting to making the ultimate "tragic and fatal mistake," TIGER 02 also draws our attention to an insight revealed by most accident investigations:[2] "There is a chain of events or circumstances which come together and lead to a tragic outcome." How best to untangle these webs of causality is indeed a sticky problem—one that I address at the end of this section. However, a necessary if not sufficient condition for even recognizing this analytical challenge is to first push beyond our natural tendency to blame the individual.

Sensemaking as analytical antidote. One way to help escape the fundamental attribution trap is to avoid framing causal questions as decisions. Graham Allison's classic analysis of the Cuban Missile Crisis is titled *Essence of Decision* (1971). Diane Vaughan's examination of the Space Shuttle *Challenger* disaster is titled *The Challenger Launch Decision* (1996). Framing such tragedies as "decisions" immediately focuses our attention on an individual making choices. Any analysis that emphasizes the ultimate human proximate cause—President Kennedy's *decision* (initially) to support the Bay of Pigs invasion or NASA managers' *decision* to launch the *Challenger*—only reinforces our natural inclination to blame the individual. Blindly accepting the assumption that individual decisions are the key to understanding such events, we logically preclude other, perhaps more fruitful possibilities. While both of these examples are exemplary in their treatment of complex untoward events, reframing the basic puzzle as one of "making sense" rather than as a "decision" radically shifts the focus of inquiry. Drucker explains:

> The Westerner and the Japanese man mean something different when they talk of "making a decision." In the West, all the emphasis is on the *answer* to the question. Indeed, our books on decision making try to develop systematic approaches to giving an answer. To the Japanese, however, the important element in decision making is *defining the question*. The important and crucial steps are to decide whether there is a need for a decision and what the decision is about. And it is in that step that the Japanese aim at attaining consensus. Indeed, it is this step that, to the Japanese, is the essence of decision. The answer to the question (what the West considers the decision) follows from its definition. (Drucker, 1974: 466–67)

I could have framed the individual-level analysis as a problem of decision making. I could have asked, "Why did they *decide* to shoot?" However, such a framing puts us squarely on a path that leads straight back to the individual decision maker, away from potentially powerful contextual features and right back into the jaws of the fundamental attribution error. "Why did they decide

---

[2] The authors of a 1993 review of friendly fire by the Office of Technology Assessment conclude that "friendly fire is often thought of as due primarily, or exclusively, to misidentification. Investigation of particular cases usually reveals that the fratricide was in fact the last link in a chain of mistakes" (U.S. Congress, Office of Technology Assessment, 1993: 3).

to shoot?" quickly becomes "Why did they make the *wrong* decision?" Hence, the attribution falls squarely onto the shoulders of the decision maker and away from potent situational factors that influence action.

Framing the individual-level puzzle as a question of meaning rather than deciding shifts the emphasis away from individual decision makers toward a point somewhere "out there" where context and individual action overlap. Individual responsibility is not ignored. However, by viewing the fateful actions of TIGERS 01 and 02 as the behaviors of actors struggling to make sense, rather than as rational attempts to decide, we level the analytical playing field toward a more complete and balanced accounting of all relevant factors, not just individual judgment.

The DUKE "couldn't believe that anybody could make that *dumb a mistake*." Such a reframing—from decision making to sensemaking—opened *my* eyes to the possibility that, given the circumstances, even *I* could have made the same "dumb mistake." This disturbing revelation, one that I was in no way looking for, underscores the importance of initially framing such senseless tragedies as "good people struggling to make sense," rather than as "bad ones making poor decisions." The fundamental attribution error is alive and well. Adopting Weick's sensemaking as a "set of explanatory possibilities" (1995: xi) offers a powerful antidote to solving such mysteries at the individual level of analysis.

Group Lessons

When it comes to understanding the puzzle behind AWACS crew inaction, once again the central lesson is a familiar one. Just as the fundamental attribution error is a well-understood phenomenon operating at the individual level of analysis, group formation and member stability are widely understood to be central considerations for high-performance teams. For a variety of reasons, our aircrew fell victim to several breaches of the most basic rules for successful group design and launch. After reviewing these, I'll briefly examine the notion of "social redundancy"—a related issue particularly relevant to the design of teams in high-hazard organizations.

Weak launch. In compelling testimony before a House National Security Subcommittee, Kaye Mounsey, widow of Army Warrant Officer Erik Mounsey (Black Hawk pilot), pleaded with Committee members to, among other things, "explain to her and other family members how in the world the crew of the AWACS *failed to put two and two together.*"[3] At the time of the shootdown, the nineteen-member crew of the AWACS had only two flights

[3] This comment was taken from witness testimony before Representative Robert Dornan's Military Personnel Subcommittee investigating the shootdown. The hearing was held on 3 August 1995.

of aircraft to track inside the TAOR: a two-ship flight of F-15s and a two-ship flight of Black Hawks. Mourning family members wanted to know why such a highly trained crew, supported by such a sophisticated system, failed to intervene in their loved ones' tragic deaths. After all, isn't that what the acronym stands for—Airborne *Warning and Control* System? Why didn't they warn? Why didn't they control?

In chapter 4 we traced this puzzling inaction on the part of the AWACS all the way back to its crew's formation in the states. A poor crew launch resulted in the deployment of an underdeveloped team. A weak team experienced confused authority relationships and diffuse responsibilities. Under a set of unusual circumstances, confused authority and diffuse responsibilities led to inaction. Inaction led to tragedy.

Once again, there is nothing new here; Air Force leadership was well aware of basic findings concerning high-performance teams. Research on groups has shown over and over again just how critical a good launch and crew-member stability is to team development and performance (Ginnett, 1987, 1990; Hackman, 1990; Bettenhausen and Murnighan, 1985; Gersick, 1988). Such findings were no secret to the military. The "Crew Resource Management" movement had made significant inroads into the Air Force during the Cold War (Prince and Salas, 1993). Concerned about improving the performance of its bomber crews carrying nuclear weapons, the Air Force was in fact a major player in the development and adoption of aircrew training and development programs.

Hence, military aircrew manning and training policies were heavily influenced by solid social psychological research, research that clearly demonstrated the benefits of successful aircrew formation and stability. Once again however, the lesson from this case is that it's not that we don't know any better; but rather it seems that hard-won lessons in theory are often overlooked in practice. For example, research by Hackman indicates that "constant changes in cockpit crew composition deprive members of the time and experience they need to build themselves into a good team" (1993: 54). The Air Force is well aware of this lesson. In fact, they adopted a personnel and training policy called "hard crewing" based on this very principle. In theory, the rule is simple: crews should be as "hard"—tight, cohesive, and stable—as possible. Every effort should be made to keep trained and experienced crews together. However, like many other theoretically informed lessons, in practice, this one often went unheeded.

During the following exchange, Major Saylor, the Assistant Deputy of Operations for Missions at the time of the accident, who also flew as an observer on the fateful AWACS flight, reveals how this lesson translated into action in OPC:

Q: Please explain the hard crew concept to the investigating officer.

A: It is very difficult to explain because we've gotten unclear guidance from higher headquarters on this. It is also different between flight crew and mission crew.

Q: Let us focus on mission crew.

A: My understanding of the hard crew is just have as many key people as you can on the crew fly as many times as possible. And the key positions being MCC, ASO, and SD. Try to schedule them to fly together as much as possible.

Q: When you said that you had received conflicting guidance, what did you mean by that?

A: I remember working with the Director of Operations in the squadron and he had received a couple of messages from Headquarters ACC [Air Combat Command] . . . and we were being levied a requirement to fly hard crews; but with the ops tempo and the manning we had, it was near impossible to make it happen. So it was one of those things that you go okay, we'll fly hard crews, but everybody knows that the percentages of flying with a real hard crew is very difficult.[4] (Headquarters, 8th Air Force, 1995: 144a.11)

The intent was clear: flying "hard crews" meant "have as many key people as you can on the crew fly as many times as possible." Unfortunately, while the guidance was clear, while it made sense in theory, flying hard crews was apparently hard to do in practice.

Once again, it's not that there was anything abnormal going on here in the sense of unexplainable behavior; all group behavior that initially appeared puzzling can be explained using familiar concepts and design tools. It's not that science hasn't offered any advice; aircrew formation and stability is important. It's not that the Air Force wasn't listening. Stated Air Combat Command and Wing policies were consistent with theory; each AWACS crew was required to complete two, full, three hour OPC simulator runs *together* prior to deploying. It's just that such apparently simple lessons are quite often very difficult to follow in practice.

In theory, it would have been nice to have had the entire crew together at Tinker Air Force Base in Oklahoma prior to deploying. In theory, it would have been nice to have had everyone train together for two complete simulator sessions before departing. In theory, it would have been nice to have had the sim-tape driving the stateside preparation exactly match the troop list and rules of engagement in force in OPC at the time. In theory, it would have been nice to have followed higher headquarters' guidance to fly "hard

---

[4] Notice Major Saylor's words: "So it [hard crews] was one of those things that you go 'okay we'll fly hard crews,' but everyone knows that the percentages of flying with a real hard crew is very difficult" (Headquarters, 8th Air Force, 1995: 144a.11). You have to wonder what other directives based on solid theory fall into this "So you go okay we'll do it, but everyone knows . . ." category.

crews." However, theory is not always easy to practice. In practice, of the three "key positions" identified above, the SD was the only leader "available" when it came time to launch our new crew in a stateside simulation. In practice, the second simulator session was canceled because it conflicted with a local Wing exercise. In practice, the sim-tape provided by Boeing was old and deemed too expensive to update. In practice, the original ASO was pulled at the last minute to attend a career school; the MCC was assigned to the crew after the scheduled sim-training; and DUKEs only linked up with AWACS crews after they arrived in Turkey. In theory, it would have been nice. In practice, however, . . .

The fallacy of social redundancy. Another theory, borrowed from technical systems designers, argues that the answer to fallible components (human beings) in high-hazard organizations is duplication and overlap—redundancy. The value of redundancy is based on the compelling logic of independent components. If the odds of one component failing are one in one hundred, then the odds of two *independent* components failing simultaneously are one in ten thousand.[5] Add a third pilot to the cockpit and the odds go up to one in a million. Unfortunately, actually meeting the required assumption of independence makes directly transferring the benefits of redundancy from theory to practice and from technical to social systems extremely difficult.

High-reliability theorists emphasize redundancy as one of the most prominent design features of unusually successful organizations (Roberts, 1990; LaPorte and Consolini, 1991). However, many of their illustrations cite only technical examples—voice backup to radar map locations, redundant computer and communications systems, backup power supplies, and multiple safety devices—not social ones (Sagan, 1993: 19–21, 39–40).

Ironically, even these technically redundant additions, designed specifically to reduce the likelihood of system failure, can in fact have just the opposite effect. Despite designers' best intentions, redundancy can unwittingly increase the chances of an accident by encouraging operators to push safety limits well beyond where they would have, had such redundancies not been installed.[6] Layered redundancy can also make system operation more difficult to understand and diagnose (Perrow, 1984). Multiple overlapping

---

[5] For example, all passenger airliners are required to have a copilot. This policy follows from the statistically compelling logic of redundancy. However, as crew resource management (CRM) scientists warn (and any experienced pilot will tell you), pilot and copilot are *not* independent components. Much CRM research is focused on untangling the safety implications of this powerful social relationship.

[6] According to aircraft designers, UH-60 Black Hawks are powered by twin turboshaft engines to reduce the likelihood of accidents caused by engine failure. Ask helicopter pilots in private about this "safety" feature and, off the record, some will tell you that the twin engines simply allow them to fly faster, to "push the envelope" twice as far as they would with only one engine. For a detailed analysis of how operators "navigate" within safety envelopes or "safety space," see Rasmussen (1990: 1190–95) and Reason (1997: 107–24).

components dramatically increase system complexity, automatically compensate for hidden weaknesses, effectively stymie attempts to locate root causes, and generally frustrate learning. Finally, the components of redundant systems are quite often much less independent than we think. While often no more than an irritating design challenge in purely technical systems, meeting the demand for independence in a social system is next to impossible.

The AWACS mission crew was designed based on the principle of redundancy. As demands for reliability increase, so does the frequency of design responses based on duplication and overlap; "duplication is a substitute for perfect parts" (Bendor, 1985). Well aware that humans are not perfect parts, as well as the potentially steep price to be paid for imperfection inside the AWACS, Weapons and Air Surveillance Section monitoring responsibilities overlapped significantly. Controllers and their supervisors monitored up to twelve different, but overlapping, radio frequencies. Supervisory responsibilities were also duplicated. The DUKE watched the MCC (and the SD and ASO), who watched the SD and ASO (and WDs and ASTs), who looked over the shoulders of the WDs and ASTs. The AWACS mission crew was a textbook case of how to design a reliable system from unreliable parts—by building in social redundancy.[7]

However, as substantial evidence presented in chapter 4 indicates, the textbook might be wrong. Instead of increased reliability, the net result of social redundancy in the AWACS mission crew was diffuse responsibility and confused authority. Everyone was responsible, hence no one was. Rather than encouraging double checking and stringing multiple safety nets to catch individual mistakes, overlap and duplication led instead to an abdication of individual responsibility both horizontally and vertically. Such diffusion of accountability for helicopter monitoring and intervention effectively paralyzed the crew. No one monitored the helicopters; no one questioned the engagement.

Realizing clear benefits from redundancy in social systems is an uphill struggle. As illustrated by our crew in the AWACS, the fundamental assumption of independence is routinely violated. The Air Surveillance Section was no more independent of the Weapons Section than the MCC was of the SD or ASO. The DUKE relied exclusively on information fed to him by the Mission Crew. Individual controller responsibilities overlapped; but with no explicit boundaries, no one knew exactly where one WD's territory ended and the next one started. Hence, activity along the boundaries went unchallenged. Helicopter activity was, by social definition, a fringe activity; as a result, it fell in the middle of no one's scope. Hence, it also fell through the cracks.

---

[7] This fundamental puzzle of how to build "reliable systems from unreliable parts" was framed by John von Neumann in Bendor (1985: 295).

We form teams in hopes (often naive) that the whole will somehow be greater than the sum of its parts. One of Alderfer's (1983) four attributes for a real group—for a collection of individuals to be considered a real social system—is that its members must be *interdependent* for some shared purpose. For our AWACS crew to climb out of Katzenbach and Smith's performance trough depicted in Figure 4.1, for them to become more than a "pseudo-team," they had to "hammer out a common working approach" (1993: 91). Given that our traditional notions of high-performance teams demand high levels of interdependence, how then can we expect them to simultaneously meet the fundamental requirement of redundancy—independent components?

They can't; hence, the fallacy of social redundancy.

Our AWACS crew got caught between two fundamentally opposing design criteria. On the one hand, Crew Resource Management literature and Air Force policies emphasize crew formation and member stability to support traditional notions of team building. On the other hand, high-reliability organizational theorists argue that "redundancy is absolutely essential if one is to produce safety and reliability inside complex and flawed organizations" (Sagan, 1993: 21). As it turns out, trying to meet both design goals at once may be worse than focusing on either one. Not only are the benefits of redundancy reduced by interdependence, but as illustrated by the poor performance of our AWACS crew, when you try to simultaneously meet both the goals of redundancy and team building within the same group, you can end up in social no man's land—a wasteland where group members are neither interdependent enough to be a "real team" nor independent enough to gain the reliability benefits of redundancy.

A weak launch and the fallacy of social redundancy combined to paralyze nineteen technically qualified individuals. You see, there was no "real crew" in the AWACS that day. Unfortunately, neither the helicopters, the fighters, nor even the individuals in the back of the AWACS realized what was missing. Everyone assumed the collection of technicians was a team; no one appreciated their absence until it was too late.

Organizational Lessons

"To organize is to assemble ongoing interdependent actions into sensible sequences that generate sensible outcomes" (Weick, 1979: 3). In Task Force Provide Comfort, on 14 April, at approximately 1030 hours local time, organizing failed. "Ongoing interdependent actions" were no longer "assembled into sensible sequences," thus generating an outcome that made no sense at all.

Once again, the fundamental lesson here is taken straight out of "Organizing 101": Whatever you divide, you have to put back together again; and its corollary: The more divided, the more effort required to rejoin. To these lessons, I add a third caution: Disorganizing forces work overtime; the work of organizers is never done.

Integration as an Ongoing Accomplishment. Key subgroups within Task Force Provide Comfort were deeply "divided"; hence, they required a great deal of effort to "rejoin." Significant differences in mission requirements demanded highly differentiated subunits. Years of autonomous Service operations created large gaps between Army and Air Force operations. Reinforced daily by intimate relationships with "the stuff of their work," AWACS controllers and F-15 and UH-60 pilots all developed fundamentally different orientations toward goals, time, and interpersonal relationships. A whole host of forces aligned to continuously increase levels of differentiation within the task force—to drive task force subunits further and further apart.

For coordinated action, highly differentiated units demand equally high levels of integration (Lawrence and Lorsch, 1967). The organization—the staff and leadership of Task Force Provide Comfort—struggled mightily to meet these demands. In their efforts to organize—to "assemble ongoing interdependent actions into sensible sequences"—they employed a wide range of coordinating mechanisms. Operations orders, daily, weekly, and monthly planning meetings, liaison officers, checklists, schedules, flow sheets, Operating Instructions, Read Files, Traffic Orders, Control Orders, Staff Directives, OIs, ARFs, ATOs, ACOs, SOPs, BSDs, ROEs, MAD DOGS, and DUKES all tried to hold together what the relentless forces of differentiation were driving apart. For over three years they succeeded; ultimately, they failed.

They failed partly because integration is an ongoing accomplishment and partly because rules, orders, directives, procedures, checklists, and instructions are largely static tools, ill-fitted to meet the ever-changing requirements of a dynamic system. The Army never got the word on Mode I IFF codes; the F-15 pilots weren't alerted to the helicopters' mission that day; the Black Hawks entered the No Fly Zone prior to it being swept; and fighters and helicopters were talking on different radio frequencies. In the end, largely rule-based organizational efforts to coordinate complex evolving actions of highly differentiated subgroups failed to keep pace with the ever-present and constantly changing face of differentiation. Rules written to coordinate today's interactions may not apply tomorrow.

In this case, organizational integration and system reliability are closely related. An organizational failure to integrate contributed to the shootdown. A series of critical coordination failures combined to decrease the reliability of the system and increase the likelihood of an accident. Similar to integration, reliability is an ongoing accomplishment. "People need to see that inertia is a complex state, that forcefield diagrams have multiple forces operating in opposed directions . . . once situations are made reliable, they will unravel if they are left unattended" (Weick, 1987: 119). Picture the various forces driving differentiation as multiple vectors pushing ever outward. To hold the organization together each of these forces must be countered with sufficient energy in the appropriate direction. What makes this task such a challenge is that both the strength and direction of these divisive forces are constantly changing, while the critical organizational outcomes—integration and reliability—remain constant.

A system where dynamic inputs create constant outcomes induces a potentially dangerous form of organizational blindness. For over three years, dynamic inputs (in this case, the ever-changing actions and interactions of task force subunits) created stable outcomes (reliability and integration). The rules written in the Spring of 1991 to *integrate* the various subunits of Task Force OPC effectively countered the forces of differentiation. Organizing was *reliable* for 1,109 days. However, such a lengthy period of constant outcomes—integration and reliability—effectively blinded task force leaders to the reality and implications of ever-changing inputs. Weick explains:

> Reliability is also invisible in the sense that reliable outcomes are constant, which means that there is nothing to pay attention to. Operators see nothing and seeing nothing, presume that nothing is happening. If nothing is happening and if they continue to act the way they have been, nothing will continue to happen. This diagnosis is deceptive and misleading because dynamic inputs create stable outcomes. (1985: 118)

Just because it isn't broken, doesn't necessarily mean that it isn't breaking. Prior to 14 April 1994, the organization wasn't broken. As a result, no one noticed that it was breaking. It was, however operating on borrowed time. The stable outcome of reliability blinded task force leadership from noticing the changing nature of its inputs, from recognizing the steadily increasing disconnect between originally designed coordinating mechanisms and evolving organizational reality within the task force.

Near Miss. Humans are notoriously bad monitors of systems that rarely fail. When it comes to monitoring reliable systems for mistakes, *we* are inherently unreliable. As Weick warns, "operators see nothing and see nothing" and hence, "presume that nothing is happening" (1985: 118)[8] Unfor-

[8] When asked by investigators what he thought was the "highest threat in the AOR," TIGER 02 didn't talk about Iraqi MIGs or enemy Surface-to-Air Missile (SAM) sites; instead, he replied:

A: The unexpected. Something that you don't expect. The fact that it's routine, day in, day out, everybody goes out there with a certain blood pressure level, a certain expectation. . . . That's, that's probably the biggest threat. And that kind of goes with complacency. It's still an unfriendly neighborhood out there and you have to have that in mind every time you go out there. If you don't have that in mind, then you're setting yourself up to be surprised.

Q: Do you think that there is a problem with complacency among the aircrews?

A: I think that the people that are down here doing this mission get very comfortable with

tunately for the members of Task Force OPC, there was plenty happening, plenty of action for them to see. Once again however, as practitioners basking in the day-to-day aura of a reliable system, they weren't very good at discerning what was important until after the fact, until it was too late. Once again, because the system wasn't broken, no one noticed that it was breaking. As is often the case with such tragedies (Vaughn, 1996: 1–32), the warning signs were there; however, at the time, no one recognized them for what they were. Only in hindsight do they grab our attention as important indicators of a breaking system.

During the accident investigation, CW2 Henson, a Black Hawk pilot for Eagle Flight, relayed the following story:

> I was doing a two-ship TAOR to Bashur with an Air Force team to look at the airfield and survey it for aircraft coming in. Prior to landing, I had a radio conversation with COUGAR to have some aircraft check us because we would be on the ground for a short period of time. COUGAR at the time had pretty much just blew us off and didn't pay no attention to us. During that time—we were on the airfield and the survey team was surveying the airfield—two F-111s flew over just at the time we were getting ready to crank. I hadn't started the engines at that time, but was getting strapped in. The F-111s flew over, did what looked like a "return to target," did a low pass, and continued on their way. I was not concerned because we already coordinated with COUGAR and just thought they were doing their job.
>
> A couple days later I was at Incirlik at the club. Another pilot with me was talking to one of the F-111 pilots that we had previously helped with a maintenance problem. He [fighter pilot] told him about two F-111s that made a pass over, popped their safety's and had returned to blow us off the face of the earth . . . they had popped their safety's and was [sic] getting ready to wax us. . . . At the last minute, the guy said those look like two Black Hawks.
>
> Nothing really happened after that. Captain Howden was the commander at the time and he was one of the pilots that was with us. As far as I know he knew about it and that was about as far as it went. (Andrus, 1994: TAB V-107)

At the club over a few drinks, an Air Force F-111 pilot tells some Army aviators, "You don't know how lucky you are. We were on the trigger when we realized it was you" (Andrus, 1994: TAB V-102, 1) and "that was about

---

the pace and what's going on . . . there's a cookie cutter type of approach that we use . . . I wouldn't use complacent, but comfortable with the pace and the tasking down here and I'm afraid that *it may lead to some assumptions that everybody knows everything they need to know about what's going on out there, when I'm not convinced they do.* (emphasis added) (Andrus, 1994: TAB V028, 56)

Notice his words, "the people that are down here [at OPC] . . . get very comfortable," which can lead to "assumptions that everyone knows everything they need to know about what's going on." TIGER 02's insights match Weick's warning about operators who "see nothing and see nothing" and hence, "assume that nothing is happening."

as far as it went." Near misses like this F-111 incident should sound organizational alarms. However, it seems that the emphasis in this case was on the "miss" and not on the "near," and nothing was done; nothing was learned.[9]

Had this particular incident with the F-111 been thoroughly examined in September of 1992 when it occurred, there is a chance that some of the disconnects discovered only after the shootdown in 1994 might have been uncovered.[10] Note the similarities between the F-111 near miss and the F-15 shootdown. In both cases, Air Force fighters could not talk directly to Army helicopters. In both cases, the fighters were unaware of the helicopters' mission/presence in the TAOR, even though both flights of aircraft had been in contact with AWACS controllers just prior to the engagements. In both cases, the AWACS failed to accurately relay the helicopters' status to the fighter pilots. In both cases, the fighter pilots followed their Rules of Engagement all the way through to a visual identification pass (VID)—the final check in the system. The only real difference between the F-111 near miss and the actual shootdown is that the F-111 pilots were able to correctly identify the helicopters as Black Hawks—and then only on their second pass, at the last minute.

Had this incident been recognized for what it was—a chance to learn, had it been passed up the chain of command, had this near miss been taken seriously by senior leaders, had it been studied with even a fraction of the organizational resources that went into the eventual shootdown investigation, perhaps someone might have noticed serious disconnects developing within the organizational system. And just maybe, having uncovered some of these coordination failures, something might have been done to correct them and possibly prevent the shootdown a year and a half later. Unfortunately, the incident was not reported; so we'll never know for sure what might have happened.

This story is disturbing for two reasons. First, and perhaps most telling of all, this near miss *was not* treated as a serious incident; it was not passed up the chain of command; it was not investigated; it was not recognized as either a warning sign or an opportunity to learn. Instead it was only by chance that the F-111 story ever came to light at all. Recognizing the near miss for what it was took a chance meeting between two members of isolated subgroups over a beer. Raising this incident to a level of visibility

---

[9] Aware of the Federal Aviation Administration's anonymous system that encourages all commercial pilots to report "near misses" so that everyone can learn from them, I asked several fighter pilots about the norm in the Air Force for reporting such incidents. While each response differed slightly, the following quotation best captures the spirit behind all of them: "Hey, you know sir [winked], no blood no harm; no harm no foul. . . . War is hell. We don't fly in the 'friendly skies of United.' "

[10] The fact that this near miss occurred as early as it did—only a year and a half into OPC—indicates that the organizational systems designed to prevent such a mishap had already deteriorated significantly by September of 1992.

where the organization could learn from it took an extraordinary event—the tragic loss of lives over a year later.

Second, even if the F-111 incident had been recognized as an important indicator of the organization's health and even if it had been raised to the highest levels and examined in some detail, I am still doubtful that the right lessons would have been learned, that appropriate action would have been taken. Given the organization's response to the eventual tragedy—treating it as a potential crime instead of as a safety mishap and then heaping stacks of new rules on top of the old ones—I am not confident that this near miss, even if it had come to light, would have generated the type of organizational learning required to identify and address the underlying fundamental conditions that increased the likelihood that such a breakdown occurred in the first place. Instead, I would predict that first, individual attributions would have been made (most likely directed toward AWACS controllers and Army aviators). And second, a list of even tighter rules would have been written—rules that directly "fix" those errant behaviors immediately antecedent to this particular incident. Deeper root causes such as interservice rivalries and the conditions that encourage practical drift would remain unexamined.[11]

Returning to Weick's forcefield analogy, if the various forces driving differentiation are seen as multiple vectors pushing ever outward and the integrative challenge for leaders of complex organizations is to identify and contain them, then the predicted organizational response to such a near miss would be to round up those few pesky vectors that momentarily escaped and drive them back under control with sufficient force to ensure that they never escape again, that this particular type of near miss never happens again.[12] Such an organizational reaction to the F-111 incident just might have pre-

---

[11] Within a year of returning to their home base at Spangdahlem, Germany, the same F-15 squadron that shot down our two Black Hawks experienced a second tragedy, the roots of which support my skepticism about organizations' willingness and ability to address underlying systemic causes. On 30 May 1995 a pilot was killed when his F-15 crashed during takeoff on a routine training mission. Within days, the cause was located. The aircraft's flight-control rods had been improperly installed, making the F-15 impossible to control. Perhaps influenced by the post-shootdown pressure to hold someone accountable, Air Force officials initiated particularly harsh criminal proceedings against the two mechanics who had made the mistake, charging each with one count of negligent homicide and four counts of dereliction of duty. During preparations for the court-martial, defense counsel uncovered evidence indicating that "the Air Force had known for ten years that flight-control rods on F-15s could be cross-connected, yet officials failed to warn mechanics in technical manuals or training courses" (Watkins, 1996: 11). By prosecuting the mechanics, the immediate proximal cause of the accident, the Air Force once again demonstrated our tendency to blame individuals and not look for deeper causal conditions. On 30 October 1996, the day his court-martial was scheduled to begin, one of the mechanics, Technical Sergeant Thomas Mueller, took his own life rather than stand trial, thus completing a string of tragedies that began in the skies over northern Iraq.

[12] I base this prediction on the *actual* organizational response to the shootdown in 1994, which was to identify the most immediate causes of the accident and "fix each of them" with a new layer of rules.

vented the tragedy that took place in April of 1994—because the two incidents are so similar in their immediate proximal causes. Unfortunately, even
though it might have prevented this particular tragedy, such an approach
entirely misses the organizational-level lesson of this case: Reliability and
integration are constant outcomes of dynamic systems. Fixing the specific set
of inputs that generated the F-111 incident might prevent a similar engagement from occurring in the short term; however, because the inputs in such a
system are forever changing, underlying fundamental design weaknesses
would continue to plague the organization unless they are addressed at a
much deeper level.

Intra-level Summary and Notions of Causality

We know quite a bit, yet we know so little. Application of individual, group,
and organizational theories to the three intra-level puzzles identified by Secretary Perry removed much of the mystery surrounding the shootdown. Solving these puzzles uncovered the following three lessons:

- Look beyond individual error by framing puzzling behavior in complex
  organizations as individuals struggling to make sense.
- Follow the basic design principles of high-performance teams and think
  twice about chasing the advantages of social redundancy.
- Treat organizational states of integration and reliability with chronic
  suspicion. Recognize them for what they are: constant outcomes of dynamic systems, ongoing accomplishments that require active preventa-
  tive maintenance.

There is little new here: Fight the urge to blame individuals for complex
incidents; apply in practice what we know in theory about the design of
high-performance teams; and be vigilant. As behavioral scientists, we are
pretty good at explaining limited behaviors at a given level of analysis.
However, when it comes to explaining complex events that cut across traditional domains and time, we don't fare nearly as well. And, when it comes to
predicting untoward incidents in complex organizations *before* they occur,
we fail miserably. Sadly, we're not alone.

Practitioners seem equally impotent when it comes to recognizing the onset of conditions that increase the likelihood of failure. Not only do they
appear largely incapable of sensing the conditions of impending doom *prior*
to such incidents, but typical organizational reaction to such tragedies *after*
they occur reveals a strong tendency to frame the problem in linear deterministic terms: What *caused* the accident?

Hopefully this study illustrates the limitations of adopting such cause-and-
effect approaches when trying to understand untoward events in complex

organizations. Return to the Causal Map (Figure 1.3). What *caused* the accident? An IFF failure? Yes. Pilot misidentification? Yes. AWACS inaction? Probably. Coordination failure? Probably. Interservice rivalry? Maybe. Shrinking defense budget and increased OPTEMPO? Maybe. The fall of the Soviet Union? Hmm. . . . How far back up the causal stream are we willing to swim? Jens Rasmussen, a longtime scholar of accidents and human error, explains the fundamental problem with this approach to causality:

> In causal explanations of an accidental occurrence, its origin will be backtracked upstream the course of events to find the "cause." No objective stop rule can be devised to terminate this search. It is always possible to go one more step backwards in the search and the decision to stop and to accept an event as "the (root) cause" depends on the discretion of the analyst. (Rasmussen, 1993b: 3)

What it depends on is *who* is conducting the search and *why*. Technicians stop when they find something broken that they can fix. Trainers stop when they find a weak skill that they can train. Lawyers stop when they find a responsible individual that they can prosecute. Political leaders stop when their constituents stop. Scientists stop when they learn something new.

Why limit ourselves to a causal model grounded primarily in the physical sciences? Rather than asking "What caused the shootdown?" why not ask instead, "What were the *general conditions* present in the task force prior to the accident *that increased the likelihood* that such a tragedy might occur?" Framing the issue in this manner allows for much more play in the system, play that we know is there.[13] Though the behavioral disciplines are primarily probabilistic sciences, when faced with the task of explaining complex events, we seem all too willing to reach for deterministic cause-and-effect models.

From the start, my intent was to fight this natural tendency. In contrast to the explicit goal given Major General Andrus's investigating team, I set out not to find "the cause or causes" (Andrus, 1994:1), but rather to uncover a set of conditions that increased the likelihood of such a tragedy occurring. Framing the study as a search for behavioral and organizational conditions rather than causes led me to look across levels of analysis and across time. That's where I found the mechanism "practical drift."

---

[13] Two complementary principles allow for such "play" in the system, but have had little impact on empirical studies. The first is the principle of equifinality, which holds that from multiple starting points, through various paths, a social system can arrive at the same outcome (Katz and Kahn, 1978). The second is multiple possibility theory, which suggests that the same situation can result in multiple outcomes (Tyler, 1983). When combined, these two propositions describe a world with much more play in it than traditional cause-and-effect models. Approaching the empirical world from such a permissive perspective promises to open new avenues of inquiry into complex social phenomena.

On Practical Drift: Or Is It Sailing?

There are many lessons here. The main one is worth repeating. Untoward events in complex organizations cannot be fully understood by limiting ourselves to any one or even a series of within-level accounts. We must step back and look across levels of analysis and across time. We must approach such low-frequency events as abnormal outcomes of normal systems. We have to analyze such cases in a way that recognizes the dynamic, integrated nature of organizational reality—one that, while acknowledging the parts, also recognizes the whole. In addition to tracking down each contributing factor, for each accident, we should also search for general sets of conditions that increase the likelihood of failure. In addition to chasing causes, we should search for mechanisms.

Practical drift—the slow, steady uncoupling of local practice from written procedure—is one such mechanism. It operates both across levels of analysis and across time. In particular, this mechanism helps us better understand accidents where failures to coordinate play a significant role. Context and history are important. Local adaptation can lead to global disconnects. As outlined in chapter 6, practical drift describes a dynamic set of conditions that increases the likelihood of serious disconnects in complex systems.

Others have uncovered novel mechanisms to account for organizational failures with systemic origins. In her historical ethnography *The Challenger Launch Decision*, Diane Vaughan offers a "nascent theory" she calls the "normalization of deviance" to account for NASA's fateful decision to launch the *Challenger* (1996: 394). According to Vaughan, technical deviations in the performance of O-rings designed to seal joints in the space shuttle's solid rocket boosters were "normalized" over time. As mechanisms, "normalization of deviance" and "practical drift" have much in common; as explanations "grounded" in substantively different case studies, they also differ in equally important ways. A brief comparison of the two accounts following the structure of Vaughan's argument deepens our understanding of the fundamental mechanisms at work in the shootdown.

According to Vaughan, "in the years preceding the *Challenger* launch, engineers and managers together developed a definition of the situation that allowed them to carry on as if nothing were wrong when they continually faced evidence that something *was* wrong. This is the problem of the normalization of deviance" (Vaughan, 1998: 36). Similarly, in the years prior to the shootdown, Operation Provide Comfort (OPC) staff and operators developed their own definitions of the situation that allowed them to carry on. However, unlike *Challenger* engineers and managers who *collectively* struggled to define acceptable risk—largely in very public and structured ways— long histories of interservice rivalries, reinforced by loose coupling and intimate relationships with differing tasks, prevented OPC subunits from ever developing a shared "definition of the situation." Instead, the shootdown story is largely one of how separate belief systems emerged over time to define work situations from multiple local perspectives. Similar to the *Challenger* tragedy, deviance from initially established expectations and procedures was being normalized; however, unlike NASA, where such deviance was centrally redefined as acceptable, in OPC the process of redefining workplace procedures was conducted locally in subunits dispersed throughout the task force.

Vaughan identifies three social forces that contributed to the normalization of deviance: the production of culture, the culture of production, and structural secrecy (1996: 394–99; 1998: 37–43). While each of these factors played a role in the shootdown, they did so in ways slightly different than those uncovered in the *Challenger* story. First, Vaughan explains how work group culture was initially defined. "As the members of the SRB (Solid Rocket Booster) work group interacted about their task, their interpretive work became the basis for an official definition of the boosters as an 'Acceptable Risk'" (1998: 37). Similarly, as the members of each subunit in OPC "interacted about their task, their interpretive work became the basis for" definitions of acceptable workplace procedure. However, unlike the *Challenger* story, culture production in OPC was largely a local process, one that produced multiple *un*official definitions of acceptable practice.

Once produced, deviant interpretations were reinforced and maintained by what Vaughan calls a culture of production—"institutionalized belief systems that shaped interpretation, meaning, and action at the local level" (1998: 39). Similarly, as OPC operator belief systems shifted from rule-based to task-based logics of action, multiple subunit cultures of production emerged to shape "interpretation, meaning, and action at the *local* level," just as Vaughan describes. Contradicting conventional interpretations of a "unidimensional NASA culture dominated by production concerns," Vaughan explains how the "culture of production incorporated three cultural imperatives: the original technical culture of excellence created during the Apollo era (methodological rigor and quantitative science), political accountability (production and cost concerns), and bureaucratic accountability (attention to rules and procedures)" (1998: 39). Applying this approach to the shootdown reveals additional insights into the complexity of OPC culture.

Not only was OPC's culture of production multidimensional in terms of its many subcultures, at a more global level, members of OPC also experienced mixed signals from several different and often-conflicting mandates. Since the end of the Cold War, U.S. military forces have been increasingly called upon to participate in what have become known as "operations other than war." Nation-building, peace-keeping, and peace-enforcement missions have largely replaced high-intensity conflict as the most common type of operation for the American military. Enforcing the no fly zone over northern Iraq is an example of this relatively new type of mission. Similar to Vaughan's analysis of NASA, the workplace in OPC was dominated by three cultural imperatives: the original warrior ethic, aviation's mandate for safety, and restrictions common to a police force. Presented in this way, the story of the shootdown becomes one of individuals and groups struggling to balance the competing demands of several powerful cultural imperatives: the violent aggression of all-out war, the tempered rationality of safe flight, and the conservative use of force required of police. Influenced by their training, parent unit cultures, and an intimate relationship with their day-to-day work, members of various subunits each resolved these contradictions in their own way. We saw how safety-conscious AWACS controllers struggled to temper the aggressive spirit of F-15 fighter pilots; how F-15 pilots fought the complacency of flying "ground hog day" lazy eights (routine, uneventful flights) for weeks on end; and how conservative rules of engagement written to control a policing action failed to prevent friendly fighters from killing twenty-six peacekeepers in an area that was technically designated as a "combat zone." Vaughan's multidimensional approach to the culture of production reveals the complexity and localized influence of institutionalized scripts—cultural meaning systems that "convey to people what is normal and acceptable in particular situations" (1998: 39).

Cultures of production help account for people's definition of the situation. But if significant deviance is being normalized over time from within, why doesn't someone from outside take notice? Why didn't someone in OPC pick up on the fact that various subunits had drifted away from globally synchronized procedures? Vaughan's answer is "structural secrecy":

> Secrecy is built into the very structure of organizations. As organizations grow large, actions that occur in one part of the organization are, for the most part, not observable in others. Division of labor between subunits, hierarchy, and geographic dispersion segregate knowledge about tasks and goals. Distance—both physical and social—interferes with the efforts of those at the top to "know" the behavior of others in the organization—and vice versa. Specialized knowledge further inhibits knowing. The language associated with a different task, even in the same organization, can conceal rather than reveal. (Vaughan, 1998: 42)

This is largely the organizational-level explanation I presented in chapter 5 when we tried to understand why Eagle Flight wasn't better integrated into task force operations. Long histories of interservice rivalry reinforced by physical and social separation led members of various subunits to develop differing orientations toward their work. These very same factors also work to inhibit the free flow of information necessary to recognize the onset of practical drift. Just as Vaughan's structural secrecy prevented outsiders from noticing the work group's emergent belief in acceptable risk, OPC's non-integration of Army helicopters into task force operations kept each major player's definition of their local situation a secret unto themselves.

In several ways, Vaughan's "normalized deviance" is similar to "practical drift." We both draw from similar disciplinary backgrounds and apply similar methods to account for tragic mistakes in complex organizations. However, the differences between our explanations can be traced back to fundamental differences in the stories themselves. The shootdown case is ultimately a story about coordination failure, how multiple subunits within complex organizations each construct their own local sense of reality, how these constructions can differ, and how such disconnects can ultimately lead to tragedy. While Vaughan's explanation of the *Challenger* disaster traces how changes in NASA's environment impacted policy decisions that trickled down (1997) from the top in a way that changed both the structure and culture of work so as to normalize the deviant performance of a critical technical component.

Across Levels

As practical drift crept into Task Force Provide Comfort, it both shaped and was shaped by factors that cut across all traditional levels of analysis. Individual, group, organizational, and environmental factors all contributed to the production of drift, just as drift in turn then influenced the behavior and fate of pilots, crews, and units.[14] If you study any single level of analysis, you miss the drift. To see both the production and influence of this mechanism, we have to widen our field of vision to take in the entire picture. Practical drift is a holistic mechanism that only makes sense when traveling *across* traditional analytical boundaries. Nature doesn't respect such artificial borders and neither should we.

Forces at each level of analysis played a significant role in the construction of drift. Because on any given day this task force was manned by continuously rotating crews and specialists from around the world, there were significant numbers of organizational members struggling to make sense of

[14] Aside from including them in the Causal Map (Figure 1.3), I don't go into any great detail in this study about the importance of broader contextual factors. This is not because I don't think they had an important influence on shaping the general conditions that eventually resulted in the shootdown. They did. However, for purely practical reasons, I cut off any detailed analysis at the Task Force level. Since the unit of analysis for this study was the shootdown—an event whose proximate cause was individual action—I decided that individual, group, intergroup, and task force organizational-level factors provided enough contextual richness to understand this event. Clearly, broader interorganizational and sociopolitical dynamics between Task Force OPC and the Army and Air Force, as well as between the U.S. military, Turkish, and Iraqi governments, substantially influenced the broader context within which this tragic event took place, just as the shootdown in turn influenced these very same factors.

their new situation. Each individual soldier and airman rotating through OPC had to learn how to act. It was this constant battle for individual sense-making and expertise that fueled the engines of drift. Where did these individuals turn to learn the "rules of the game?"

The first place an incoming member of OPC expected to find some answers was from the organization itself. As part of their formal in-processing, each pilot, mechanic, and staff officer attended a series of "spin-up briefings" presented by permanent party cadre. They also received stacks of organizational documents designed to teach them exactly what was expected. However, no matter how well designed or written, such formal procedures simply could not answer every question or cover all of the often subtle details necessary to successfully make it through a day in OPC. Therefore, in their search for additional clues, "newbies" also turned to other individuals, such as "experts" from previous rotations, permanent party staff instructors, and formal leaders. They also turned toward each other.

Constructing norms of acceptable behavior is largely a social process. Therefore, not surprisingly, group and intergroup phenomena also played a central role in the production of drift. Few if any servicemen in OPC worked alone. Aircrews, shift teams, two- and four-ship fighter flights, work details, staff sections, and guard watches all contributed to the social construction of locally acceptable procedure. Many of these small groups interacted frequently and together they colluded to refine parochial standards of conduct. However, others did not. For instance, Army aviators and Air Force fighters rarely interacted, either on the job or off. Task independence, physical separation,[15] social isolation, and long histories of separate services encouraged the development of disparate views of the world, creating disconnects the seriousness of which was not recognized until it was too late.

Ironically, the sensed omniscience of an omnipresent organization also contributed to this tragedy. You couldn't do anything within OPC without running into visible reminders that there was indeed a larger plan. Exceptions to policy had to be approved by higher headquarters; you had to get AWACS's permission to enter the TAOR; operational changes required copies furnished to all sorts of people; each subunit passed up daily SIT-REPs to keep everyone informed. There were hundreds of subtle everyday

[15] Ironically, strict altitude separation rules—restrictions that required Air Force fixed-wing aircraft to fly above an artificial "hard deck" and Army helicopters to remain well below it—designed explicitly to prevent mid-air collisions, in fact contributed to the mutual isolation and ignorance of these two units. In the end, it was this forced separation that greatly contributed to an ignorance of each other's operations. Since fast movers and helicopters were prohibited from ever flying anywhere near each other, they never saw each other and they had no reason to talk to each other. This enforced isolation bred a deep ignorance of each other's operations so that when in fact they were eventually thrown together in a rare occurrence, neither party understood the other. Perversely, the very rule that was designed to avoid one type of accident perhaps increased the likelihood of another.

reminders that someone, somewhere knew what was going on. Detailed Task Force rules and schedules dominated the rhythm and flow of daily life. From occasional curfews to training schedules, these organizational artifacts were reassuring evidence that coordination was happening, that organizing was going on.

Perhaps the most visible reassurance that everything was working according to plan came in the form of periodic visits by the Task Force Commander. Brigadier General Pilkington was an extremely active and visible leader. He flew routine sorties into the TAOR as an F-16 pilot. He was a frequent passenger on Eagle Flight missions. And he also flew regularly in the AWACS. Each time the boss shows up, subordinates perceive the visit as an inspection. Whether intended or not, each time General Pilkington visited a unit and made no correction, the message received was, "Everything is OK. Drive on." Commanders' visits validate the legitimacy of local practices making them powerful, if unwitting, accomplices to the crimes of practical drift.

Senior leader actions, formal organizational rules, intergroup isolation, intra-group norms, and individual sense-making all play a part in the development of practical drift. As a mechanism, drift cuts across all levels of analysis. Focus solely at any one level and you'll miss it. A second way to miss drift is to take a snapshot. As a dynamic process, it cuts across time just as surely as it does levels of analysis. Like an animal in the wild that remains hidden until it moves, drift can't be seen in a single glance. To notice drift requires system movement; movement requires the passage of time.

Across Time

If practical drift involves a "slow, steady uncoupling of local practice from written procedure," then a necessary condition to detect its presence is the passage of time. The very word "drift" implies movement—subtle movement, but movement nonetheless. To detect such movement requires a sensitivity to the passage of time. Single snapshots won't do. Some form of longitudinal data is required to uncover the secrets of such dynamic mechanisms.[16]

Technically, there are no purely cross-sectional analyses of accidents. All explanations at least implicitly assume the passage of time. Linear cause-and-effect models rest on temporal assumptions. Even the most descriptive treatments of accidents include antecedents. However, none of the "conventional explanations for accidents—design, equipment, procedures, operators,

---

[16] Fortunately, accident investigators made a heroic effort to interview many of the original members of OPC and included their testimony in the final report. These interviews along with an extensive record of organizational archives tell a fairly complete story of OPC rules and practice during the first three years of the operation prior to the shootdown.

supplies and materials, or environment" (Perrow, 1984: 63)—explicitly include the passage of time as a central element. Practical drift does.

As a mechanism, drift is but one piece of the shootdown puzzle. At the center of my model lies a cycle (see Figure 6.1). Practical drift is the novel muscle that moves us from quadrant 2 to 3 in the matrix; however, to fully understand the shootdown as the perverse outcome of a complex system, the dynamic process must be seen in its entirety. One complete cycle involves stepping through all four organizational states. Each transition explicitly recognizes the passage of time. Vertical movements ($1 = >2$ and $3 = >4$) are driven by changes in the situation. Horizontal movements ($2 = >3$ and $4 = >1'$) capture changes in the predominant logic of action. Without seeing the organization across significant periods of time—in this case, three years—such cycles remain hidden.

Time is important. In recent reviews, prominent organizational scholars have called for an increased sensitivity to the temporal aspects of social systems. Two of these lines of thought had a strong influence on my approach to this case study. In his review of research studying work groups in organizations, Hackman (1990) identified four unanticipated crosscutting themes. Two of them centered explicitly on the passage of time:

> *Time and Rhythm.* Temporal phenomena were everywhere in the groups we studied, and they significantly affected what happened within them . . . time limits, cycles, and rhythms not only affected how groups went about their work, but also shaped group climate and the quality of members' experiences. . . . *Self-fueling Spirals.* We found considerable evidence to support the dictum that, over time, the rich get richer and the poor get poorer. Groups that somehow got onto a good track tended to perform better as time passed, while those that got into difficulty found that their problems compounded over time. (480–82)

Social systems never stand still. At any given moment, they are either getting better or getting worse; they are either spiraling upward on a path toward ever better performance or downward on a path toward failure. Once again, Hackman offers some insight into what sets these spirals in motion: "Our evidence suggests a two-factor hypothesis. One factor is the quality of the group's initial design. The other is the occurrence of positive or negative events that trigger the spiral" (1990: 482).

If Hackman is right, then our AWACS crew should offer a strong test of his hypothesis. A weak launch and poor design was followed by an extremely negative event early in the group's life. Such combinations should send the group spiraling off into a negative spin. Unfortunately (or fortunately) we weren't able to test Hackman's hypothesis on this particular crew. Due to the seriousness of the accident and resulting criminal investigations, the crew on duty during the shootdown never flew again intact. Both crew composition and mission requirements changed dramatically as a result of the shootdown. However, I did incorporate Hackman's two factors into my broader theory of practical drift. Both the quality of the organization's initial design (quad 1) and the occurrence of a negative event (quad 4) combine to trigger a negative spiral—the hypothesized second cycle of 1' through 4'.

In their review of the concept of "organizations as loosely coupled systems," Orton and Weick (1990) called for a "reconceptualization" of the concept away from a unidimensional towards a more dialectical interpretation.[17] Central to this reinterpretation is a more dynamic treatment of coupling, one that explicitly addresses the passage of time:

> The concept of loose coupling is simplified when researchers use it for flat, static descriptions, rather than detailed, dynamic descriptions. Weick (1979: 44) argued that nouns focus attention on reified objects, whereas verbs focus attention on dynamic processes. Researchers who see systems as static objects to be labeled ("this is a loosely coupled system") are less likely to capture loose coupling than are researchers who see systems as an arena for complex, ongoing processes ("loose coupling in this system occurs when . . ."). (Orton and Weick: 1990: 218–19)

Taking the hint, when I looked across levels, I viewed the system "as an arena for complex, ongoing processes" rather than as a "static object to be labeled." Instead of categorizing the Task Force as either loosely or tightly coupled (Perrow, 1984: 97), I considered the possibility that the situation could change along this dimension, that in fact it might not be the presence or lack of coupling that was important, but rather the pattern of coupling over time. Once again, to see "complex, ongoing processes," you have to gather longitudinal data; you have to look across time.

Practical Sailing[18]

On a beautiful spring day the surface of Boston Harbor is dotted with dozens of sailboats. From the stern of each boat, from the perspective of each captain, progress is technically rational—there are desired destinations and captains maneuver their boats accordingly. However, from the perspective of an airline passenger on final approach to Logan Airport, the paths struck by

---

[17] According to the authors, adopting a dialectical interpretation allows us to think simultaneously about both rationality and indeterminacy, "to combine the contradictory concepts of connection and autonomy . . . by juxtaposing both forces, simultaneously, within the same system" (Orton and Weick, 1990: 216). Adopting such a position is precisely the leverage I needed to illustrate one of the central dimensions of the shootdown—loose coupling not as a static label, but rather as a dynamic state with serious implications for organizational performance.

[18] While reviewing drafts of this book, Charles Perrow suggested I use the term "practical sailing" to capture the functional aspects of local adaptation.

hundreds of boats look chaotic and random; boats appear to be drifting in all directions. From the local perspective of each captain, progress could be described as practical sailing—the result of continuous intelligent adjustments and adaptations to changing local conditions and goals. From the more global perspective of 10,000 feet, it appears that no one is in charge and boat traffic seems to be drifting out of control.

Practical drift and practical sailing are two sides of the same coin. Depending on your perspective, the slow steady uncoupling of local practice from global procedures can appear either rational and effective or random and dangerous. From the local perspective of pilots in F-15s and helicopters, and individual crew members inside the AWACs, organizing emerges out of the very practical demands of work. Rasmussen explains:

> In most work situations, the individual actor is faced with many degrees of freedom with respect to the composition of normally successful work procedures. The flexibility and speed of professional expertise evolve through a process of adaptation to the peculiarities of the work environment. . . . During this adaptation, performance will be optimized according to the individual actor's subjective process criteria within the boundaries of his individual resources. (Rasmussen, 1993b: 10)

Successful adaptation to local conditions is often the mark of professional expertise. To the operator, this adaptive process is rational and makes sense. From the local perspective such progress is practical sailing—one side of the coin.

> Unfortunately, perception of the qualities of the work process itself is immediate and unconditional and the benefit from local adaptation to subjective performance criteria is perceived in the situation. In contrast, the effect of activities on the ultimate product of work (and on side effects) of local adaptive trials can be considerably delayed, obscure and frequently conditional with respect to multiple other factors. Shortcuts and tricks-of-the trade will frequently evolve and be very efficient under normal conditions while they will be judged serious human errors when they, under special circumstances, lead to severe accidents. (Rasmussen, 1993b: 10)

This insight describes the other side of the coin. From the global perspective at the task force level, in hindsight, local sailing of multiple subunits within Operation Provide Comfort looks like chaotic drift; each subunit cutting random paths away from centrally established rules and procedures.

As Rasmussen points out, "shortcuts and tricks-of-the trade will frequently evolve and be very efficient under normal conditions" (1993b: 10). This is what makes this mechanism so seductive. For three years "under normal conditions," many "shortcuts and tricks-of-the-trade" evolved within OPC subunits. Some of them, such as the practice of helicopters not switching controllers while attempting to land at Zakhu, no doubt resulted in increased reliability and help to account for the 1,109 days of safe operations. "Even for activities in familiar situations for which normative work procedures exist, there will be ample opportunities for modification of such procedures. The development of expert know-how and rules-of-thumb depends on adaptation governed by an empirical correlation of cues to successful acts" (Rasmussen, 1993b: 11). Staying on the enroute frequency and talking to the enroute controller became a "rule-of-thumb" even though "normative work procedures" dictated otherwise—an example of practical sailing at its best. Unfortunately, "when situations change, e.g., due to disturbances or faults in the system to be controlled, reliance will continue to be placed on the usual cues which are no longer valid, and error will be likely" (Rasmussen, 1993b: 11). Practical sailing turned into practical drift when the "situation changed" from loosely to tightly coupled and all parties continued to rely "on the usual cues which [were] no longer valid."

Practical sailing and practical drift—two sides of the same coin. For organizational leaders, the challenge of this dynamic is illustrated by the metaphor: At any given moment you can only see one side of a coin. Original designers only saw the global imperative to synchronize subunits under the most extreme conditions of tight coupling. In practice, operators only saw local adaptation as sailing. Unfortunately, task force leaders never gained the global vantage point of our airline passenger over Boston Harbor; they never saw the drift from globally synchronized rules; they never recognized the situation for what it was—conditions ripe for failure.

General Conditions

So what *were* the general conditions present in the Task Force that increased the likelihood of an accident happening? In summary, there were three:

- A complex high-hazard organization that couldn't afford to learn from trial and error; hence, the tendency to *overdesign*, and a bias to *overcontrol*;
- A long enough period of loosely coupled *time* sufficient to generate substantial gaps between globally synchronized rules and local subgroup practice; and
- A *reasonable chance* that isolated subgroups would become *tightly coupled* at some point in the future.

After a brief discussion of two of these ("time" has already been covered), I conclude with some final thoughts for both practitioners and scientists.

First, Task Force OPC was a high-hazard organization—one that couldn't afford to learn from trial-and-error because it couldn't afford that first error. Such organizations are unusually susceptible to what I call the "control trap." Simply put, this pitfall manifests itself as, "Because we must [control], we may [control]; because we may/can [control], we will [control]."

Traditionally, when an organization accepts responsibility to manage hazardous technologies or systems—to run nuclear power plants, to transport hazardous chemicals, to build dams, to fly commercial aircraft, to control disease, to pilot giant fuel tankers, to safeguard weapons of mass destruction, to defend the country—society has been willing to grant them additional latitude when it comes to controlling member behavior—all in the name of safety. The rationale here is that the collective costs to society for failure in such organizations is so high, that we are willing to allow management extra leeway when it comes to controlling employee behavior. Because we must, we may.

Members of the Armed Forces give up many personal freedoms and Constitutional rights for the "privilege" of being entrusted with weapons of mass destruction. The Uniform Code of Military Justice (UCMJ) is much more restrictive than laws that govern private citizens. Many restrictions on service member behavior have been upheld in the name of "maintaining good order and discipline" and in the "interests of national security." Mandatory HIV testing, invasive personal security background checks, legal restrictions on place of duty and travel (AWOL), mandatory height and weight standards, unquestioned subordination to legal orders of superiors, and numerous restrictions on personal appearance and freedom of speech are just a few examples of how our society has allowed the military unusual leeway when it comes to controlling member behavior.

This privilege can be abused in two ways. First, granted unusual authority to control its members, leaders of such organizations are naturally tempted to extend such power into areas not even remotely related to the sustainment of reliability. Given extraordinary control, why not use it to ease the burdens of everyday managerial problems—even those not remotely tied to safety or national security? With over twenty years in uniform, I have witnessed many such abuses. My favorite (harmless) example is the post commander who dictated the limits of Christmas decorations in family housing areas—when they could be put up ("not earlier than . . ."), when they had to be taken down ("not later than . . ."), how many strings of lights ("not more than . . ."), and even the color ("white!"). Because he could (control), he did (control).

I tell this story to illustrate just how easy it is for leaders in such organizations to get carried away on the control trip. If commanders feel free to dictate family decorations at Christmas, you can only imagine how freely they exercise control in the name of vital mission requirements. This suggests a second way control is abused—not by overextending the privilege, but rather by overusing it. The logic flows something like this: if a little control is good, and more control is better, then a lot of control must be best.

After all, complete control of these hazardous technologies is society's mandate—the very reason such organizations are granted extensive invasive rights in the first place. Because we must, we may; *because we may, we do*. Consistent with this logic, managers of high-hazard organizations tend to overdesign their systems and overcontrol their people—sometimes with unexpected results.

Unexpected results from human attempts to (over)control complex systems are beginning to surface almost everywhere. Fiscal solutions/controls to one economic ill often generate another. No matter how many dams we build or how high we build them, flooding still occurs—not as frequently perhaps, but almost always with greater devastation. Pesticides designed to control the spread of harmful insects often lose their strength and end up causing more harm than good. Antibiotics designed to control the spread of disease become ineffective over time and can even weaken our natural immune systems. We spend the majority of our health care resources on patients during their last ten days of life and still they die. Because we are not willing to tolerate depressions, disease, bankruptcies, natural disasters, and even death; and, because we seem to enjoy a limited ability to control the onset of such evils at least in the short run; hence, we feel a moral imperative to rush in and control. Because we have the ability to interrupt the natural flow of things, we do—quite often in a big way.

Perhaps we shouldn't. When it comes to control, less is sometimes more. Many environmentalists argue for adopting natural solutions to "control" pests. Most naturalists now agree that many forest fires are natural disasters that we should let burn; even though we can put them out, perhaps we shouldn't. Others feel the same way about flood control; instead of building ever-higher and longer dams, perhaps we should expect occasional flooding, plan for it, and allow it to happen—rather than trying to completely prevent it. Even with death, many find living wills more appropriate than Herculean attempts to control life in its final stages.

While there seems to be some precedent for moving in the opposite direction—and there are no doubt lessons to be learned here—our natural inclination when it comes to managing hazardous systems is still to control. And if that doesn't work, control some more. We tend to hang onto most tightly that which we can't afford to lose. Unfortunately, well-intentioned efforts to prevent failure through tight control often produce just the opposite effect.

This is what I suggest happened in OPC. This is the general set of conditions present in the Task Force that increased the likelihood of failure: As a result of the phenomenon I just described, original coordination rules were overdesigned (quad 1). This is the first condition. In practice, they didn't match reality in a primarily loosely coupled world (quad 2). This is the second condition. The combination of these two conditions encouraged practical drift—a mechanism that set the stage for the final ingredient—chance.

In addition to overcontrol and time, there had to be a reasonable chance that the system would become tightly coupled again. If there was no physical way that our helicopters, fighters, and AWACS could come together, if the system remained loosely coupled forever, no amount of control or time could result in a shootdown. The third necessary condition, whose presence increased the likelihood of tragedy, was the reasonable chance that these subgroups would interact in a significant way.

Even though the Airspace Control Order directed a zone of altitude separation between fighters and helicopters, even though fighters and helicopters had very different unit missions requiring no direct interaction, and even though there is some truth to aviators' safety catch-all, "big sky, little planes," there was always a reasonable chance—no matter how remote—that fate would have its way and at some place and some time, all three aircraft would be thrown together. The presence of this reasonable chance in OPC is the third necessary condition that increased the likelihood of an accident.

What were the odds that the Black Hawks would drop down into a deep valley causing the AWACS to lose line-of-sight just as the F-15s crossed into Iraq? Very small indeed. Phrases such as "s--t happens," Murphy's Law, and "it was their day" are all colorful attempts to acknowledge the significant role that chance plays in our lives.[19] I explicitly include this stochastic element in my theory by recognizing the significant role that it plays in changing the situation from loose to tight coupling (quad $3 = >4$). There had to be a reasonable chance for this shift to occur; this is the third and final condition that increased the likelihood of an accident.

Implications: Let's Build a Library

What does all this mean for practitioners, for managers of complex, high-hazard organizations? Does admitting to the role that chance plays in our

---

[19] I don't intend for the mechanical-looking progression of states in the theoretical matrix (Figure 6.1) to imply an overly deterministic explanation for this accident. By all accounts, this was a very rare event. "Chance—the fortuitous combination of causal elements at a particular place and time" (Reason, 1997: 108) played a significant role in the birth of this tragedy. "The large random component in accident causation means that 'safe' organizations can still have bad accidents, and 'unsafe' organizations can escape them for long periods. Bad luck can bring down the deserving, while good luck can protect the unworthy" (Reason, 1997: 108). Based on this logic, the simple fact that a tragic accident occurred in OPC does not, in and of itself, indicate that this was an unsafe organization. It also does not imply that practical drift must result in failure. What the matrix in Figure 6.1 does suggest is that organizations with multiple subunits operating largely in loosely coupled worlds are vulnerable to a particular type of coordination failure. Understanding this dynamic draws our attention to *chance* encounters between subunits as the stochastic trigger for failure. The question for leaders then becomes one of creating conditions that reduce the likelihood of such unexpected shifts into the tightly coupled mode.

lives doom us to accept the inevitability of such failures? If so, what are the implications for leaders who openly admit to the inherent fallibility of their organizations? What are the implications when they don't? If the answer to practical drift is not more rules and tighter control, then what? For both scientists and practitioners, where do we go from here?

The following passage from a congressional study commissioned to investigate the unusually high rates of fratricide during the Persian Gulf War nicely summarizes my findings from this study:

> Reducing fratricide is desirable and feasible, but eliminating it is not. Although programs to reduce fratricide are certainly needed, setting a goal of eliminating fratricide is unrealistic and probably even counterproductive. Overly restrictive rules of engagement, for example, may so reduce combat effectiveness that casualties inflicted by the enemy increase more than friendly fire losses are reduced. (U.S. Congress, Office of Technology Assessment, 1993: 2)

Similarly, reducing serious accidents in high-hazard organizations is desirable and feasible, but eliminating them is not. "No system can completely avoid errors. Any discussion of reliability must start with that as axiomatic" (Weick, 1987: 122). These are strong statements coming from various academic circles. However, how do these same admissions sound when they're coming from the leaders of our high-hazard organizations?

How would we feel if the head of the Nuclear Regulatory Agency declared that "eliminating accidents is 'unrealistic and probably even counterproductive?'" How would you feel if the Chairman of the Federal Aviation Administration or your favorite airline admitted that "no system can completely avoid errors." How would you feel if you had just lost a loved one in a friendly fire accident and his leader admitted that war is hell and "reducing fratricide is desirable, but eliminating it is not?"

There is a fundamental dilemma faced by leaders in all high-hazard organizations. If not publicly, at least in their guts they know that airplanes are going to continue to crash; terrorists are going to continue to blow up buildings; accidents will continue to plague nuclear power plants; and additional soldiers will continue to die from friendly fire. And yet, how should they reconcile this reality with their responsibility to safeguard thousands of lives each day? How do you admit that accidents will happen while simultaneously struggling to eliminate them?

In the military, no training accidents are "acceptable." And yet, we know that hundreds of soldiers will die in the peacetime Army each year.[20] During hearings into an unusual rash of military accidents, Senator Sam Nunn, ranking Democrat on the Senate Armed Services Committee, emphasized this very dilemma: "Training accidents are going to happen. We try to minimize

---

[20] For example, out of the 1,054 total active duty military deaths in 1995, 565 of them died as the result of accidents. Only 6 died from hostile action and all of those were from terrorist attacks. Similarly, 203 out of 385 deaths in the Army were caused by accidents (Maze, 1996).

those, but it is in the effort to train that we reduce overall casualties" (Maze, 1996: 30). Senator Nunn's approach is consistent with the Office of Technology Assessment's conclusion that "eliminating fratricide is unrealistic and probably even counterproductive." Once again, Senator Nunn: "I hope we don't come to a conclusion that zero casualties is possible in the military. It is just impossible." Defense Secretary Perry and General Shalikashvili responded to Nunn by nodding their heads in agreement[21] (Maze, 1996: 30).

Training accidents are going to happen no matter how many safeguards are implemented. The goal of zero casualties is simply unattainable. Eliminating fratricide is unrealistic. And "no system can completely avoid errors." Yet no accidents, zero casualties, eliminating fratricide, and avoiding errors are all noble objectives. Trying to reach them is like chasing an asymptote; you can get closer and closer, but you'll never get there. Accepting this fact is the necessary first step for organizational leaders. Tempered by the knowledge that you'll never get there, chasing these goals can be healthy.[22] "Reducing fratricide is desirable and feasible" but only if, and this is the lesson from this case, we understand the potential downsides of

---

[21] In an article titled "The Military's Getting Queasier About Death" (Schmitt, 1995), General Shalikashvili acknowledged the potential downside of pushing too hard for "zero casualties":

> I'm concerned we do not start in our young leaders this notion that it's better to be hesitant and timid. The result will not be that they will take fewer casualties. The result will be they will take more. We need to guard against that. (Schmitt, 1995: 2)

He went on to warn of the "chilling effect" that constant second guessing can have "on troops in the field":

> Commanders up and down the chain of command are saying, "Oops!" from now on every time something like this [accident] happens, when a sergeant goes out on a patrol and comes to a fork, takes a right fork and later on, it turns out he should have taken the left fork, we have hearings on why the sergeant took the wrong turn. . . . We need to understand what impact that has. (Schmitt, 1995: 2)

Following the shootdown in Northern Iraq, senior DOD officials faced intense pressure to hold someone accountable for the twenty-six lost lives. General Shalikashvili's remarks highlight leaders' need to temper accountability with an eye toward the broader impact that such actions could have on the future effectiveness of the fighting force. How many lives will be lost in the next war if we have an Air Force filled with timid fighter pilots?

[22] James Reason, longtime scholar of "safety wars," turns to a military analogy to capture the nature of this chase:

> Cognisant [sic] organizations understand the true nature of the "safety war." They see it for what it really is—a long guerrilla struggle with no final conclusive victory. For them, a lengthy period without a bad accident does not signal the coming of peace. They see it, correctly, as a period of heightened danger and so reform and strengthen their defenses accordingly. In any case, since entropy wins in the end, a more appropriate metaphor for the conclusion of the safety war might be likened to the last helicopter out of Saigon rather than a decisive Yorktown, Waterloo or Appomatox. (Reason, 1997: 114)

pushing too hard. Vicious cycles like the one driven by practical drift are fueled by ignorance of their underlying dynamics. Blindly throwing more and more rules at the symptoms of a broken system without fully understanding the underlying structure that created them often makes matters worse.[23]

If not more control, if not tighter rules, then what? How *do* you solve the problem of practical drift? First, the answer is clearly not more rules or additional layers of coordinating mechanisms. Second, directly attacking practical drift isn't the answer either. While a powerful mechanism, drift is only one more symptom of deeper problems. The first step is to reframe the question: Where do you attack cycles like the one at the heart of this shoot-down? Systems theorists have demonstrated the general ineffectiveness of intervening at any particular point in a cycle (Senge, 1990). The lesson from studying spirals is that starting conditions and system structure are the key points of leverage. This all leads to the second step which involves a general reframing of the entire research problem.

I started out by framing the puzzle at individual, group, and organizational levels of analysis. Existing behavioral science theories adequately addressed each of these issues. Not fully satisfied, I looked across levels and time to gain a holistic perspective of the entire system. Uncovering the mechanism of practical drift was key; it was the missing piece of the systems puzzle, but still only a piece. With drift in hand, I could step back even further and make out a complete cycle for the complex event that was the shootdown. Seeing this cycle I now realize that the important question is not how to fix pilot misidentification, crew inaction, organizational non-integration, or even practical drift; the more fundamental question for both theory and practice is: What are the critical design features of a hyper-complex, multilevel, multi-task, organizational system that will increase the likelihood of accomplishing the "total task" consistently?

---

[23] I have nothing against rules. We need them in complex organizations. However, this case study reveals a few insights into the nature of rules in complex organizations. First, we have a tendency to write too many of them. We cannot write a rule for every contingency, and yet, the nature of rational design and technical accountability in large bureaucracies encourages us to try. Periodic review and pruning is required to fight such tendencies to meet each new contingency with a formal rule. Second, too many formal rules encourages practical drift (or is it sailing?). In order to accomplish the mission, well-meaning workers will always subvert globally established rules that don't seem to make sense locally. These "make it happen" employees are invaluable. Such discretions only become *in*discretions when they result in unintended outcomes. Hence, if we want employees to pay attention to the rules we do write, we have to limit their number to the absolute bare minimum and then vigorously enforce them without exception. A few inviolable rules unconditionally enforced trumps volumes of take-your-pick guidance any day. For example, the altitude separation rule might be one such rule that no one violates without extraordinary approval, a rule that, if enforced, might have prevented the shootdown.

I don't have the answers.[24] However, each part of this study contains some hints. Although this is only one case, I am convinced that similar behaviorally based analyses of other complex organizational failures hold the key to identifying these critical design features. As caring humans we pray that such tragedies never occur. As pragmatic practitioners we know that they will. As behavioral theorists we must be ready to rush in and mine them for all they're worth, because dramatic organizational incidents such as this shootdown are rare scientific treasures—natural breaching experiments (Garfinkel, 1963) that unlock exciting behavioral mysteries normally hidden by the thick crust of day-to-day routines. If we could put together a library of such treasures, thick behavioral descriptions of complex untoward events, I'm confident that such studies will move us closer to unlocking the fundamental design mysteries of hyper-complex organizations.

[24] In the final chapter of his book *Managing the Risks of Organizational Accidents*, James Reason ends on an optimistic note: "Workplaces and organizations are easier to manage than the minds of individual workers. You cannot change the human condition, but you can change the *conditions* under which people work" (emphasis added) (1997: 223). Identifying a robust set of conditions for hypercomplex organizational systems that decreases the likelihood of tragic failures should be the target of future research. A single case study can only hint at the theoretical and practical treasures to be gained from constructing a library of similar in-depth behavioral analyses.

Appendix 1

Method

MY GENERAL research strategy was to conduct a qualitative analysis of this single explanatory embedded case study (Yin, 1994) for the purpose of building grounded theory (Strauss and Corbin, 1990).

Why this approach?

Yin tells us that "case studies are the preferred strategy when 'how' and 'why' questions are being posed, when the investigator has little control over events, and when the focus is on a contemporary phenomenon within some real-life context" (1994: 1). My empirical question—"How in the world could this accident happen?"—clearly fit Yin's "how" criteria. The theoretical puzzle—"What are the organizational and behavioral conditions that resulted in such an organizational tragedy?"—fits equally well with Yin's "why" criteria. I obviously have "no control over the events" and the "real-life context" within which the event takes place is of central importance— hence, my selection of the case study as a research strategy.

My analysis was qualitative and grounded in the tradition of Glaser and Strauss (1967). "Formulating theoretical interpretations of data grounded in reality provides a powerful means both for understanding the world 'out there' and for developing action strategies that will allow for some measure of control over it" (Strauss and Corbin, 1990: 9). I wanted to understand how and why this accident happened by building theory grounded in the contextually rich data of the real-world event.

Why a single case study?

Yin suggests three rationales for conducting single-case designs. The first is when the case represents *the* "critical case" in the sense that it tests a well-formulated theory—similar to a critical experiment. I had no theory to test. However, Yin's second two rationales for conducting a single-case design apply. The shootdown is both an "extreme or unique case" and also a potentially "revelatory one." It is unique in the sense that such accidents rarely happen. Not only is such a tragedy rare, but the fact that no simple compelling explanation presented itself also argued for further inquiry. It was potentially revelatory in the sense that I had gained rather unique access to an extensive set of data, including internal departmental communications not readily accessible or interpretable to the nonmilitary social scientist.

Why embedded?

This question begs the fundamental challenge of defining what the case is all about. What is the case? What is the unit of analysis? The unit of analysis must be consistent with the research question. Cases can be about almost anything: individuals, groups, companies, and even countries can be the main unit of analysis. However, as Yin reminds us, "the 'case' also can be some event" (1994: 22).

The main unit of analysis in this study is "the shootdown"—an event. However, in contrast to a holistic design, my approach was emphatically embedded. The event was studied as it occurred, embedded in the interaction of several important subunits. Key individual behaviors—such as those of the F-15 pilots, the AWACS controllers and supervisor, and the task force commander—were all studied, each as it related to the main unit of analysis which is the accident itself. Important dyads and subgroups were also studied. The relationship between the lead and his wingman in the F-15 flight, the performance of the mission crew in the AWACS, and the organizational cultures of the three parent organizations were all units worthy of explicit consideration. Finally, the actions of subunits and individual members could not be fully understood in isolation from the general context. Task Force Provide Comfort, its mission, procedures, and history were all important contextual considerations within which the main unit of analysis—the shootdown—was embedded and without which the central event could not be fully understood.

Once again Yin recommends using "the case study method because you deliberately want to cover contextual conditions—believing that they might be highly pertinent to your phenomenon of study" (1994: 13). This is decidedly the case with the shootdown, where "the boundaries between phenomenon and context are not clearly evident" (Yin, 1994: 13). Where the shootdown ends is clear; where it begins is not. As complex explanatory case studies move further and further away from the proximal causes of an event, connections become more and more tenuous as the causal field becomes increasingly diffuse. Rasmussen raises this issue as the fundamental difficulty of causal explanations: "No objective stop rule can be devised to terminate this search. It is always possible to go one more step backwards in the search . . ." (1993b:3). By explicitly stating the theoretical research question as a search for "organizational and behavioral *conditions*" that resulted in the tragedy, I dealt with this epistemological challenge head-on.

Appendix 2

Friendly Fire Applied: Lessons for Your Organization?

- Have you shot down any friendly helicopters lately?

- Who are the "fighter pilots" and who are the "bus drivers" in your organization? Do you listen to "radar heads" and "techno-geeks?"

- Do you have any DUKEs that might be "pigs looking at watches?"

- Do you have any collections of individuals that should be "real teams" instead? How "hard" are your crews?

- Do you have any important tasks for which everyone is responsible, and yet no one is? Would anyone call 911 if a Kitty Genovese was attacked in your organization?

- Are there any powerful situations that might make friendly Black Hawks look like enemy Hinds?

- Do you have any long histories of interservice rivalries in your organization?

- What do you do with your "command climate surveys?" Employee satisfaction surveys? Sensing session results?

- What are you missing by "being involved the way you are" in your organization? What do you miss by flying F-16s instead of F-15s?

- How do you learn from such tragedies? Do you learn? Is the focus on learning or on the "politics of blame?"

References _____

Abbott, A. (1990). "Conceptions of Time and Events in Social Science Methods: Causal and Narrative Approaches." *Historical Methods* 23: 140–50.

Adkin, M. (1989). *Urgent Fury: The Battle for Grenada.* Lexington, Mass.: Lexington Books.

Aerospace Daily. (1994). "IFF Still a Deadly Problem as U.S. F-15s Shoot Down U.S. UH-60s." April 15: 81.

Alderfer, C. P. (1983). "Intergroup Relations and Organizations." In J. R. Hackman, E. Lawler, and L. Porter, eds., *Perspectives on Behavior in Organizations.* New York: McGraw-Hill.

Allard, C. K. (1990). *Command, Control, and the Common Defense.* New Haven: Yale University Press.

———. (1995). *Somalia Operations: Lessons Learned.* Washington, D.C.: National Defense University Press.

Allison, G. T. (1971). *Essence of Decision: Explaining the Cuban Missile Crisis.* Boston: Little, Brown and Company.

Altshwager, H. R. (1995). "Instructions for Deliberation, U.S. v. Captain Wang, General Court-Martial." HQs, 8th Air Force.

Amin, A. M. (1994). Ground-to-Air Video, 14 April 1994. Zakhu, Iraq: KDP K.TV.

Andrus, J. G. (1994). *AFR 110-14 Aircraft Accident Investigation Board Report of Investigation: U.S. Army Black Hawk Helicopters 87-26000 and 88-26060.* U.S. Air Force.

Anonymous. (1994). *Quality of Life Survey, AWACS Unit.* 552 ACW/CC.

Argyris, C., and Schon, D. (1974). *Theory in Practice.* San Francisco: Jossey-Bass.

Army Times. (1996). "Getting It Together." April: 29.

Beckwith, C. A., and Knox, D. (1983). *Delta Force.* New York and San Diego: Harcourt Brace Jovanovich.

Bender, J. B. (1985). *Parallel Systems: Redundancy in Government.* Berkeley: University of California Press.

Bettenhausen, K., and Murnighan, J. K. (1985). "The Emergence of Norms in Competitive Decision-Making Groups." *Administrative Science Quarterly* 30: 350–72.

Bliss, T. F. (1994). *Memorandum for Record: Subject: AWACS Readiness Status.* 552 ACW/CC.

Boykin, K. S. (1994a). "Memorandum for 8 AF/CC: Subject: Over Taping of Portion of AWACS Mission Videotape." 8 AF/DS, Inquiry Officer.

———. (1994b). *RCM 303 Inquiry Officer Report: Subject: Rules for Courts Martial 303 Inquiry into the Shoot-Down of Two U.S. Army UH-60 Black Hawk Helicopters in Northern Iraq on 14 April 1994.* 8AF/DS, Barksdale AFB, LA.

Brown, R. (1986). *Social Psychology.* (2d ed.) New York: Free Press.

Bruner, J. (1986). *Actual Minds, Possible Worlds.* Cambridge, Mass.: Harvard University Press.

Burrell, G., and Morgan, G. (1979). *Sociological Paradigms and Organizational Analysis*. London: Heinemann.

Carroll, J. S. (1995). *Incident Reviews in High Hazard Production Systems: A Proposal for a Multidisciplinary Workshop*. National Science Foundation proposal, Massachusetts Institute of Technology, Cambridge.

Cohen, E. A., and Gooch, J. (1990). *Military Misfortunes: The Anatomy of Failure in War*. New York: The Free Press.

Cooper, H. S. (1973). *Thirteen: The Flight that Failed*. New York: Dial Press.

Cristol, A. J. (1995). *The Liberty Incident* (No. IPI483). Program on Information Resources Policy, Harvard University.

Curry, D. (1995). *Congressional Hearing Summary: Friendly Fire Incident Over Iraq (Black Hawk Shootdown)* Military Personnel Subcommittee, House National Security Council. Department of the Army, Office, Chief of Legislative Liaison.

DiMaggio, P. (1994). "Culture and Economy." In N. J. Smelser and R. Swedberg, eds., *The Handbook of Sociology*. Princeton, NJ: Princeton University Press.

DOD Joint Combat Camera Center. (1994). *AWACS Mission Tape, 14 April, 1994*. Incirlik Air Base, Turkey.

Dornan, R. K. (1995). "Dornan Announces 'Friendly Fire' Hearing: National Security Subcommittee to Investigate Iraq Shoot Down." In P. Morrell, ed., News Release, Washington, D.C.: U.S. House of Representatives.

Doyle, A. C., Sir (1905). *The Complete Sherlock Holmes*. New York: Doubleday.

Drucker, P. E. (1974). *Management: Tasks, Responsibilities, Practices*. New York: Harper & Row.

Elster, J. (1989). *Nuts and Bolts for the Social Sciences*. Cambridge: Cambridge University Press.

English, H. B., and English, A. C. (1958). *A Comprehensive Dictionary of Psychological and Psychoanalytical Terms*. New York: Longmans, Green.

Eysenck, M. W. (1982). *Attention and Arousal: Cognition and Performance*. New York: Springer-Verlag.

Fayol, H. (1949). "General Principles of Management." In D. S. Pugh, ed., *Organization Theory*. New York: Penguin Books.

Fiedler, F. (1977). "The Leadership Game: Matching the Man to the Situation." In J. R. Hackman, E. Lawler, and L. Porter, eds., *Perspectives on Behavior in Organizations*. New York: McGraw-Hill.

Firth, R. (1936). *We, The Tikopia*. London: Unwin, Ltd.

Foushee, H. C., Lauber, J. K., Baetge, M. M., and Acomb, D. B. (1986). *Crew Factors in Flight Operations III: The Operational Significance of Exposure to Short-Haul Air Transport Operations* (Technical Memorandum #88342). Moffett Field, Calif.: NASA-Ames Research Center.

Friedland, R., and Alford, R. R. (1991). "Bringing Society Back In: Symbols, Practices, and Institutional Contradictions." In W. W. Powell and P. J. DiMaggio, eds., *The New Institutionalism in Organizational Analysis*. Chicago: University of Chicago Press.

Fuller, J.F.C. (1933). *Generalship: Its Diseases and Their Cures*. London: Faber & Faber, Ltd.

Garfinkel, H. (1963). "A Conception of, and Experiments with, Trust as a Condition of Stable Concerted Actions." In O. J. Harvey, ed., *Motivation and Social Interaction*. New York: Ronald Press.

Geertz, C. (1973). *The Interpretation of Cultures*. New York: Basic Books.

Gersick, C. J. (1988). "Time and Transition in Work Teams: Toward a New Model of Group Development." *Academy of Management Journal* 41: 9–41.

Gersick, C. J., and Hackman, J. R. (1990). "Habitual Routines in Task-Performing Teams." *Organizational Behavior and Human Decision Processes* 47: 65–97.

Gilbert, R. K. (1988). "Psychological Factors Inhibiting Arms Control Activism." *American Psychologist* 43:*10*: 755–64.

Ginnett, R. C. (1987). *First Encounters of the Close Kind: The Formation Process of Airline Flight Crews*. Unpublished doctoral dissertation, Yale University: New Haven, Conn.

———. (1990). "Airline Cockpit Crews." In J. Richard Hackman, ed., *Groups That Work*. San Francisco: Jossey-Bass.

———. (1993). "Crews as Groups: Their Formation and Their Leadership." In E. L. Wiener, R. L. Helmreich, and B. G. Kanki, eds., *Cockpit Resource Management*. San Diego: Academic Press.

Glaser, B., and Strauss, A. (1967). *The Discovery of Grounded Theory*. Chicago: Aldine.

Glassman, R. B. (1973). "Persistence and Loose Coupling in Living Systems." *Behavioral Science* 18: 83–98.

Goffman, E. (1961). *Asylums: Essays on the Social Situation of Mental Patients and Other Inmates*. New York: Doubleday.

———. (1973). *The Presentation of Self in Everyday Life*. New York: Overlook Press.

Graham, P., ed. (1995). *Mary Parker Follett—Prophet of Management*. Boston: Harvard Business School Press.

Griffin, L. J. (1992). "Temporality, Events, and Explanation in Historical Sociology: an Introduction." *Sociological Research Methods* 20: 403–27.

———. (1993). "Narrative, Event-Structure Analysis, and Causal Interpretation in Historical Sociology." *American Journal of Sociology* 98(5): 1094–1133.

Gulick, L., and Urwick, L. (1937). *Papers on the Science of Administration*. Institute of Public Administration, Columbia University.

Hackman, J. R., ed. (1990). *Groups That Work (And Those That Don't): Creating Conditions for Effective Teamwork*. San Francisco: Jossey-Bass.

———. (1993). "Teams, Leaders, and Organizations: New Directions for Crew-Oriented Flight Training." In E. L. Wiener, R. L. Helmreich, and B. G. Kanki, eds., *Cockpit Resource Management*. San Diego: Academic Press.

Hackworth, D. H. (1990). *About Face*. New York: Simon & Schuster.

Hall, J. B. (1994). "Memorandum for MG Andrus, Chairman, Accident Investigation Board: Subject: My Unresolved Concerns Regarding Investigation of Aircraft Accident," 14 April 1994. U.S. Army.

Hannan, M., and Freeman, J. (1989). *Organizational Ecology*. Cambridge, Mass.: Harvard University Press.

Hatch, D. L. (1948). *Changes in the Structure and Function of a Rural New England Community Since 1900*. Unpublished doctoral thesis, Harvard University.

Headquarters 8th Air Force. (1995). "Record of Trial, General Court Martial, U.S. v. Captain Jim Wang." Maureen A. Nation, ed., Tinker Air Force Base, Oklahoma.

Hill, M. (1989). "The Vincennes: Seven Minutes in July." *San Diego Magazine*. February: 108–205.

Homans, G. C. (1950). *The Human Group*. New York: Harcourt, Brace & World.

Janis, I. L. (1982). *Groupthink: Psychological Studies of Policy Decisions and Fiascoes* (2d ed.) Boston: Houghton Mifflin.

Joulwan, G. A. (1994). "Memorandum for the Secretary of Defense: Subject: Endorsement of Report of Investigation into the Accidental Shoot-Down of Two U.S. Army UH-60 Helicopters by Two Operation Provide Comfort F-15 Aircraft Which Occurred on 14 April 1994." Office of the Commander in Chief, U.S. European Command.

Kanki, B. G., and Palmer, M. T. (1993). "Communication and Crew Resource Management." In E. L. Wiener, R. L. Helmreich, and B. G. Kanki, eds., *Cockpit Resource Management*. San Diego: Academic Press.

Katz, D., and Khan, R. L. (1978). *The Social Psychology of Organizations*. New York: Wiley.

Katzenbach, J. R., and Smith, D. S. (1993). *The Wisdom of Teams*. Boston: Harvard Business School Press.

Kerr, S., and Jermier, J. M. (1978). "Substitutes for Leadership: Their Meaning and Measurement." *Organizational Behavior and Human Performance* 22: 375–403.

Kyle, J. H. (1990). *The Guts to Try: The Untold Story of the Iran Hostage Rescue Mission*. New York: Orion Books.

Langer, E. J. (1989). "Minding Matters: The Consequences of Mindlessness-Mindfulness." In L. Berkowitz, ed., *Advances in Experimental Social Psychology* 22: 137–73, New York: Academic Press.

LaPorte, T. R., and Consolini, P. M. (1991). "Working in Practice But Not in Theory: Theoretical Challenges of 'High-Reliability Organizations.'" *Journal of Public Administration Research and Theory* 1: 19–47.

LaPorte, T. R., Roberts, K., and Rochlin, G. I. (1989). *High Reliability Organizations: The Research Challenge*. Institute of Governmental Studies, University of California, Berkeley (April).

Latané, B. (1981). "The Psychology of Social Impact." *American Psychologist* 36: 343–56.

Latané, B., and Darley, J. M. (1970). *The Unresponsive Bystander: Why Doesn't He Help?* New York: Appleton-Century-Crofts.

Latané, B., and Nida, S. A. (1981). "Ten Years of Research on Group Size and Helping." *Psychological Bulletin* 89: 308–24.

Latané, B., K. Williams, and S. Harkins. (1979). "Many Hands Make Light Work: The Causes and Consequences of Social Loafing." *Journal of Personality and Social Psychology* 37: 822–32.

Lauber, J. K. (1984). "Resource Management in the Cockpit." *Airline Pilot* 53: 20–23.

Lawrence, P. R., and Lorsch, J. W. (1967). *Organization and Environment*. Boston: Harvard Business School Press.

Leavitt, H. J. (1975). "Suppose We Took Groups More Seriously." In E. L. Cass and F. G. Zimmer, eds., *Man and Work in Society*. New York: Van Nostrand Reinhold.

Louis, M. (1980). "Surprise and Sensemaking: What Newcomers Experience in Entering Unfamiliar Organizational Settings." *Administrative Science Quarterly* 25: 226–51.

Maddox, D. M. (1994). "Memorandum for General Joulwan: Subject: Report of Aircraft Accident Investigation." Department of the Army, HQs, U.S. Army Europe, and Seventh Army, the Commander in Chief.

Maruyama, M. (1963). "The Second Cybernetics: Deviation-Amplifying Mutual Causal Processes." *American Scientist* 51: 164–79.

May, R. (1994). "Gun Target Video—F-15." Incirlik AB, Turkey: DOD Joint Combat Camera Center.

Maze, R. (1996). Nunn: " 'Zero Casualty' Military Is Not Possible." *Army Times*. July 29: 30.

Metcalf, H. C., and Urwick, L., eds. (1941). *Dynamic Administration: The Collected Papers of Mary Parker Follett*. London: Pitman.

Meyer, J. W., and Rowan, B. (1977). "Institutionalized Organizations: Formal Structure as Myth and Ceremony." *American Journal of Sociology* 83: 340–63.

Milgram, S. (1963). "Behavioral Study of Obedience." *Journal of Abnormal and Social Psychology* 67: 371–78.

Moorman, W. A. (1994). "Memorandum for CINCUSAFE/CC: Subject: Legal Review—AFR 110–14 Report of Accident Investigation; the 14 April 1994 Shootdown of Two UH-60 Helicopters in Iraq." Department of the Air Force, HQs U.S. Air Forces in Europe.

Morgan, C. J. (1978). "Bystander Intervention: Experimental Test of a Formal Model. *Journal of Personality and Social Psychology* 36: 43–55.

Mounsey, K. (1995). "Testimony Before National Security Subcommittee to Investigate Iraq Shoot Down." U.S. Congress: Washington, D.C.

Oaks, R. C. (1994). "Memorandum for General Joulwan: Subject: Report of Aircraft Accident Investigation." Department of the Air Force, United States Air Forces in Europe.

Oettinger, A. G. (1990). *Whence and Whither Intelligence, Command and Control? The Certainty of Uncertainty* (No. P-90–1). Program on Information Resources Policy, Harvard University.

Office of the Assistant Secretary of Defense for Public Affairs. (1994). *Helicopter Shootdown Report Released* (News Release No. 417–94). Department of Defense.

Office of the Chief of Staff, U.S. Air Force. (1994). *Report to the Secretary of Defense: Black Hawk Shootdown Corrective Actions*.

Office of the Joint Chiefs of Staff. (1994). "Helicopter Shootdown: Lessons Learned." CINCs' Conference.

Orlady, H. W., and Foushee, H. C. (1986). "Cockpit Resource Management Training." In H. W. Orlady and H. C. Foushee, ed., *NASA/MAC Workshop*. San Francisco: NASA Scientific and Technical Information Branch.

Orton, D. J., and Weick, K. E. (1990). "Loosely Coupled Systems: A Reconceptualization." *Academy of Management Review* 15:2: 203–23.

Patton, M. Q. (1987). *How to Use Qualitative Methods in Evaluation*. Newbury Park, Calif.: Sage.

Perrow, C. (1984). *Normal Accidents*. New York: Basic Books.

Perry, W. (1994). "Memorandum for the Secretaries of the Army, Navy, Air Force, Chairman of the Joint Chiefs of Staff, and Chiefs of Staff of the Army, Air Force, and Chief of Naval Operations: Subject: Aircraft Accident and Corrective Action." Office of the Secretary of Defense.

Phillips, H. (1995). *Avoidable Errors*. New York: ABC News—*Prime Time Live*.

Prince, C., and Salas, E. (1993). "Training and Research for Teamwork in the Military Aircrew." In E. L. Wiener, R. L. Helmreich, and B. G. Kanki, eds., *Cockpit Resource Management*. San Diego: Academic Press.

Rasmussen, J. (1990). *Human Error and the Problem of Causality in Analysis of Accidents*. Phil. Trans. R. Soc. Lond. B327: 449–62.

———. (1993a). "Risk Management, Adaptation, and Design for Safety." In N. E. Sahlin and B. Brehmer, eds., *Future Risks and Risk Management*. Dordrecht: Klower.

———. (1993b). *What Can Be Learned from Disasters in Other Endeavors? Perspectives on the Concept of Human Error*. Manuscript for invited contributions to: Human Performance and Anesthesia Technology, Society for Technology in Anesthesia Conference: New Orleans, February 1993 and the First Danish Conference on Cognitive Science Research: Roskilde, October 1992.

Reason, J. T. (1990). *Human Error*. Cambridge: Cambridge University Press.

———. (1997). *Managing the Risks of Organizational Accidents*. Aldershot, England: Ashgate.

Roberts, K. (1989). "New Challenges to Organizational Research: High Reliability Organizations." *Industrial Crisis Quarterly* 3:3: 111–25.

———. (1990). "Some characteristics of One Type of High Reliability Organization." *Organization Science* 1:2: 160–76.

———. (1993). *New Challenges to Understanding Organizations*. New York: Macmillan.

Roethlisberger, F. J., and Dickson, W. J. (1939). *Management and the Worker*. Cambridge, Mass.: Harvard University Press.

Rosenberger, J. D. (1994). *Protecting the Force: The Neglected Element of Combat Power*. Fort Irwin, Calif.: National Training Center.

Rousseau, Denise, M. (1996). "Book Review: The Limits of Safety: Organizations, Accidents, and Nuclear Weapons." *Administrative Science Quarterly* 41: 200–203.

Ryan, P. B. (1985). *The Iranian Rescue Mission: Why It Failed*. Annapolis, Md.: Naval Institute Press.

Sagan, Scott D. (1993). *The Limits of Safety: Organizations, Accidents, and Nuclear Weapons*. Princeton, N.J.: Princeton University Press.

Scales, R. H. (1994). *Certain Victory: The U.S. Army in the Gulf War*. Washington, D.C.: U.S. Army Command and General Staff College Press, A Select Reprint.

Schmitt, E. (1995). The Military's Getting Queasier About Death. *New York Times*. August 7: 2.

Schutz, A. (1967). *The Phenomenology of the Social World*. Evanston, Ill.: Northwestern University Press.

Schwartz, S. H., and Clausen, G. T. (1970). Responsibility, Norms, and Helping in an Emergency. *Journal of Personality and Social Psychology* 16: 299–310.

Scott, E. R. (1992). *Organizations: Rational, Natural, and Open Systems* (3d ed.). Englewood Cliffs, N.J.: Prentice Hall.

Seligman, M.E.P., Maier, S. F., and Geer, J. (1968). "The Alleviation of Learned Helplessness in the Dog." *Journal of Abnormal Psychology* 78: 256–62.

Selznick, P. (1949). *TVA and the Grass Roots*. Berkeley: University of California Press.

Senge, P. M. (1990). *The Fifth Discipline: The Art and Practice of the Learning Organization*. New York: Currency Doubleday.

Senge, P. M., Roberts, C., Ross, R., Smith, B., and Kleiner, A. (1994). *The Fifth Discipline Fieldbook: Strategies and Tools for Building a Learning Organization*. New York: Currency Doubleday.

Shalikashvili, J. M. (1994a). Memorandum for the Secretary of Defense: Subject: Transmittal of Report of Investigation into the Accidental Shootdown of Two U.S. Army UH-60 Helicopters by Two Operation Provide Comfort F-15 Aircraft Which Occurred on 14 April 1994. Office of the Chairman, Joint Chiefs of Staff.

————. (1994b). Memorandum for the Secretary of Defense: Subject: Final Report on the Status of Corrective Actions Taken on the Report of the Shootdown of Helicopters Over Iraq. Office of the Chairman, Joint Chiefs of Staff.

Sherif, M. (1935). "A Study of Some Social Factors in Perception." *Archives of Psychology* 187: 45.

Shrader, C. R. (1982). *Amicicide: The Problem of Friendly Fire in Modern War*. Fort Leavenworth, Kan.: U.S. Army Command and General Staff College Press.

Simon, H. A. "A Behavioral Model of Rational Choice." *Quarterly Journal of Economics* 69: February 1955.

Spence, K. W. (1956). *Behavior Theory and Conditioning*. New Haven, Conn.: Yale University Press.

Spencer, H. (1904). *Autobiography*. Vol. 2. New York.

Starr, E. M. (1994). *Investigating Officer's Report: United States v. May, Article 32, UCMJ*. HQs, Seventeenth Air Force.

Stockton, W. (March 27, 1988). "Trouble in the Cockpit." *The New York Times Magazine*, p. 38.

Strauss, A., and Corbin, J. (1990). *Basics of Qualitative Research: Grounded Theory Procedures and Techniques*. Newbury Park, Calif.: Sage.

Sutton, R. I., and Staw, B. M. (1995). "What Theory Is Not." *Administrative Science Quarterly* 40: 371–84.

Tamuz, M. (1994). "Developing Organizational Safety Information Systems for Monitoring Potential Dangers." In G. F. Apostolakis and J. S. Wu, eds., *Proceedings of PSAM* 2. Los Angeles: University of California Press.

Thompson, J. D. (1967). *Organizations in Action*. New York: McGraw-Hill.

Tuckman, B. W. (1965). "Developmental Sequence in Small Groups." *Psychological Bulletin* 63: 384–99.

Turner, B. A. (1976). "The Organizational and Interorganizational Development of Disasters." *Administrative Science Quarterly* 21: 378–97.

Tyler, L. E. (1983). *Thinking Creatively: A New Approach to Psychology and Individual Lives*. San Francisco: Jossey-Bass.

U.S. Air Force. (1993). Multi-Command Regulation 55–33, *E-3 Operating Procedures—Aircrew*. Washington. Headquarters, Department of the Air Force.

U.S. Air Force. (1994). *Black Hawk Shootdown Corrective Actions: Report to the Secretary of Defense*, dated 30 September 1994. Washington: Department of the Air Force.

U.S. Army. (1985). Field Circular 101–55. *Corps and Division Command and Control*. Fort Leavenworth, Kan.: Department of the Army.

U.S. Army. (1987). Field Manual 22–103. *Leadership and Command at Senior Levels*. Washington: Headquarters, Department of the Army.

U.S. Congress, Office of Technology Assessment. (1993). *Who Goes There: Friend or Foe?* OTA-ISC-537, Washington: U.S. Government Printing Office.

U.S. General Accounting Office, Office of Special Investigations. (1997). *Operation Provide Comfort: Review of U.S. Air Force Investigation of Black Hawk Fratricide Incident (GAO/OSI-98–4)*. Washington: U.S. Government Printing Office.

U.S. Joint Chiefs of Staff. (1986). *JCS Pub. 1: Dictionary of Military and Associated Terms*. Washington: Office of the Joint Chiefs of Staff.

Varela, F. J., Thompson, E., and Rosch E. (1991). *The Embodied Mind: Cognitive Science and Human Experience*. Cambridge, Mass.: MIT Press.

Vaughan, D. (1996). *The Challenger Launch Decision*. Chicago: University of Chicago Press.

———. (1997). "The Trickle-Down Effect: Policy Decisions, Risky Work, and the *Challenger* Tragedy." *California Management Review* 39: 1–23.

———. (1998). "Rational Choice, Situated Action, and the Social Control of Organizations." *Law & Society Review* 32: 23–61.

Wagner, M. (1990). *Task II Report: The Organization, Development, and Management of Army Doctrine*. Alexandria, Va.: Dynamics Research Corporation Systems Division.

Washington Times. (1996). "Poor English Eyed in Air Crash." April 17: A6.

Watkins, S. (1996). The High Cost of Accountability. *Air Force Times*. December 23: 10–14.

Weber, M. (1949/1905). *The Methodology of Social Sciences*. New York: Free Press.

Weick, K. E. (1976). "Educational Organizations as Loosely Coupled Systems." *Administrative Science Quarterly* 21: 1–19.

———. (1979). *The Social Psychology of Organizing*. (2d ed.) New York: McGraw-Hill.

———. (1985). "A Stress Analysis of Future Battlefields." In J. G. Hunt and J. D. Blair, eds., *Leadership on the Future Battlefield*. Washington: Pergamon Brassey's.

———. (1987). "Organizational Culture as a Source of High Reliability." *California Management Review* 29: 112–27.

———. (1993a). "Sensemaking in Organizations: Small Structures with Large Consequences." In J. K. Murnighan, ed., *Social Psychology in Organizations*, pp. 10–37. Englewood Cliffs, N.J.: Prentice Hall.

———. (1993b). "The Collapse of Sensemaking in Organizations: The Mann Gulch Disaster." *Administrative Science Quarterly* 38: 628–52.

———. (1995a). *Sensemaking in Organizations*. Thousand Oaks, Calif.: Sage.

———. (1995b). "What Theory Is Not, Theorizing Is." *Administrative Science Quarterly* 40: 385–90.

Weick, K. E., and Roberts, K. H. (1993). "Collective Mind in Organizations: Heedful Interrelating on Flight Decks." *Administrative Science Quarterly* 38: 357–81.

Westrum, R. (1982). "Social Intelligence about Hidden Events." *Knowledge* 3:3: 381–400.

Whyte, W. F. (1943). *Street Corner Society*. Chicago: University of Chicago Press.

Wiener, E. L., Helmreich, R. L., and Kanki, B. G., ed.. (1993). *Cockpit Resource Management*. San Diego: Academic Press.

Yin, R. K. (1994). *Case Study Research: Design and Methods*. (2d ed.) Thousand Oaks, Calif.: Sage.

Zimbardo, P. G., Haney, C., Banks, W. C., and Jaffe, D. (1972). *The Psychology of*

Imprisonment: Privation, Power, and Pathology. Unpublished paper, Stanford University.

Zimbardo, P. G., Haney, C., and Banks, W. C. (1973). "A Pirandellian Prison." *New York Times Magazine*, pp. 38–60.

Zucker, L. G. (1991). "The Role of Institutionalization in Cultural Persistence." In W. W. Powell and P. J. DiMaggio, eds., *The New Institutionalism in Organizational Analysis*. Chicago: University of Chicago Press.

Author Index _____